The Longman Textbook Reader

without Answers

Second Edition

Compiled by

Cheryl Novins

PEARSON
Longman

New York   Boston   San Francisco
London   Toronto   Sydney   Tokyo   Singapore   Madrid
Mexico City   Munich   Paris   Cape Town   Hong Kong   Montreal

Acquisitions Editor: Kate Edwards
Senior Supplements Editor: Donna Campion
Marketing Manager: Thomas DeMarco
Electronic Page Makeup: Grapevine Publishing Services, Inc.
Cover Designer: Teresa M. Ward
Cover Images: iStockphoto

The Longman Textbook Reader with Answers, Second Edition, compiled by Cheryl Novins.

Copyright © 2008 Pearson Education, Inc.

ISBN: 0-205-51924-5

1 2 3 4 5 6 7 8 9 10—OPM—10 09 08 07

Contents

Introduction for Instructors

Reading courses offer college students many opportunities. In addition to helping them increase literal comprehension skills, such courses provide a basis for further college study in a wide variety of disciplines. Students who master the skills taught in their reading courses are well on their way to success in college and in the workplace.

A large part of success in any endeavor involves understanding the expectations of the situation. College students are expected to be independent learners, to take charge of their studies, and to find motivation from within. They are expected to attend lectures, take exams, and read their textbooks. Developmental reading texts often stress the importance of attending class and usually offer some tips on how to prepare for and take tests. They also include various excerpts from college texts to prepare students for the material they will encounter in their other college courses.

Unfortunately, such textbook excerpts (which often beautifully illustrate such important concepts as main idea, supporting details, and patterns of organization) tend to be fairly short—no more than a paragraph or two, or three or four pages at most. Such material tends to give ample drill and practice in the all-important reading skills, but often does not match the assignments that students will receive in their other courses, where they will be expected to read one or two complete textbook chapters per week.

In the interests of providing students with longer, chapter-length readings, Longman is pleased to offer *The Longman Textbook Reader*, 2/e. This paperback volume features complete textbook chapters from freshman textbooks representing six different course areas. The six course areas are:

- **Business:** Chapter 3, "Communicating Interculturally." From Bovée, Courtland L., and John V. Thill. *Business Communication Today*, 8/e. © 2005, Prentice Hall.
- **Natural and Life Sciences:** Chapter 21, "Nutrition and Digestion." From Campbell, Neil A., et al. *Biology: Concepts & Connections*, 5/e. © 2006, Benjamin/Cummings.
- **Mathematics:** Chapter 10, "Statistics." From Lial, Margaret K., Stanley A. Salzman, and Diana L. Hestwood. *Basic College Mathematics*, 7/e. © 2006, Addison-Wesley.
- **History:** Chapter 16, "Global Encounters: Europe and the New World Economy, 1400–1650." From Brummett, Palmira, et al. *Civilization Past & Present (Volume I: To 1650)*, 11/e. © 2006, Longman.
- **Humanities and the Visual Arts:** "Salvation," by Langston Hughes, and "The Masque of the Red Death," by Edgar Allan Poe. From Sisko, Yvonne Collioud. *American 24-Karat Gold: 24 Classic American Short Stories*, 2/e. © 2006, Longman. Works of Art: Chapter 16, "Global Encounters: Europe and the New World Economy, 1400–1650." From Brummett, Palmira, et al. *Civilization Past & Present (Volume I: To 1650)*, 11/e. © 2006, Longman.
- **Social Sciences:** Chapter 10, "Health and Stress." From Wood, Samuel E., Ellen Green Wood, and Denise Boyd. *Mastering the World of Psychology*, 2/e. © 2006, Allyn and Bacon.

These chapters were also chosen to represent the most commonly required and/or selected courses taken by incoming college freshmen. Each chapter is reproduced in its entirety; the complete original text, all photographs and graphic art, and pedagogical features are included. In addition, a series of exercises, group activities, and critical thinking activities have been prepared specially for this edition.

We hope *The Longman Textbook Reader*, 2/e will be an asset to you and your students.

Kate Edwards
Acquisitions Editor, Reading and Study Skills
Longman Publishers
Kate.Edwards@ablongman.com

Unit I

From

Courtland L. Bovée

John V. Thill

Business Communication Today

Eighth Edition

Chapter 3:
Communicating Interculturally

An Introduction to Business Communications

Business communication focuses on the unique communication processes that are at work in business environments. Many factors influence the effectiveness of business communications. Factors such as diversity, technology, organizational structures, and communication barriers are faced by companies in today's global environment. It is critical in business to ensure that all communications, whether written or verbal, are subject to appropriate business etiquette.

Business communication is offered as a major in many business programs and is also offered as an elective course in business administration programs. There are many career opportunities for this field including advertising, marketing, international business, mass media, and public administration.

Strategies for Reading Business Communications

When reading a business communications textbook, take the time to preview, annotate, take notes, and outline the material. Pay attention to any technical concepts and terminology. It is very important that as you read you distinguish between the facts and opinions of the authors. In addition, take the time to carefully interpret supporting graphic material including examples of business correspondence and documents.

chapter 3

Communicating Interculturally

COMMUNICATION CLOSE-UP AT E-SOFTSYS

www.e-softsys.com

It's tough enough to schedule meetings and coordinate team efforts when your partners work across the hall. Imagine what it's like when they work on the other side of the planet. The potential for misunderstandings, missed assignments, and mistrust could easily derail any project. And these are just some of the obstacles facing Kat Shenoy, president and CEO of E-SoftSys. His company employs offshore teams of engineers in two development centers located in Bangalore and Mangalore India, to develop software for other companies.

When potential customers think about using E-SoftSys for offshore software development, most need reassurance that the firm can successfully manage and monitor its far-flung team. As one customer asks: "How will it operate from so far away? Will we be able to communicate effectively?" To address their concerns and ensure effective teamwork, Shenoy offers customers a mix of human interaction and electronic collaboration (tools such as e-mail, instant messaging, and NetMeeting online software).

Keeping the project on track requires plenty of communication with the customer and within the team. Team members in the United States and India rely on frequent, informal communication to avoid misunderstanding one another, missing assignments, and forcing the project off schedule.

To succeed in today's marketplace, E-SoftSys relies on its team of programmers, who are spread across the globe, from the United States to Russia to India. Everyone in the company recognizes the challenges of communicating across cultures.

5

The project manager uses regular, formal communication with the customer—typically through daily/weekly status reports—to build trust and provide reassurance that the international team is making progress toward timely completion of the software.

However, technology can't address all the communication challenges. E-SoftSys teams often pull together people from diverse cultural backgrounds with different language abilities, and the company has found that face-to-face communication is critical when these teams are forming. For instance, during the early stages of most projects, either an India-based project manager travels to a customer's location in the United States, or a U.S.-based project manager travels to the E-SoftSys office in Bangalore, India, to collaborate with the Indian staff in designing the software and planning the work. By working side by side, even temporarily, these intercontinental colleagues establish a rapport that bridges time and space when the personnel return to their home office.[1]

---

1 LEARNING OBJECTIVE

Discuss the opportunities and challenges of intercultural communication

Effective intercultural communication
- Opens up business opportunities around the world
- Improves the contributions of employees in a diverse workforce

You will probably communicate with people in other countries at some time in your career.

UNDERSTANDING THE OPPORTUNITIES AND CHALLENGES OF INTERCULTURAL COMMUNICATION

E-SoftSys's experience illustrates both the challenges of intercultural communication and the opportunities available for business professionals who know how to communicate across cultures. **Intercultural communication** is the process of sending and receiving messages between people whose cultural background could lead them to interpret verbal and nonverbal signs differently. Every attempt to send and receive messages is influenced by culture, so to communicate successfully, you'll need a basic grasp of the cultural differences you may encounter and how you might overcome them. Your efforts to recognize and surmount cultural differences will open up business opportunities throughout the world and maximize the contribution of all the employees in a diverse workforce.

The Opportunities in a Global Marketplace

You might be a business manager looking for new customers or new sources of labor. Or you might be an employee looking for new work opportunities. Either way, chances are good that you'll be looking across international borders sometime in your career.

Thousands of U.S. businesses depend on exports for significant portions of their revenues. Every year, these companies export roughly $700 billion in materials and merchandise, along with billions more in personal and professional services. If you work in one of these companies, you may well be called on to visit or at least communicate with a wide variety of people who speak languages other than English and who live in cultures quite different from what you're used to. Of the top ten export markets for U.S. goods, only two (Canada and Great Britain) speak English as an official language, and Canada has two official languages, English and French.

In the global marketplace, most natural boundaries and national borders are no longer the impassible barriers they once were. Domestic markets are opening to worldwide competition as businesses of all sizes look for new growth opportunities outside their own countries. Automotive giant Ford markets to customers in more than 125 countries with websites that offer local information, usually in the local language.[2]

Even small companies in remote locations can sell and support their products on a global scale, thanks to e-mail, the Internet, and worldwide delivery services. Pygmy Boats is a small manufacturer of kayak kits in the equally small town of Port Townsend, Washington, and yet it reaches customers all over the world via its website.[3] Similarly, Pens.it, an Italian retailer of fountain pens, sells its products globally online as well.[4] Large or small, companies know that in the global marketplace, they face cultural and language barriers among customers and employees (see Figure 3.1).

The Advantages of a Multicultural Workforce

Even if you never visit another country or transact business on a global scale, you will interact with colleagues from a variety of cultural backgrounds. Smart business leaders recog-

Communication Solution

E-SoftSys's Kat Shenoy recognizes the economic advantages of employing the large pool of talented computer professionals in India and other countries, but he also understands that successful intercultural communication requires extra effort by everyone involved.

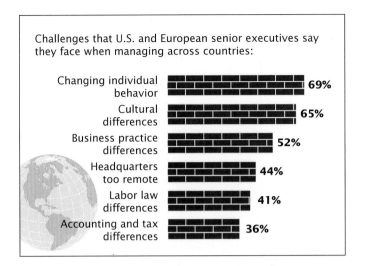

FIGURE 3.1
**Going Global Has
Its Barriers**

Challenges that U.S. and European senior executives say they face when managing across countries:

Challenge	Percentage
Changing individual behavior	69%
Cultural differences	65%
Business practice differences	52%
Headquarters too remote	44%
Labor law differences	41%
Accounting and tax differences	36%

nize the competitive advantages of a diverse workforce that has employees of different national, religious, and ethnic backgrounds—as well as different gender and age groups. Diverse workforces bring a broader range of viewpoints and ideas, help companies understand and identify with diverse markets, and enable companies to tap into the broadest possible pool of talent.

When Louis Gerstner, Jr., took over as CEO of IBM, workplace diversity became one of his top priorities—and it played a supporting role in the turnaround of IBM's faltering business. Under Gerstner's direction, IBM established executive-led task forces to represent women, Asian Americans, African Americans, Hispanic Americans, Native Americans, people with disabilities, and individuals who are gay, lesbian, bisexual, and transgender. Recommendations from these task forces helped transform IBM's recruiting, training, leadership, and development practices. Today, diversity is fostered at the employee level through 133 networking groups that unite people with a variety of talents and interests.[5]

Diversity is simply a fact of life for all companies. The United States has been a nation of immigrants from the beginning, and that trend continues today. The Western and Northern Europeans who made up the bulk of immigrants during the nation's early years now share space with people from across Asia, Africa, Eastern Europe, and other parts of the world. By 2010 recent immigrants will account for half of all new U.S. workers.[6] Nor is this pattern of immigration unique to the United States: Workers from Africa, Asia, and the Middle East are moving to Europe in search of new opportunities, while workers from India, the Philippines, and Southeast Asia contribute to the employment base of the Middle East.[7]

However, you and your colleagues don't need to be recent immigrants to constitute a diverse workforce. Differences in everything from age and gender to religion and ethnic heritage to geography and military experience enrich the workplace. Both immigration and workforce diversity create advantages—and challenges—for business communicators throughout the world.

The diversity of today's workforce brings distinct advantages to businesses:
- A broader range of views and ideas
- An understanding of diverse markets
- A broad pool of talent from which to recruit

Putting more people of various ethnicities on the floor—and in executive positions—is commonplace for Wal-Mart, which was recently ranked by *Fortune* magazine as one of America's 50 best companies for Asian, African, and Hispanic Americans. This diverse group of Wal-Mart managers clearly understand the importance of being sensitive to others' cultures.

The Challenges of Intercultural Communication

Cultural diversity affects how business messages are conceived, planned, sent, received, and interpreted in the workplace. Today's increasingly diverse workforce brings with it a wide

A company's cultural diversity affects how its business messages are conceived, composed, delivered, received, and interpreted.

range of skills, traditions, backgrounds, experiences, outlooks, and attitudes toward work—all of which can affect employee behavior on the job. Supervisors face the challenge of communicating with these diverse employees, motivating them, and fostering cooperation and harmony among them. Teams face the challenge of working together closely, and companies are challenged to coexist peacefully with business partners and with the community as a whole.

The interaction of culture and communication is so pervasive that separating the two is virtually impossible. The way you communicate—from the language you speak and the nonverbal signals you send to the way you perceive other people—is influenced by the culture in which you were raised. The meaning of words, the significance of gestures, the importance of time and space, the rules of human relationships—these and many other aspects of communication are defined by culture. To a large degree, your culture influences the way you think, which naturally affects the way you communicate as both a sender and a receiver.[8] So you can see how intercultural communication is much more complicated than simply matching language between sender and receiver. It goes beyond mere words to beliefs, values, and emotions.

Throughout this chapter, you'll see numerous examples of how communication styles and habits vary from one culture to another. These examples are intended to illustrate the major themes of intercultural communication, not to give an exhaustive list of styles and habits of any particular culture. With an understanding of these major themes, you'll then be prepared to explore the specifics of any culture.

> Culture influences everything about communication, including
> • Language
> • Nonverbal signals
> • Word meaning
> • Time and space issues
> • Rules of human relationships

ENHANCING YOUR INTERCULTURAL SENSITIVITY

> Your communication tends to be automatic.

The good news is that you're already an expert in culture, at least in the culture you grew up with. You understand how your society works, how people are expected to communicate, what common gestures and facial expressions mean, and so on. The bad news is that because you're such an expert in your own culture, your communication is largely automatic; that is, you rarely stop to think about the communication rules you're following. An important step toward successful intercultural communication is becoming more aware of these rules and of the way they influence your communication. A good place to start is to understand what culture is.

2 LEARNING OBJECTIVE

Define culture and explain how culture is learned

> Culture is a shared system of symbols, beliefs, attitudes, values, expectations, and behavior norms.

> You belong to several cultures.

Understanding the Concept of Culture

For the purposes of communication, **culture** can be defined as a shared system of symbols, beliefs, attitudes, values, expectations, and norms for behavior. In other words, your cultural background influences the way you prioritize what is important in life, helps define your attitude toward what is appropriate in any given situation, and establishes rules of behavior.[9]

Actually, you belong to several cultures. The most obvious is the culture you share with all the people who live in your own country. In addition, you belong to other cultural groups, including an ethnic group, probably a religious group, and perhaps a profession that has its own special language and customs. All members of a culture have similar assumptions about how people should think, behave, and communicate, and they all tend to act on those assumptions in much the same way. However, cultures differ widely from group to group and may vary in their rate of change, their degree of complexity, and their tolerance toward outsiders. These differences affect the level of trust and openness that you can achieve when communicating with people of other cultures.

Within a major culture such as the United States are other cultural groups, such as Mexican Americans, Californians, and science fiction fans. In fact, as a country with a large population and a long history of immigration, the United States is home to a vast array of cultures. Similarly, Indonesia is home to a wide variety of ethnic and religious cultures, whereas Japan is much more homogeneous, having only a few separate cultural groups.[10]

> People learn about culture directly and indirectly from members of their group.

People learn culture directly and indirectly from other members of their group. As you grow up in a culture, you are taught who you are and how best to function in that culture by the group's members. For example, you might've been raised to address parental figures as "Ma'am and Sir," "Mother and Father," "Mom and Dad," or simply "Marge and Bob," depending on the degree of respect and formality that your culture expects of children.

Sometimes you are explicitly told which behaviors are acceptable; at other times you learn by observing which values work best in a particular group. This double-edged format for learning ensures that culture is passed on from person to person and from generation to generation.[11] It also ensures that, as stated earlier, you are often unaware of the influence of your own culture, acting and reacting automatically.

In addition to being automatic, established cultures tend to be coherent; that is, they are fairly logical and consistent throughout. For instance, the notion of progress is deeply embedded in the culture of the United States. From the country's early westward expansion to its support and admiration of entrepreneurs and innovators, U.S. culture generally views progress as a positive factor, and it rewards those who achieve it. Conversely, those who don't progress are sometimes considered underachievers, even if they live perfectly happy and contented lives. Such coherence generally helps a culture function more smoothly internally.

Cultures tend to be coherent.

Cultures also tend to be complete; that is, they provide most of their members with most of the answers to life's big questions. This idea of completeness dulls or even suppresses curiosity about life in other cultures. Therefore, such completeness can complicate communication with other cultures.[12]

Cultures tend to be complete.

Overcoming Ethnocentrism and Stereotyping

The very nature of culture being automatic, coherent, and complete can lead the members of one culture to form negative attitudes about—and rigid, oversimplified views of—other cultures. **Ethnocentrism** is the tendency to judge all other groups according to your own group's standards, behaviors, and customs. When making such comparisons, people too often decide that their own group is superior.[13] An even more extreme reaction is **xenophobia**, a fear of strangers and foreigners. Clearly, businesspeople who take these views will not interpret messages from other cultures correctly, nor are they likely to send successful messages.

As you recall from Chapter 1, selective perception leads people to rearrange incoming information to fit their existing beliefs. Thus, someone with a negative view of another culture is likely to continue holding that view, even if he or she sees evidence to the contrary.

Distorted views of other cultures or groups also result from **stereotyping**, assigning a wide range of generalized attributes to an individual on the basis of membership in a particular culture or social group, without considering the individual's unique characteristics. Whereas ethnocentrism and xenophobia represent negative views of everyone in a particular group, stereotyping is more a matter of oversimplifying and of failing to acknowledge individuality. For instance, assuming that an older colleague will be out of touch with the youth market or that a younger colleague can't be an inspiring leader is an example of stereotyping age groups. Many people in the United States have stereotypical views both of co-cultures within the United States and of cultures in other countries. Likewise, the people in these other countries sometimes exhibit stereotypical views of U.S. residents as well.

To show respect for other people and to communicate effectively in business, adopt a more positive viewpoint: **Cultural pluralism** is the practice of accepting multiple cultures on their own terms. When crossing cultural boundaries, you'll be even more effective if you move beyond simple acceptance and adapt your own communication style to that of the new cultures you encounter—even integrating aspects of those cultures into your own.[14] A few simple habits can help you avoid both the negativity of ethnocentrism and the oversimplification of stereotyping:

- **Avoid assumptions.** Don't assume that others will act the same way you do, that they will operate from the same values and beliefs, or that they will use language and symbols the same way you do.
- **Avoid judgments.** When people act differently, don't conclude that they are in error, that their way is invalid, or that their customs are inferior to your own.
- **Acknowledge distinctions.** Don't ignore the differences between another person's culture and your own.

3 LEARNING OBJECTIVE

Define ethnocentrism and stereotyping; then give three suggestions for overcoming these limiting mindsets

Ethnocentrism is the tendency to judge all other groups according to the standards, behaviors, and customs of one's own group.

Xenophobia is a fear of strangers.

Stereotyping is assigning generalized attributes to an individual on the basis of membership in a particular group.

Cultural pluralism is the acceptance of multiple cultures on their own terms.

To avoid ethnocentrism and stereotyping, develop a few simple habits.

4 **LEARNING OBJECTIVE**

Explain the importance of recognizing cultural variations, and list six categories of cultural differences

Cultural differences lead to miscommunication.

Recognizing Cultural Variations

When you communicate with someone from another culture, you encode your message using the assumptions of your own culture. However, members of your audience decode your message according to the assumptions of their culture, so your meaning may be misunderstood. The greater the difference between cultures, the greater the chance for misunderstanding.[15] Consider the differences in communication styles, personal values, and nonverbal symbols that led to the following cultural mishaps:

- When Hewlett-Packard (HP) brought its U.S. engineers together with its French engineers to design software, the U.S. engineers sent long, detailed e-mails to their counterparts in France. But the engineers in France viewed the lengthy messages as patronizing and replied with quick, concise e-mails. That response made the U.S. engineers believe that French engineers were withholding information. The situation spiraled out of control until HP hired a consulting firm to provide cultural training so that both sides could learn to work through their differences.[16]

- A Canadian employer rewarded a Polish-born engineer for his excellent job performance over the years with every possible award it could give him and a salary on the same level as many senior managers. However, in the engineer's view, the company should have rewarded him by putting him in charge of a large number of subordinates—as top performers are typically rewarded in his native Poland. Even though the company thought it was communicating its gratitude with pay and awards, the talented engineer left the company.[17]

- Exhibitors at a trade show could not understand why Chinese visitors were not stopping by their booth. The exhibitors were wearing green hats and giving them away as promotional items. They soon discovered that for many Chinese people, green hats are associated with infidelity: the Chinese expression "He wears a green hat" indicates that a man's wife has been cheating on him. As soon as the exhibitors discarded the green hats and started giving out T-shirts instead, the Chinese attendees began visiting the booth.[18]

Communication breakdowns such as these arise when we assume, wrongly, that other people's attitudes and lives are like ours (see "Communicating Across Cultures: Test Your Intercultural Knowledge"). Part of the problem stems from treating others the way *you* want to be treated. The best approach when communicating with people from other cultures is to treat them the way *they* want to be treated.

Treat people the way they expect to be treated.

You can begin to learn how people in other cultures want to be treated by recognizing and accommodating six main types of cultural differences: contextual, legal and ethical, social, nonverbal, age, and gender.

Contextual Differences

Cultural context is the pattern of physical cues, environmental stimuli, and implicit understanding that conveys meaning between members of the same culture.

Every attempt at communication occurs within a **cultural context**, the pattern of physical cues, environmental stimuli, and implicit understanding that convey meaning between two members of the same culture. However, cultures around the world vary widely in the role that context plays in communication (see Figure 3.2).

In a **high-context culture** such as South Korea or Taiwan, people rely less on verbal communication and more on the context of nonverbal actions and environmental setting to convey meaning. A Chinese speaker expects the receiver to discover the essence of a message and uses indirectness and metaphor to provide a web of meaning.[19] In high-context cultures, the rules of everyday life are rarely explicit; instead, as individuals grow up, they learn how to recognize situational cues (such as gestures and tone of voice) and how to respond as expected.[20] Also, in a high-context culture, the primary role of communication is building relationships, not exchanging information.[21]

High-context cultures rely on implicit nonverbal actions and environmental setting to convey meaning, unlike low-context cultures, which rely heavily on explicit verbal communication.

In a **low-context culture** such as the United States or Germany, people rely more on verbal communication and less on circumstances and cues to convey meaning. An English speaker feels responsible for transmitting the meaning of the message and often places sentences in chronological sequence to establish a cause-and-effect pattern.[22] In a low-context culture, rules and expectations are usually spelled out through explicit state-

Communicating Across Cultures

Test Your Intercultural Knowledge

Never take anything for granted when you're doing business in a foreign country. Here are several examples based on true stories about businesspeople who blundered by overlooking some simple but important cultural differences. Can you spot the erroneous assumptions?

1. You're tired of the discussion and you want to move on to a new topic. You ask your Australian business associate, "Can we table this for a while?" To your dismay, your colleague ignores the request and keeps right on discussing the topic.
2. You finally made the long trip overseas to meet the new German director of your division. Despite slow traffic, you arrive only four minutes late. His door is shut, so you knock on it and walk in. The chair is too far away from the desk, so you pick it up and move it closer. Then you lean over the desk, stick out your hand and say, "Good morning, Hans, it's nice to meet you." Why is his reaction so chilly?
3. Your meeting went better than you'd ever expected. In fact, you found the Japanese representative for your new advertising agency to be very agreeable; she said yes to just about everything. When you share your enthusiasm with your boss, he doesn't appear very excited. Why?

Here's what went wrong in each situation:

1. To "table" something in Australia means to bring it forward for discussion, the opposite of the usual U.S. meaning. The English that's spoken in Australia is closer to British than to U.S. English.
2. You've just broken four rules of German polite behavior: punctuality, privacy, personal space, and proper greetings. In time-conscious Germany, you should never arrive even a few minutes late. Also, Germans like their privacy and space, and they adhere to formal greetings of "Frau" and "Herr," even if the business association has lasted for years.
3. The word *yes* may not always mean "yes" in the Western sense. Japanese people may say *yes* to confirm they have heard or understood something but not necessarily to indicate that they agree with it. You'll seldom get a direct no. Some of the ways that Japanese people say no indirectly include "It will be difficult," "I will ask my supervisor," "I'm not sure," "We will think about it," and "I see."

ments such as "Please wait until I'm finished" or "You're welcome to browse."[23] Exchanging information is the primary task of communication in low-context cultures.[24]

Contextual differences are apparent in the way cultures approach situations such as decision making, problem solving, and negotiating:

- **Decision-making practices.** In lower-context cultures, businesspeople tend to focus on the results of the decisions they face, a reflection of the cultural emphasis on logic and progress. Will this be good for our company? For my career? In comparison, higher-context cultures emphasize the means or the method by which the decision will be made. Building or protecting relationships can be as important as the facts and information used in making the decisions.[25] For example, executives negotiating in a high-context culture such as China may spend most of their time together building relationships, rather than hammering out contractual details.

  Low-context cultures concentrate on every detail of a decision, whereas high-context cultures build relationships and trust.

- **Problem-solving techniques.** In low-context cultures, businesspeople usually bring a problem out in the open, look for causes, and then often assign blame. Both problems and solutions can be handled in a highly individualized manner, assigning blame to those who cause problems and heaping credit on troubleshooters and problem solvers. However, in higher-context cultures businesspeople view problems more as part of the context in which the business is operating and less as the fault of any particular individual. The group works together to solve the problem.[26] Similarly, the tolerance for open conflict differs widely across cultures. Low-context U.S. businesspeople tolerate and sometimes even expect confrontation and debate, but high-context Japanese executives shun such tactics, even using an intermediary to avoid the unpleasant feelings that might result from open conflict.

  Low-context cultures encourage open disagreement, whereas high-context cultures avoid confrontation and debate.

- **Negotiating styles.** A business negotiation is a complicated exchange of messages. Although the two sides are willing to work together, each is also asking the other to make concessions. Complex negotiations may involve many players on both sides, may

FIGURE 3.2 How Cultural Context Affects Business Communication

IN LOW-CONTEXT COMPANIES	IN HIGH-CONTEXT COMPANIES
Executive offices are separate with controlled access.	Executive offices are shared and open to all.
Workers rely on detailed background information.	Workers do not expect or want detailed information.
Information is highly centralized and controlled.	Information is shared with everyone.
Objective data are valued over subjective relationships.	Subjective relationship are valued over objective data.
Business and social relationships are discrete.	Business and social relationships overlap.
Competence is valued as much as position and status.	Position and status are valued much more than competence.
Meetings have fixed agendas and plenty of advance notice.	Meetings are often called on short notice, and key people always accept.

Low-Context Cultures ← Swiss German · German · Scandinavian · U.S. American · French · British · Italian · Spanish · Greek · Arab · Chinese · Japanese → High-Context Cultures

Note: These are generalized assessments of each culture; contextual variations can be found within each culture between individuals.

When negotiating, whereas low-context cultures view negotiations impersonally as a series of problems to be overcome. High-context cultures emphasize harmony and agreement, even when points remain to be worked out.

drag out over months, may cover a wide range of technical and financial details, and may require translation services. Negotiators from low-context cultures expect negotiations to be an impersonal affair and view the process as a series of problems to be overcome until mutual satisfaction is reached. This style conflicts with the high-context style of emphasizing harmony and agreement, even when all the points of the negotiation aren't yet settled. Open disagreement about a business issue can be perceived by people in a high-context culture as an attack on the businessperson.[27]

Whether you're making a decision, solving a problem, or negotiating a business deal, the communication tactics that work well in a high-context culture may backfire in a low-context culture, and vice versa. The key to success is understanding why the other party is saying and doing particular things and then adapting your approach accordingly.

Legal and Ethical Differences

Low-context cultures tend to value written agreements and interpret laws strictly, whereas high-context cultures view adherence to laws as being more flexible.

Legal systems differ from culture to culture.

Cultural context also influences legal and ethical behavior. For example, because low-context cultures value the written word, they consider written agreements binding. But high-context cultures put less emphasis on the written word and consider personal pledges more important than contracts. They also tend to take a more flexible approach regarding adherence to the law, whereas low-context cultures would adhere to the law strictly.[28]

As you conduct business around the world, you'll find that legal systems differ from culture to culture. In the United Kingdom and the United States, someone is presumed innocent until proved guilty, a principle rooted in English common law. However, in Mexico and Turkey, someone is presumed guilty until proved innocent, a principle rooted in the Napoleonic code.[29]

As discussed in Chapter 1, making ethical choices can be difficult, even within your own culture. When communicating across cultures, ethics can be even more complicated. What does it mean for a business to do the right thing in Thailand? In Nigeria? In Norway? What happens when a certain behavior is unethical in the United States but an accepted practice in another culture?

For example, in the United States, bribing officials is illegal, but Kenyans consider paying such bribes a part of life. To get something done right, they pay *kitu kidogo* (or "something small"). In China businesses pay *huilu,* in Russia they pay *vzyatka,* in the Middle East it's *baksheesh,* and in Mexico it's *una mordida* ("a small bite").[30]

The United States enacted the Foreign Corrupt Practices Act in 1977, making it illegal for U.S. companies to pay bribes, even in countries where the practice is accepted (or expected). To help level the playing field for U.S. businesses, the U.S. government lobbied other nations to also outlaw bribery. After nearly 20 years, the 29 member nations of the Organization for Economic Cooperation and Development, along with five nonmembers, finally signed a treaty that made payoffs to foreign officials a criminal offense. Of course, bribery won't end just because a treaty has been signed, but many of the signatory countries have ratified the treaty and passed supporting legislation.[31]

Making ethical choices across cultures can seem incredibly complicated, but doing so actually differs little from the way you choose the most ethical path in your own culture (see Chapter 1). When communicating across cultures, keep your messages ethical by applying four basic principles:[32]

- **Actively seek mutual ground.** To allow the clearest possible exchange of information, both parties must be flexible and avoid insisting that an interaction take place strictly in terms of one culture or another.
- **Send and receive messages without judgment.** To allow information to flow freely, both parties must recognize that values vary from culture to culture, and they must trust each other.
- **Send messages that are honest.** To ensure that the information is true, both parties must see things as they are—not as they would like them to be. Both parties must be fully aware of their personal and cultural biases.
- **Show respect for cultural differences.** To protect the basic human rights of both parties, each must understand and acknowledge the other's needs and preserve each other's dignity by communicating without deception.

Social Differences

The nature of social behavior varies among cultures, sometimes dramatically. These behaviors are guided by rules. Some rules are formal and specifically articulated (table manners are a good example), and some are informal, learned over time (such as the comfortable standing distance between two speakers in an office or whether it's acceptable for male and female employees to socialize outside of work). The combination of both types of rules influences the overall behavior of everyone in a society, or at least most of the people most of the time. In addition to the factors already discussed, social rules can vary from culture to culture in the following areas:

- **Attitudes toward work and success.** Although the United States is home to millions of people having different religions and values, the major social influence is still the Puritan work ethic. Many U.S. citizens hold the view that material comfort earned by individual effort is a sign of superiority, and that people who work hard are better than those who don't. This view is reflected in the number of hours that U.S. employees work every year (see Figure 3.3). Workers in Australia, Japan, and Spain also average at least 1,800 hours of work per year, significantly more than workers in France, Germany, and Norway.
- **Roles and status.** Culture dictates, or at least tries to dictate, the roles that people play, including who communicates with whom, what they communicate, and in what way. For example, in many countries women still don't play a prominent role in business, so women executives who visit these countries may find that they're not taken seriously as businesspeople.[33] Culture also dictates how people show respect and signify rank. For example, people in the United States show respect by addressing top managers as "Mr. Roberts" or "Ms. Gutierrez." However, people in China are addressed according to their official titles, such as "President" or "Manager."[34]
- **Use of manners.** What is polite in one culture may be considered rude in another. For instance, asking a colleague "How was your weekend?" is a common way of making small talk in the United States, but the question sounds intrusive to people in cultures where business and private lives are seen as totally separate. In Arab countries it's

Ethical choices can be even more complicated when communicating across cultures; for example, bribing officials is viewed differently from culture to culture.

Keep your messages ethical by actively applying four principles.

Formal rules of etiquette are explicit and well defined, but informal rules are learned through observation and imitation.

People from the United States emphasize hard work and individual effort more than many people in other countries do.

Respect and rank are reflected differently from culture to culture in the way people are addressed and in their working environment.

The rules of polite behavior vary from country to country.

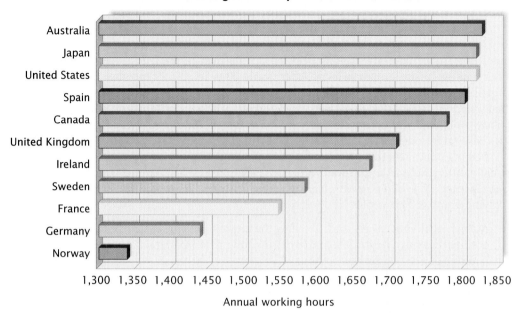

FIGURE 3.3 Working Hours Vary from Culture to Culture

impolite to take gifts to a man's wife, but it's acceptable to take gifts to his children. In India, if you're invited to visit someone's home "any time," you should make an unexpected visit without waiting for a definite invitation. Failure to take the "any time" invitation literally would be an insult, a sign that you don't care to develop the friendship. Read about a country's expectations before you visit, then watch carefully and learn after you arrive.

- **Concepts of time.** Business runs on schedules, deadlines, and appointments, but these matters are regarded differently from culture to culture. People in high-context cultures see time as a way to plan the business day efficiently, often focusing on only one task during each scheduled period and viewing time as a limited resource. However, executives from low-context cultures often see time as more flexible. Meeting a deadline is less important than building a business relationship. So the workday isn't expected to follow a rigid, preset schedule.[35] Trying to coax a team into staying on a strict schedule would be an attractive attribute in U.S. companies but could be viewed as pushy and overbearing in other cultures.

> Although businesspeople in the United States, Germany, and some other nations see time as a way to organize the business day efficiently, other cultures see time as more flexible.

Nonverbal Differences

As discussed in Chapter 2, nonverbal communication can be a reliable guide to determining the meaning of a message. However, this notion of reliability is valid only when the communicators belong to the same culture. For instance, the simplest hand gestures change meaning from culture to culture. A gesture that communicates good luck in Brazil is the equivalent of giving someone "the finger" in Colombia.[36] In fact, the area of gestures is so complicated that entire books have been written about it. Don't assume that the gestures you grew up with will translate to another culture; doing so could lead to embarrassing mistakes (see Figure 3.4).

From colors to facial expression, nonverbal elements add yet another layer of richness and complexity to intercultural communication. When you have the opportunity to interact with people in another culture, the best advice is to study the culture in advance, then observe the way people behave in the following areas:

> Nonverbal differences may be observed in numerous areas.

- **Greetings.** Do people shake hands, bow, or kiss lightly (on one side of the face or both)?
- **Personal space.** When people are conversing, do they stand closer together or farther away than you are accustomed to?
- **Touching.** Do people touch each other on the arm to emphasize a point or slap each other on the back to show congratulation? Or do they refrain from touching altogether?

FIGURE 3.4 Avoiding Nonverbal Mishaps

In the United States	A firm grip should last for several seconds.	Direct, sustained eye contact is considered a sign of friendliness, strength, and trustworthiness.	This gesture expresses a variety of positive meanings, from "yes" to "nice job."	The "OK" sign indicates approval or assurance.	A genuine smile indicates happiness, agreement, or friendliness.
In Other Cultures	Japanese traditionally prefer a slight bow of the head; some Southeast Asians prefer to press their palms together in a slight praying motion; when people do shake hands in the Middle East and Far East, gentle pressure is preferred (a firm handshake is considered aggressive).	In countries such as Japan and South Korea, eye contact can be considered aggressive.	This gesture means "one" in Germany and "five" in Japan; it's an obscene gesture in Australia and some other countries.	The "OK" sign means "zero" or "worthless" in France; indicates money in Japan; is an obscene gesture in Germany, Brazil, and some other countries.	Good news: A simple smile works everywhere in the world!

- **Facial expressions.** Do people shake their heads to indicate "no" and nod them to indicate "yes"? This is what people are accustomed to in the United States, but it's not universal.
- **Eye contact.** Do people make frequent eye contact or avoid it? Frequent eye contact is often taken as a sign of honesty and openness in the United States, but in other cultures it can be a sign of aggressiveness or lack of respect.
- **Posture.** Do people slouch and relax in the office and in public, or do they sit up straight?
- **Formality.** In general, does the culture seem more or less formal than yours?

Following the lead of people who grew up in the culture is not only a great way to learn but a good way to show respect as well.

Age Differences

The United States celebrates youth in general and successful young businesspeople in particular. The emphasis on youth is so strong that millions of older people spend millions of dollars every year trying to look or feel younger, whether it's dying that gray hair back to its original color or surgically reversing the effects of aging. Business publications frequently publish lists of successful young executives who are making their mark before age 30 or 40. Youth is associated with strength, energy, possibilities, and freedom, whereas age is too often associated with declining powers and a loss of respect and authority.[37] As a result, younger employees in U.S. companies often communicate with older colleagues as equals, even to the point of openly disagreeing with them.

However, in cultures that value age and seniority, longevity earns respect and increasing power and freedom. For instance, in many Asian societies, the oldest employees hold the most powerful jobs, the most impressive titles, and the

Expectations of personal space vary from culture to culture; not everyone is comfortable working in close quarters such as these.

Communication styles and expectations can vary widely between age groups, putting extra demands on teams that include workers of varying ages.

greatest degree of freedom and decision-making authority. If a younger employee disagrees with one of these senior executives, the discussion is never conducted in public. The notion of "saving face," of avoiding public embarrassment, is too strong. Instead, if a senior person seems to be in error about something, other employees will find a quiet, private way to communicate whatever information they feel is necessary.[38]

Communicating between a youth-oriented culture and a seniority-oriented culture can require flexibility on both sides. For example, if you work for a U.S. company that is trying to influence a group of senior managers in Japan or China, they'll probably expect to communicate with peers of equivalent seniority or status. Sending the young hotshot over to close the deal may be viewed as a sign of disrespect.

Gender Differences

In the United States, women are finding more opportunities in business than ever before.

The perception of men and women in business also varies from culture to culture. In the United States today, women find a much wider range of business opportunities than existed just a few decades ago (even though differences in pay and access to top management positions still exist—with women holding fewer than 5 percent of the top executive positions in *Fortune 500* companies).[39] However, such opportunity is not the case in more tradition-oriented societies, where men tend to hold most or all of the positions of authority and women are expected to play a more subservient role. Female executives who visit other cultures may not be taken seriously until they successfully handle challenges to their knowledge, capabilities, and patience.[40]

As more women enter the workforce and take on positions of increasing responsibility, it's important for company leaders to revisit assumptions and practices.[41] For instance, company cultures that have been dominated by men for years may have adopted communication habits that some women have difficulty relating to—such as the constant use of sports metaphors or the acceptance of coarse language.

Whatever the culture, evidence suggests that men and women tend to have slightly different communication styles. Although the following broad generalizations might not apply in every case, understanding them can serve as a useful starting point for improving communication with the opposite sex:[42]

The communication styles of men and women differ on several points.

- **Workplace hierarchy influences communication.** Regardless of your opinions or beliefs, the simple fact remains that most businesses in most countries have been dominated by men for years; therefore, women face the challenge of finding a place for themselves within this hierarchy. When communicating within such a context, women may feel more pressure to adapt their communication styles to the prevailing style in the male-dominated environment.
- **Decision-making styles influence communication.** When making a decision, the differences between men and women are similar to the differences between low-context and high-context cultures. Men tend to value decisiveness over relationship quality, and their communication therefore emphasizes content—facts and figures, tasks, and results. In contrast, women tend to emphasize collaboration and the maintenance of positive business relationships, and their communication efforts generally reflect this concern. Even when a man and a woman reach the same conclusion in a given situation, their communication on the subject may differ as a result of these stylistic difference.
- **Problem-solving styles influence communication.** Particularly in the U.S. culture of success and progress, most men place great value on their ability to solve problems. In both their personal and professional lives, they have been conditioned to judge themselves by their ability to fix things. This conditioning can lead to misunderstandings when a woman voices frustration over a problem at work and a male colleague jumps

in with a potential solution. The woman may not have been asking her colleague for a solution, but merely trying to share her feelings. She may find her colleague's response to be controlling, misguided, even insulting.

IMPROVING INTERCULTURAL COMMUNICATION SKILLS

The better you are at intercultural communication, the more successful you'll be in today's business environment. However, communicating successfully from one culture to another requires a variety of skills (see Figure 3.5). You can improve your intercultural skills throughout your entire career. Begin now by studying other cultures and languages, respecting preferences for communication styles, learning to write and speak clearly, listening carefully, knowing when to use interpreters and translators, and helping others adapt to your culture.

Studying Other Cultures

Learning all you can about a particular culture will help you send and receive intercultural messages effectively. Unfortunately, a thorough knowledge of another culture and its language—or languages—can take years to acquire. Fortunately, you don't need to learn about the whole world all at once. Many companies appoint specialists for specific countries or regions, giving you a chance to focus on fewer cultures at a time.

Improving intercultural skills is a career-long effort.

5 LEARNING OBJECTIVE

Outline strategies for studying other cultures

Communication Solution

The teams at E-SoftSys realize that successful communication requires an understanding of cultural influences. To promote effective intercultural communication, the company encourages employees to learn more about each other's cultures through international assignments and constant communication.

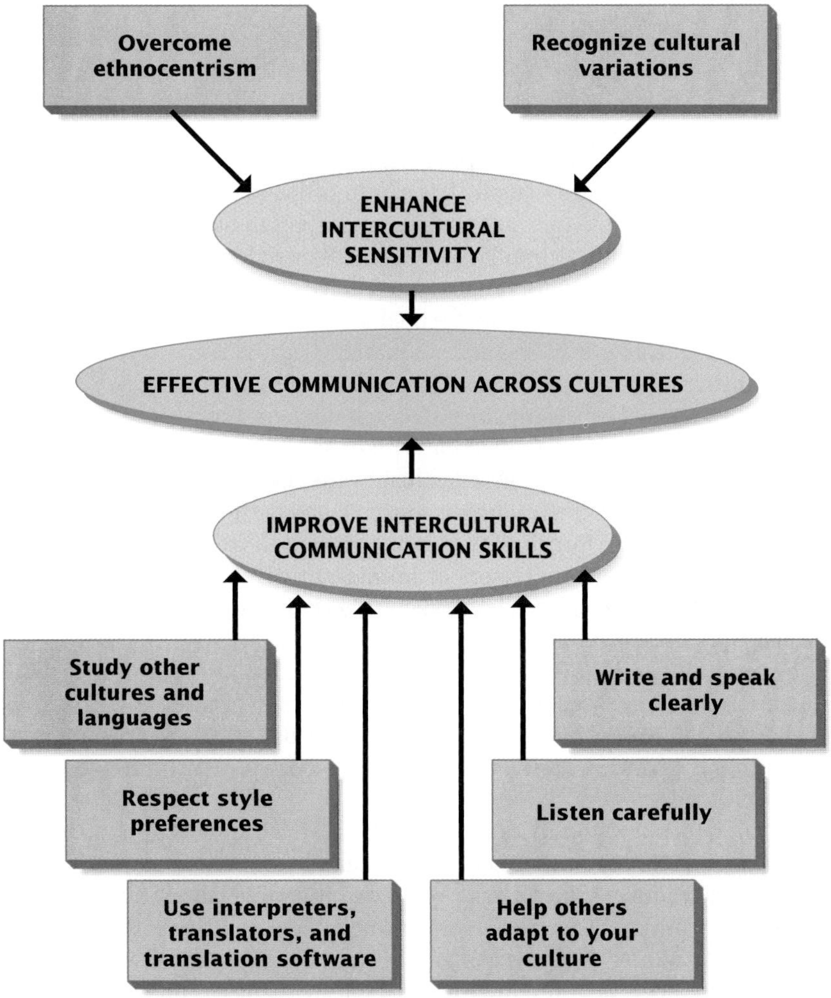

FIGURE 3.5
Components of Successful Intercultural Communication

Just a little research can help you grasp the basics of another culture.

Nor do you need to learn everything about a culture to ensure some level of communication success. Even a small amount of research will help you grasp the big picture and recognize enough communication basics to get through most business situations. In addition, most people respond positively to honest effort and good intentions, and many business associates will help you along if you show an interest in learning more about their cultures.

Mistakes will happen, and when they do, apologize (if appropriate), ask about the accepted way, and move on.

Try to approach situations with an open mind and a healthy sense of humor. You will make a mistake or two; at one point or another, everybody who tries to communicate across cultures makes mistakes. When it happens, simply apologize if appropriate, ask the other person to explain the accepted way, and then move on. As business becomes ever more global, even the most tradition-bound cultures are learning to deal with outsiders more patiently and overlook the occasional cultural blunder.[43]

If you try to learn nonverbal customs from a movie, remember that your resource is intended as entertainment.

Numerous websites and books offer advice on traveling to and working in specific cultures; they're a great place to start. Also try to sample newspapers, magazines, and even the music and movies of another country. For instance, a movie can demonstrate nonverbal customs even if you don't grasp the language. (However, be careful not to read too much into entertainment products. If people in other countries based their opinions of U.S. customs only on the silly teen flicks and violent action movies that the United States exports around the globe, what sort of impression do you imagine they'd get?) For some of the key issues to research before doing business in another country, refer to Table 3.1.

Studying Other Languages

English is the most prevalent language in international business, but it's a mistake to assume that everyone understands it.

With so many businesses stretched across national borders, successful employees commonly possess multilingual skills. Some countries have emphasized language diversity more than others over the years. For instance, businesspeople in the United States and United Kingdom often assume that people in other nations can speak enough English to get by in business, so there is less emphasis on learning other languages. In contrast, in a country such as the Netherlands, with its long history of international trade, fluency in multiple languages is considered an essential business skill.[44] The European Union, the international community of nations stretching across Europe, designated English as its official working language, but it actually has eleven official languages.[45] To simplify matters, some multinational companies ask all their employees to use English when communicating with employees in other countries, wherever they're located. Employees of Nissan, Japan's third-largest automaker, use English for internal e-mail and memos to colleagues around the world. When the company formed a strategic relationship with Renault, a French carmaker, the situation at Nissan headquarters became even more interesting, since English is not the native language of either Japanese or French employees.[46]

Many companies find that they must be able to conduct business in languages other than English.

Similarly, a number of U.S. companies are teaching their English-speaking employees a second language to facilitate communication with their co-workers. One out of every seven people in the United States now speaks a language other than English when at home. After English, Spanish is by far the most common spoken language, followed by French, German, Italian, and Chinese.[47] The Target retail chain is among those sponsoring basic Spanish classes for English-speaking supervisors of immigrant employees. Around the country, enrollment is growing in specialized classes such as health-care Spanish, firefighter Spanish, and Spanish for professionals.[48]

If you have a long-term business relationship with people of another culture, it is helpful to learn their language.

Even if your colleagues or customers in another country do speak your language, it's worth the time and energy to learn common phrases in theirs. Learning the basics not only helps you get through everyday business and social situations but also demonstrates your commitment to the business relationship. After all, the other person probably spent years learning your language.

Even if the same language is spoken in another country, don't assume that it is spoken the same way.

Don't assume that two countries speaking the same language speak it the same way. The French spoken in Quebec and other parts of Canada is often noticeably different from the French spoken in France. Similarly, it's often said that the United States and the United Kingdom are two countries divided by a common language (see Table 3.2 on p. 76.). Another complication to watch for is words that seem similar in different languages but in fact convey different degrees of intensity or different meanings entirely. The English word *formidable* (pronounced FOR-mid-a-bull or for-MID-a-bull) usually refers to something

TABLE 3.1 Doing Business Abroad

ACTION	DETAILS TO CONSIDER
Understand social customs	• How do people react to strangers? Are they friendly? Hostile? Reserved? • How do people greet each other? Should you bow? Nod? Shake hands? • How do you express appreciation for an invitation to lunch, dinner, or someone's home? Should you bring a gift? Send flowers? Write a thank-you note? • Are any phrases, facial expressions, or hand gestures considered rude? • How do you attract the attention of a waiter? Do you tip the waiter? • When is it rude to refuse an invitation? How do you refuse politely? • What topics may or may not be discussed in a social setting? In a business setting?
Learn about clothing and food preferences	• What occasions require special clothing? • What colors are associated with mourning? Love? Joy? • Are some types of clothing considered taboo for one gender or the other? • How many times a day do people eat? • How are hands or utensils used when eating? • Where is the seat of honor at a table?
Assess political patterns	• How stable is the political situation? • Does the political situation affect businesses in and out of the country? • What are the traditional government institutions? • Is it appropriate to talk politics in social or business situations?
Understand religious and folk beliefs	• To which religious groups do people belong? • Which places, objects, actions, and events are sacred? • Is there a tolerance for minority religions? • How do religious holidays affect business and government activities? • Does religion require or prohibit eating specific foods? At specific times?
Learn about economic and business institutions	• Is the society homogeneous or heterogeneous? • What languages are spoken? • What are the primary resources and principal products? • Are businesses generally large? Family controlled? Government controlled? • Is it appropriate to do business by telephone? By fax? By e-mail? • What are the generally accepted working hours? • How do people view scheduled appointments? • Are people expected to socialize before conducting business?
Appraise the nature of ethics, values, and laws	• Is money or a gift expected in exchange for arranging business transactions? • Do people value competitiveness or cooperation? • What are the attitudes toward work? Toward money? • Is politeness more important than factual honesty?

that is difficult or that arouses fear or dread. The identically spelled French word (pronounced for-mee-DAH-bluh) means terrific or wonderful.

Respecting Preferences for Communication Style

Communication style—including the level of directness, the degree of formality, preferences for written versus spoken communication, and other factors—varies widely from culture to culture. Knowing what your communication partners expect can help you adapt to their particular style. Once again, watching and learning is the best way to improve your skills; however, you can infer some generalities from what you already know about a culture. For instance, U.S. workers typically prefer an open and direct communication style; they find other styles frustrating or suspect. Directness is also valued in Sweden as a sign of efficiency, but unlike discussions in the United States, heated debates and confrontations are unusual. Italian, German, and French executives don't soften up colleagues with praise before they criticize—doing so seems manipulative to Europeans. However, professionals from high-context cultures, such as Japan or China, tend to be less direct.[49]

Communication style varies from culture to culture.

TABLE 3.2 U.S. Versus British English

U.S. ENGLISH	BRITISH ENGLISH
apartment	flat
eggplant	aubergine
cleaning lady	charwoman
elevator	lift
first floor	ground level
long-distance call	trunk call
organization	organisation
pharmacist	chemist
rare	underdone
roast	joint
string bean	French bean
sweater	pullover

International correspondence is often more formal than what U.S. businesspeople are used to.

In international correspondence, U.S. businesspeople will generally want to be somewhat more formal than they would be when writing to people in their own country. In many cultures, writers use a more elaborate style, so your audience will expect more formal language in your letter. The letter in Figure 3.6 was written by a supplier in Germany to a nearby retailer. The tone is more formal than would be used in the United States, but the writer clearly focuses on his audience. In Germany, business letters usually open with a reference to the business relationship and close with a compliment to the recipient. Of course, if you carry formality to extremes, you'll sound unnatural.

6 **LEARNING OBJECTIVE**

List seven recommendations for writing clearly in multilanguage business environments

Writing Clearly

In addition to learning the preferred style of your communication partners, you can help ensure successful messages by taking extra care with your writing. When sending written communication to businesspeople from another culture, familiarize yourself with their written communication preferences and adapt your approach, style, and tone to meet their expectations. To help you prepare effective written communications for multicultural audiences, follow these recommendations:[50]

- **Use simple, clear language.** Use precise words that don't have the potential to convey multiple meanings. For instance, the word *rich* has at least half a dozen different meanings, whereas *wealthy* has exactly one, leaving no room for ambiguity.
- **Be brief.** Use simple sentences and short paragraphs, breaking information into smaller chunks that are easier for your reader to capture and translate.
- **Use transitional elements.** Help readers follow your train of thought by using transitional words and phrases. Precede related points with expressions such as *in addition* and *first, second,* and *third*.
- **Address international correspondence properly.** Refer to Table 1.2 in Appendix A for an explanation of different address elements and salutations commonly used in certain foreign countries.
- **Cite numbers and dates carefully.** In the United States, 12-05-06 means December 5, 2006, but in France, Germany, and many other countries, it means May 12, 2006. Dates in Japan and China are usually expressed with the year first, followed by the month and then the day; therefore, to write December 5, 2006, in Japan, write it as 2006-12-05. Similarly, 1.000 means one with three decimal places in the United States and Great Britain, but it means one thousand in many European countries.

FIGURE 3.6 Effective German Business Letter (translated)

Literal translation of *Geschäfts-fürer* (Common English translation would be "managing director")

Refers to the ongoing business relationship

Uses language a bit more formally than U.S. letters do

Uses a complimentary close typical of German business letters

Shows concern for the audience

Ends with a compliment to the receiver

Includes no title in the typed name

> **Furtwangen Handcrafts**
> Kussenhofstrasse 150
> Furtwangen, Germany
>
> Mister
> Karl Wieland
> Business Leader
> Black Forest Gifts
> Friedrichstrasse 98
> 70174 Stuttgart
> GERMANY
>
> 15.5.2005
>
> Very honorable Mister Wieland,
>
> Because the tourist season will begin soon, we would like to seize the opportunity to introduce our new line of hand-carved cuckoo clocks to you. Last year you were so friendly as to buy two dozen of our clocks. In recognition of our good business relationship, we now offer you the opportunity to select the new models before we offer this line to other businesses for purchase.
>
> As you know, our artisans use only the best wood. According to time-honored patterns that are passed on from generation to generation, they carefully carve every detail by hand. Our clockworks are of superior quality, and we test every clock before it is painted and shipped. We give you a guarantee of five years on all Furtwangen Handcrafts clocks.
>
> Enclosed you will find a copy of our newest brochure and an order form. To express our appreciation, we will take over the shipping costs if you order before 15 June.
>
> We continue to wish you a lot of success in your new Stuttgart location. We are convinced that you will satisfy your regular clientele with your larger exhibition area and expanded stock and will gain many new visitors.
>
> With friendly greetings
>
> *Frederick Semper*
>
> Frederick Semper

- **Avoid slang, idiomatic phrases, and business jargon.** Everyday speech and writing is full of slang and **idiomatic phrases**, phrases that mean more than the sum of their literal parts. Many of these informal usages are so deeply ingrained that you may not even be aware that you're using them. Examples from U.S. English include phrases like "Off the top of my head," "Crossing the finish line," "More bang for the buck," and "Face the music." Your foreign correspondent may have no idea what you're talking about when you use such phrases.
- **Avoid humor and other references to popular culture.** If your everyday business correspondence is sprinkled with jokes, references to TV shows, and other cultural tidbits, make a conscious effort to avoid these when writing to people from another culture.

The correspondence shown in Figures 3.7 and 3.8 illustrates how intercultural correspondence can be improved by paying close attention to the guidelines offered in this chapter.

Speaking Clearly

Whether you're traveling to another country or teaming up with someone who is visiting or immigrating to your country, chances are good that sometime in your career you'll need

To gain insight into speaking more effectively in intercultural situations, think about what it's like to listen to someone whose native language is different from yours.

FIGURE 3.7 Ineffective Intercultural Letter

La Cristallerie

Troy Halford, U.S. Sales Representative
163 Pico Boulevard
Los Angeles, CA 90032
Voice: (213) 975-8924
Fax: (213) 860-3489
halford@home.com

Uses the U.S. format for the date, rather than the international format typically used by French writers

April 5, 2005

Mr. Pierre Coll
Director of Accounting
La Cristallerie
22 Marne Blvd.
Beaune, France 21200

Fails to follow French preferences for title and address format

Dear Pierre:

Uses reader's first name, which is much too informal for most French business correspondence

I know you've had gorgeous spring weather, with sunny skies and balmy days. But here in the States, it's been a spring of another color. We've been hammered with storms, flooding, and even late snow. Travel over here has been a nightmare, which is why you'll find my expenses a bit elevated this month.

Wastes reader's time with unnecessarily dramatic and long description of weather problems

I realize that you've asked all the reps to reduce rather than increase our expenses, but there were extenuating circumstances this last month. All the bad weather we've been having has caused major bottlenecks, with flights canceled and people forced to sleep in the terminals wherever they could find a spot.

Uses slang and idioms throughout the message, risking confusion from simple vocabulary choices (e.g., spring of another color, hammered, bottlenecks, spot, shuteye, crunch, struck out)

After being stuck in the Chicago airport for 18 hours straight, I was desperate for a hot shower and some shut-eye, so I decided to wait out the crunch in a hotel. I know that hotels near airports are expensive, but I struck out trying to book a cheaper room in town. The bottom line is I had to spend extra funds for a hotel at $877; meals, which came to some $175; $72 just in transportation from the terminal to the hotel, and extra phone calls totaling $38.

Buries specific information in awkward phrasing that ignores the directness and simplicity of using lists and parallelism

Fails to provide a total of the "extra" expenses

I appreciate your understanding these unique circumstances. I was really in a jam.

Closes with a self-centered tone rather than trying to help the reader

Sincerely,

Troy Halford

Troy Halford
U.S. Sales Rep

Fails to include enclosure notation

---

to converse with people whose native language is different from yours. You can gain some great insights into *speaking* more effectively in these situations by remembering what it's like trying to *listen* in these situations.

Every year, thousands of people around the world venture to other countries on business or personal travel, many of them eager to try the language skills they've been studying in a classroom. The result is often immediate confusion. You might ask where your hotel is or what time the meeting starts and get a response that is incomprehensible. All those words and phrases that made perfect sense in the classroom suddenly sound like an endless string of noise and gibberish.

Even when you know the vocabulary and grammar of another language, the ability to process everyday conversation can take years to master. People from the United States are notorious for stringing together multiple words into a single pseudo-word that mystifies non-native English speakers. "Did you eat yet?" becomes "Jeat yet?" and "Can I help you?" becomes "Cannahepya?" Similarly, the French language frequently uses a concept known as *liaison*, in which one word is intentionally joined with the next. Without a lot of practice, new French speakers have a hard time telling when one word ends and the next one begins.

FIGURE 3.8 Effective Intercultural Letter

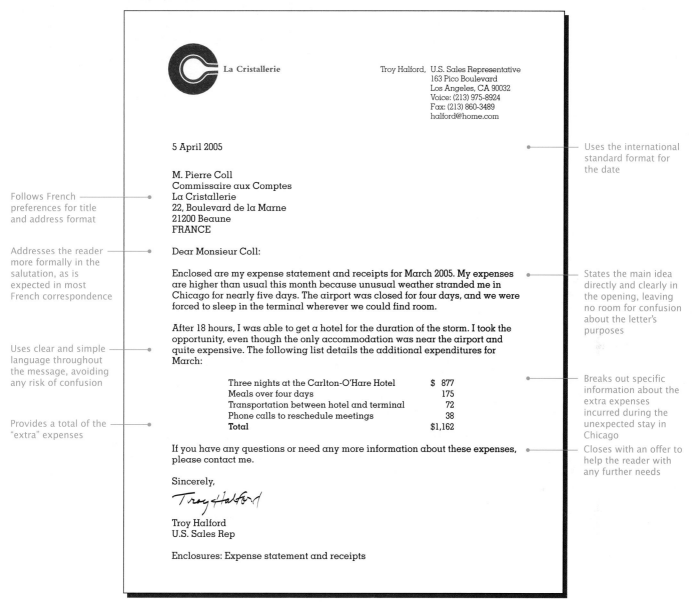

In addition to the advice provided in the preceding section on writing clearly, these guidelines will help you be more effective with intercultural conversations:

- **Speak slowly and clearly.** Your listener may need time to consciously work through several steps—steps that you do automatically and nearly instantly in your language—from deciding what the sounds mean to translating individual words to even rearranging the order of words in a sentence, if necessary. Pronounce each word clearly, stop at distinct punctuation points, and make one point at a time. This pattern of speech might sound odd and even uncomfortable to you, but it's more sensitive to the needs of your conversation partner and faster and more effective in the long run.

- **Don't rephrase until it's necessary.** A common mistake is quickly rephrasing a statement or question if you think the other person doesn't immediately grasp what you've just said. Rather than helping, this often makes the situation worse because your listener now has two sets of words to translate and comprehend. Be patient while he or she tries to extract the meaning from your message. If you get a clear sign that he or she doesn't understand what you've said, then try another angle. And when you rephrase, choose simpler words and more concrete language if possible; don't fall into the common mistake of simply saying the same thing again but louder.

To speak more clearly in intercultural conversations, follow six guidelines.

- **Look for—and ask for—feedback.** Be alert to signs of confusion in your listener. Realize that nods and smiles don't necessarily mean understanding. If the other person's body language seems at odds with the flow of the conversation, ask questions to see if your message is getting through.
- **Don't talk down to the other person.** Try not to overenunciate, don't simplify sentences to the point of spouting gibberish, and don't get frustrated with the listener for not understanding. Use phrases such as "Am I going too fast?" rather than "Is this too difficult for you?"
- **Learn foreign phrases.** Learn common greetings and a few basic phrases in the other person's native language. Even something as simple as knowing how to say "please" and "thank you" in the other language will show your good intentions and respect for others.
- **Clarify what will happen next.** At the end of the conversation, be sure that you and the other person agree on what has been said and decided. If appropriate, follow up by writing a letter or a memo that summarizes the conversation and thanks the person for meeting with you.

Listening Carefully

Languages vary considerably in the significance of tone, pitch, speed, and volume. The English word *progress* can be a noun or a verb, depending on which syllable you accent. In Chinese, the meaning of the word *mà* changes depending on the speaker's tone; it can mean *mother, pileup, horse,* or *scold.* Arabic speech can sound excited or angry to an English-speaking U.S. listener, even though the speaker is simply asking a question without being either excited or angry.[51] Businesspeople from Japan tend to speak more softly than Westerners, a characteristic that implies politeness or humility to a Western listener.

Experienced international speakers, such as Dell's CEO Michael Dell, are careful to incorporate cultural and language variations into their communication efforts.

With some practice, you can start to get a sense of vocal patterns. The key is simply to accept what you hear first, without jumping to conclusions about meaning or motivation. Let other people finish what they have to say. If you interrupt, you may miss something important. You'll also show a lack of respect. If you do not understand a comment, ask the person to repeat it. Any momentary awkwardness you might feel in asking for extra help is less important than the risk of unsuccessful communication.

To listen more effectively in intercultural situations, accept what you hear without judgment and let people finish what they have to say.

Certain documents and situations require the use of an interpreter, translator, or translation software.

Using Interpreters, Translators, and Translation Software

You may encounter business situations that require using an interpreter (for spoken communication) or a translator (for written communications). In addition, most customers expect to be addressed in their native language, particularly concerning advertising, warranties, repair and maintenance manuals, and product labels. These documents certainly require the services of a translator. Microsoft spends several hundred million dollars a year to make virtually all of its software products, websites, and help documents available in dozens of languages; the company is believed by some to be the world's largest purchaser of translation services.[52]

Professional interpreters and translators can be expensive (translators can earn up to $150 an hour or more for some languages), but skilled professionals provide invaluable assistance in business communication. For instance, an experienced translator can analyze a message, understand its meaning in the cultural context, consider how to convey the meaning in another language, and then use verbal and nonverbal signals to encode or decode the message for someone from another culture. If you use translators, you should meet with them ahead of time to give them a sense of what you are presenting and to discuss specific words or concepts that could be confusing.[53] Some companies use *back-translation* to ensure accuracy. Once a translator encodes a message into another language, a different translator retranslates the same message into the original language. This back-translation is then compared with the original message to discover any errors or discrepancies.

Back-translation is having a second translator decode the first translator's work back to the original language.

Connecting with Technology

The Gist of Machine Translation

What is the writer trying to say in the following sentence?

We have the need to balance for the barriers on this one or the market could draw well after us.

Can you figure it out? Here's the original sentence, which uses a tone that is overly casual and colloquial—a common problem in U.S. business documents:

We need to swing for the fences on this one or the market could shoot right past us.

When this sentence was run through a simple computerized translation service, from English to French and back to English, the software clearly had trouble with the "swing for the fences" and "shoot right past us" figures of speech.

Without hands-on intervention from experienced human translators, machine translation systems can produce results that are anywhere from amusing to nonsensical to downright dangerous. Whether you're using one of the automatic website translation services available from such sites as Alta Vista and Google, or a text translator such as the one available at WorldLingo (www.worldlingo.com), keep in mind that you won't get the same quality that you'd get from a human translator.

However, you won't always have the luxury of waiting for, or paying for, a human translator. For example, your sales department might receive an unexpected e-mail message from somebody who appears to be a potential customer in another country. You don't want the expense of hiring a translator this early in the relationship, but you don't want to let a big deal slip away either. By running the message through a basic machine translator, chances are you can get a basic idea of the

message almost instantly. At the very least, you'll probably be able to tell whether the message is important enough to warrant the time and expense of a translator. And if you get results that make you scratch your head or laugh out loud, do call in a translator to make sure that you and the sender understand one another correctly.

CAREER APPLICATIONS

1. Why do you think a computer might have trouble translating "swing for the fences" (a baseball phrase for trying as hard as one can to hit the ball out of the park)?
2. What are some examples of business documents that would probably be safe to read via machine translation? What are some that would be dangerous to trust to software?

The time and cost required for professional translation has encouraged the development of **machine translation**, any form of computerized intelligence used to translate one language to another. Dedicated software tools and online services such as WorldLingo (www.worldlingo.com) and Alis Technologies (www.alis.com) offer some form of automated translation. Major search engines such as Alta Vista and Google let you request a translated version of the websites you find. Although none of these tools promises translation quality on a par with human translators, they can be quite useful with individual words and short phrases, and they can give you the overall gist of a message (see "Connecting with Technology: The Gist of Machine Translation").[54]

Even though translation technology is getting better, frequent errors make it risky to use for important business communications. A computer could translate every word perfectly and still present you with a new message that is wildly inaccurate, given differences in sentence structure, idiomatic usage, and other factors. If you want to create business documents that are accurate and truly localized, the only sure solution is using human translators who are native speakers of the target language.[55]

Machine translation uses computerized intelligence to translate material from one language to another.

Don't rely on machine translation for important messages.

Helping Others Adapt to Your Culture

Now that you have a good appreciation for the complexity of getting your message across to someone in another culture, you can also appreciate the challenge faced by people from

When people from other cultures try to communicate with you, try to help them by suggesting media such as e-mail, IM, or intranet sites.

CHECKLIST: Improving Intercultural Communication Skills

- Study other cultures so that you can appreciate cultural variations.
- Study other languages.
- Help nonnative English speakers learn English.
- Respect cultural preferences for communication style.
- Write clearly, using brief messages, simple language, generous transitions, and appropriate international conventions.

- Avoid slang, humor, and references to popular culture.
- Speak clearly and slowly, giving listeners time to translate your words.
- Ask for feedback to ensure successful communication.
- Listen carefully and ask speakers to repeat anything you don't understand.
- Use interpreters and translators for important messages.

other cultures when they try to communicate with you. Whether a younger person is unaccustomed to the formalities of a large corporation or a colleague from another country is working on a team with you, look for opportunities to help people fit in and adapt their communication style. For more ideas on how to improve communication in the workplace, see "Checklist: Improving Intercultural Communication Skills."

Remember that speaking and listening are usually much harder in a second language than writing and reading. Oral communication requires participants to process sound in addition to meaning, and it doesn't provide any time to go back and reread or rewrite. So instead of asking a foreign colleague to provide information in a conference call, you could set up an intranet site where the person can file a written report. Similarly, using instant messaging and e-mail is often easier for colleagues with different native languages than participating in live conversations. An added plus with many of these technologies is overcoming the barrier of time zones. You can simply carry on a written conversation online, rather than participating in phone calls early in the morning or late at night.

Whatever assistance you can provide will be greatly appreciated. Smart businesspeople recognize the value of intercultural communication skills. Moreover, chances are that while you're helping others, you'll learn something about other cultures, too.

DOCUMENT MAKEOVER

IMPROVE THIS LETTER

To practice correcting drafts of actual documents, visit www.prenhall.com/onekey on the web. Click "Document Makeovers," then click Chapter 3. You will find a letter that contains problems and errors relating to what you've learned in this chapter about developing effective intercultural communication skills. Use the Final Draft decision tool to create an improved version of this letter. Check the message for a communication style that keeps the message brief, does not become too familiar or informal, uses transitional elements appropriately, and avoids slang, idioms, jargon, and technical language.

COMMUNICATION CHALLENGES AT E-SOFTSYS

 After contributing to several successful projects, you were recently promoted to the position of project manager. You're now managing your first project, and Kat Shenoy has told you it's time to visit the office in Bangalore, India, to complete the software design, organize the work, and get acquainted with the local team. You're already nervous about leading your first project, and that feeling is compounded by your apprehension about working with an international team.

Individual Challenge: You have two weeks to prepare for the trip. Several of your U.S. co-workers have ample experience working with the Bangalore office, and several have traveled there for launch meetings. You also learn that a recently hired software engineer, Mahesh, is originally from Jaipur, a city about 945 miles (1,524 km) north of Bangalore. He has spent the last 6 years in the United States, earning his degree from the local university. Who would you ask for advice on communicating with Indian team members? Please explain your answer. Explain how you would approach Mahesh to ask for his help in learning about the Indian business culture.

Team Challenge: Mahesh is flattered that you approached him and agrees to help, even though he is quite busy. In a small group, create a prioritized list of the topics you should explore and the questions you would like to ask both Mahesh and your U.S. colleagues about your upcoming 6-week assignment in India.

SUMMARY OF LEARNING OBJECTIVES

1 Discuss the opportunities and challenges of intercultural communication. The global marketplace spans natural boundaries and national borders, allowing worldwide competition between businesses of all sizes. Therefore, today's businesspeople are likely to communicate across international borders with people who live in different cultures. Moreover, the world's domestic workforces are becoming more and more diverse, with employees having different national, religious, and ethnic backgrounds. Therefore today's companies benefit from a broader range of viewpoints and ideas, they have a better understanding of diverse markets, and they recruit workers from the broadest possible pool of talent. However, whether communicating with people around the world or at home, intercultural communication presents challenges as well, including motivating diverse employees to cooperate and to work together in teams, as well as understanding enough about how culture affects language to prevent miscommunication.

2 Define culture and explain how culture is learned. Culture is a shared system of symbols, beliefs, attitudes, values, expectations, and norms for behavior. Culture is learned by listening to advice from other members of a society and by observing their behaviors. This double-edged method uses direct and indirect learning to ensure that culture is passed from person to person and from generation to generation.

3 Define *ethnocentrism* and *stereotyping*; then give three suggestions for overcoming these limiting mindsets. Ethnocentrism is the tendency to judge all other groups according to the standards, behaviors, and customs of one's own group. Stereotyping is assigning a wide range of generalized attributes to individuals on the basis of their membership in a particular culture or social group, without considering an individual's unique characteristics. To overcome ethnocentrism and stereotyping, follow three suggestions: (1) avoid assumptions, (2) avoid judgments, and (3) acknowledge distinctions.

4 Explain the importance of recognizing cultural variations, and list six categories of cultural differences. People from different cultures encode and decode messages differently, increasing the chances of misunderstanding. By recognizing and accommodating cultural differences, we avoid automatically assuming that everyone's thoughts and actions are just like ours. Begin by focusing on six categories of cultural differences: contextual differences (the degree to which a culture relies on verbal or nonverbal actions to convey meaning), legal and ethical differences (the degree to which laws and ethics are regarded and obeyed), social differences (how members value work and success, recognize status, define manners, and think about time), nonverbal differences (differing attitudes toward greetings, personal space, touching, facial expression, eye contact, posture, and formality), and age differences (how members think about youth, seniority, and longevity).

5 Outline strategies for studying other cultures. Although a thorough knowledge of another culture and its language(s) can take years to acquire, conducting research will help you grasp the big picture and recognize enough basics to get through most business situations. Find websites and books that offer advice on traveling to and working in specific cultures. Also sample newspapers, magazines, music, and movies of the culture you're interested in to get an idea of dress, nonverbal customs, manners, and so on—always being careful not to read too much into entertainment products.

6 List seven recommendations for writing clearly in multilanguage business environments. Take extra care with your writing, adapting your approach, style, and tone to meet audience expectations. To write effectively to multicultural audiences, follow these recommendations: (1) use simple, clear language; (2) be brief; (3) use transitional elements; (4) address international correspondence properly; (5) cite numbers and dates carefully, (6) avoid slang, idiomatic phrases, and business jargon, (7) avoid humor and other references to popular culture.

Test Your Knowledge

1. How have market globalization and cultural diversity contributed to the increased importance of intercultural communication?
2. What are the potential advantages of a multicultural workforce?
3. How do high-context cultures differ from low-context cultures?
4. In addition to contextual differences, what other categories of cultural differences exist?
5. What is ethnocentrism, and how can it be overcome in communication?
6. What four principles apply to ethical intercultural communication?
7. Why is it a good idea to avoid slang and idioms when addressing a multicultural audience?
8. What are some ways to improve oral skills when communicating with people of other cultures?
9. What are the risks of using computerized translation when you need to read a document written in another language?

10. What steps can you take to help someone from another culture adapt to your culture?

Apply Your Knowledge

1. What are some of the intercultural differences that managers of a U.S.-based firm might encounter during a series of business meetings with a China-based company whose managers speak English fairly well?
2. What are some of the intercultural communication issues to consider when deciding whether to accept an overseas job with a firm whose headquarters are in the United States? A job in the United States with a local branch of a foreign-owned firm? Explain.
3. How do you think company managers from a country that has a relatively homogeneous culture might react when they do business with the culturally diverse staff of a company based in a less homogeneous country? Explain your answer.
4. Your company has relocated to a U.S. city where Vietnamese culture is strongly established. Many of your employees will be from this culture. What can you do to improve communication between your management and the Vietnamese Americans you are currently hiring?
5. **Ethical Choices** Your office in Turkey desperately needs the supplies that have been sitting in Turkish customs for a month. Should you bribe a customs official to speed up delivery? Explain your decision.

Practice Your Knowledge

Document for Analysis

Your boss wants to send a brief e-mail message welcoming employees recently transferred to your department from your Hong Kong branch. They all speak English, but your boss asks you to review his message for clarity. What would you suggest your boss change in the following e-mail message—and why? Would you consider this message to be audience centered? Why or why not?

I wanted to welcome you ASAP to our little family here in the States. It's high time we shook hands in person and not just across the sea. I'm pleased as punch about getting to know you all, and I for one will do my level best to sell you on America.

Exercises

For live links to all websites discussed in this chapter, visit this text's website at www.prenhall.com/bovee. Just log on, select Chapter 3, and click on "Featured Websites." Locate the page or the URL related to the material in the text.

3.1 **Intercultural Sensitivity: Recognizing Variations** You represent a Canadian toy company that's negotiating to buy miniature truck wheels from a manufacturer in Osaka, Japan. In your first meeting, you explain that your company expects to control the design of the wheels as well as the materials that are used to make them. The manufacturer's representative looks down and says softly, "Perhaps that will be difficult." You press for agreement, and to emphasize your willingness to buy, you show the prepared contract you've brought with you. However, the manufacturer seems increasingly vague and uninterested. What cultural differences may be interfering with effective communication in this situation? Explain.

3.2 **Ethical Choices** A U.S. manager wants to export T-shirts to a West African country, but a West African official expects a special payment before allowing the shipment into his country. How can the two sides resolve their different approaches without violating U.S. rules against bribing foreign officials? On the basis of the information presented in Chapter 1, would you consider this situation an ethical dilemma or an ethical lapse? Please explain.

3.3 **Teamwork** Working with two other students, prepare a list of 10 examples of slang (in your own language) that might be misinterpreted or misunderstood during a business conversation with someone from another culture. Next to each example, suggest other words you might use to convey the same message. Do the alternatives mean *exactly* the same as the original slang or idiom?

3.4 **Intercultural Communication: Studying Cultures** Choose a specific country, such as India, Portugal, Bolivia, Thailand, or Nigeria, with which you are not familiar. Research the culture and write a brief summary of what a U.S. manager would need to know about concepts of personal space and rules of social behavior in order to conduct business successfully in that country.

3.5 **Multicultural Workforce: Bridging Differences** Differences in gender, age, and physical abilities contribute to the diversity of today's workforce. Working with a classmate, role-play a conversation in which
   a. A woman is being interviewed for a job by a male personnel manager
   b. An older person is being interviewed for a job by a younger personnel manager
   c. An employee who is a native speaker of English is being interviewed for a job by a hiring manager who is a recent immigrant with relatively poor English skills
   How did differences between the applicant and the interviewer shape the communication? What can you do to improve communication in such situations?

3.6 **Intercultural Sensitivity: Understanding Attitudes** As the director of marketing for a telecommunications firm based in Germany, you're negotiating with an official in Guangzhou, China, who's in charge of selecting a new telephone system for the city. You insist that the specifications be spelled out in the contract. However, your Chinese counterpart seems to have little interest in technical and financial details. What can you do or say to break this intercultural deadlock and obtain the contract so that both parties are comfortable?

3.7 **Cultural Variations: Ability Differences** You are a new manager at K & J Brick, a masonry products company that is now run by the two sons of the man who founded it 50 years ago. For years, the co-owners have invited the management team to a wilderness lodge for a combination of outdoor sports and annual business planning meetings.

You don't want to miss the event, but you know that the outdoor activities weren't designed for someone with your physical impairments. Draft a short memo to the rest of the management team, suggesting changes to the annual event that will allow all managers to participate.

3.8   Culture and Time: Dealing with Variations When a company knows that a scheduled delivery time given by an overseas firm is likely to be flexible, managers may buy in larger quantities or may order more often to avoid running out of product before the next delivery. Identify three other management decisions that may be influenced by differing cultural concepts of time, and make notes for a short (two-minute) presentation to your class.

3.9   Intercultural Communication: Using Interpreters Imagine that you're the lead negotiator for a company that's trying to buy a factory in Prague, capital of the Czech Republic. Although you haven't spent much time in the country in the past decade, your parents grew up near Prague, so you understand and speak the language fairly well. However, you wonder about the advantages and disadvantages of using an interpreter anyway. For example, you may have more time to think if you wait for an intermediary to translate the other side's position. Decide whether to hire an interpreter, and then write a brief (two- or three-paragraph) explanation of your decision.

3.10   Internet: Translation Software Explore the powers and limitations of computer translation at AltaVista, www.altavista.com. Click on "translate" and enter a sentence such as "We are enclosing a purchase order for four dozen computer monitors." Select "English to Spanish" and click to complete the translation. Once you've read the Spanish version, cut and paste it into the "text for translation" box, select "Spanish to English," and click to translate. Try translating the same English sentence into German, French, or Italian and then back into English. How do the results of each translation differ? What are the implications for the use of automated translation services and back-translation? How could you use this website to sharpen your intercultural communication skills?

3.11   Intercultural Communication: Improving Skills You've been assigned to host a group of Swedish college students who are visiting your college for the next two weeks. They've all studied English but this is their first trip to your area. Make a list of at least eight slang terms and idioms they are likely to hear on campus. How will you explain each phrase? When speaking with the Swedish students, what word or words might you substitute for each slang term or idiom?

Expand Your Knowledge

For live links to the websites that follow, visit this text's website at www.prenhall.com/bovee. When you log on, select Chapter 3, then select "Student Resources," click on the URL of the featured website, and review the website to complete these exercises.

Exploring the Best of the Web

Cultural Savvy for Competitive Advantage
www.executiveplanet.com
Want to be more competitive when doing business across borders? Executive Planet offers quick introductions to expected business practices in a number of countries, from setting up appointments to giving gifts to negotiating deals. Visit www.executiveplanet.com and browse the country reports to answer the following questions.

1. What sort of clothes should you pack for a business trip to Mexico that will include both meetings and social events?
2. You've been trying to sell your products to a Saudi Arabian company whose executives treat you to an extravagant evening of dining and entertainment. Can you take this as a positive sign that they're likely to buy from you?
3. You collect antique clocks as a hobby, and you plan to give one of your favorites to the president of a Chinese company you plan to visit. Would such a gift likely help or hurt your relationship with this person?

Exploring the Web on Your Own

Review these chapter-related websites on your own to learn more about intercultural communication.

1. Background Notes, www.state.gov, provides helpful background information on every country with which the United States has an official relationship. This site is published by the U.S. State Department. Just click on Country Background Notes in the Travel and Living Abroad section.
2. Geert Hofstede Analysis, www.cyborlink.com/besite/hofstede.htm, offers insight into how various countries differ—sometimes widely—in the personal and social values that affect business.
3. Travlang, www3.travlang.com, can help you learn a foreign language. Check out the site's translating dictionaries and learn a new word in a foreign language every day.

Learn Interactively

Interactive Study Guide

Go to the Companion Website at www.prenhall.com/bovee. For Chapter 3, take advantage of the interactive "Study Guide" to test your knowledge of the chapter. Get instant feedback on whether you need additional studying.

Also, visit this site's "Study Hall," where you'll find an abundance of valuable resources that will help you succeed in this course.

Peak Performance Grammar and Mechanics

To improve your skill with verbs, visit www.prenhall.com/onekey, click "Peak Performance Grammar and Mechanics," click "Grammar Basics," then click "Verbs." Take the Pretest to determine whether you have any weak areas. Then review those areas in the Refresher Course. Take the Follow-Up Test to check your grasp of verbs. For an extra challenge or advanced practice, take the Advanced Test. Finally, for additional reinforcement in verbs, go to www.prenhall.com/bovee, where you'll find "Improve Your Grammar, Mechanics, and Usage" exercises.

Testing Your Understanding—Unit I

Business Communication Today,
Chapter 3: Communicating Interculturally

 Pages 4–12
CHECKING YOUR COMPREHENSION

Identify the following statements as true or false.

1. People learn culture directly and indirectly from other members of their group.

2. In a high-context culture people rely more on verbal communication and less on circumstances and cues to convey meaning.

3. The best approach when communicating with people in other cultures is to treat others the way you want to be treated.

Choose the best answer for each of the following questions.

4. Culture influences everything about communication, except
   a. the meaning of words.
   b. significance of gestures.
   c. skills.
   d. importance of time and space.

5. According to the chapter, what is deeply embedded in the culture of the United States?
   a. notion of progress
   b. completeness
   c. coherence
   d. ethnocentrism

6. According to the chapter, which of the following is considered a cultural group?
   a. professional group
   b. religious group
   c. country
   d. all of the above

7. Which of the following cultural contexts affects business communication in high-context companies?
   a. Position and status are valued much more than competence.
   b. Workers rely on detailed background information.
   c. Meetings have fixed agendas and plenty of advance notice.
   d. Information is highly centralized and controlled.

Answer each of the following questions.

8. List the three contextual differences that cultures use to approach situations.

9. What are the advantages of a diverse workforce?

10. What is meant by the statement "A culture tends to be complete"?

11. List six challenges that U.S. and European executives encounter when managing across countries.

Define each term as it is used in the chapter.

12. cultural pluralism

13. cultural context

14. xenophobia

Discussion and Critical Thinking Questions

1. Discuss the interaction of culture and communication.

2. Based on the strategies E-Softsys utilizes to manage its diverse workforce, what suggestions do you have for companies with global workforces?

3. To what category does the United States belong in terms of cultural context? What does this mean in terms of decision making, problem solving, and negotiating?

Pages 13–19
CHECKING YOUR COMPREHENSION

Identify the following statements as true or false.

1. In Kenya, paying bribes is considered a way of life.

2. Non-verbal communication is a reliable guide for communicators in other cultures to determine the meaning of a message.

3. According to the chapter, English is the language most often used in international business.

Choose the best answer for each of the following questions.

4. In Asian culture, the oldest employees
   a. earn the most respect.
   b. hold the most impressive titles.
   c. hold the most powerful jobs.
   d. all of the above.

5. In which of the following countries do workers not meet 1,800 annual working hours?
   a. United States
   b. Sweden
   c. Spain
   d. Australia

6. According to the chapter, women's communication style in decision making is to emphasize
   a. results.
   b. tasks.
   c. facts and figures.
   d. collaboration and the maintenance of positive business relationships.

7. The authors suggest that you should do the following to improve intercultural communication skills in another culture except
   a. conduct research on the culture.
   b. apologize for making cultural mistakes.
   c. become fluent in the language.
   d. read newspapers and magazines from the country.

Answer each of the following questions.

8. List the four areas in which social rules can vary from culture to culture.

9. In which countries is direct eye contact considered aggressive?

10. When observing non-verbal behaviors in a culture, what behaviors should you look for?

11. List the communication style differences between men and women.

Define each term as it is used in the chapter.

12. Napoleonic code

13. social behavior

14. gender differences

Discussion and Critical Thinking Questions

1. Discuss the impact of the Foreign Corrupt Practices Act in 1977 enacted by the United States government.

2. What challenges do older workers face in the United States?

3. What advice would you give a new company that was intending to do business internationally?

Pages 20–29
CHECKING YOUR COMPREHENSION

Identify the following statements as true or false.

1. When sending written communication to businesspeople from another culture, you should prepare the communication to meet their expectations.

2. If you do not understand a comment made by a non-native English speaker, it is disrespectful to ask the person to repeat what he or she has said.

3. You should not rely on machine translations for important messages.

4. Writing and reading are harder in a second language than speaking and listening.

Choose the best answer for each of the following questions.

5. When addressing a letter to a company in Japan, the date would be expressed as
   a. July 3, 2006.
   b. 2006-07-03.
   c. 07-03-06.
   d. 2006-03-07.

6. To be more effective in intercultural conversations, you should not
   a. clarify what will happen next.
   b. learn foreign phrases.
   c. talk down to the other person.
   d. speak slowly and clearly.

7. Which of the following should a person do to listen more effectively in intercultural situations?
   a. Interrupt a conversation to ask for clarification.
   b. Jump to conclusions.
   c. Demand to have an interpreter.
   d. Let people finish what they have to say.

Answer each of the following questions.

8. List the six guidelines for speaking more clearly in intercultural conversations.

9. According to the chapter, what is the benefit of employing professional interpreters and translators?

10. Identify the benefits of using machine translation.

11. Explain Figure 3.7 and identify what type of correspondence it illustrates.

Define each term as it is used in the chapter.

12. idiomatic phrases

13. back-translation

14. machine translation

Discussion and Critical Thinking Questions

1. Based on the information provided in the chapter, what are the advantages of technologies in communicating with foreign colleagues?

2. What is the greatest challenge in learning conversational English in the United States? What does this indicate about the difficulties in learning to converse in other languages?

3. According to the chapter, communication styles vary from culture to culture. What is suggested regarding how to overcome the differing communication styles, including level of directness, the degree of formality, and preferences for written versus spoken communication?

Chapter Review
END OF CHAPTER ANALYSIS

Choose the best answer for each of the following questions.

1. The author employs all of the following techniques for making the material easier to read except
   a. boldface.
   b. marginal notations.
   c. graphics.
   d. chapter outline.

2. What is the overall purpose of this chapter?
   a. To understand the challenges and potential opportunities of intercultural communication.
   b. To learn how to help others adapt to other cultures.
   c. To understand the importance of customizing verbal and written correspondence for international companies.
   d. To provide an analysis of the ethical and legal issues of doing business globally.

3. The chapter addresses all of the following areas except
   a. strategies for studying other cultures.
   b. overcoming ethnocentrism and stereotyping.
   c. respecting different communication styles.
   d. giving and responding to constructive feedback.

Group Project

1. Create a communications plan for a company based in the United States that has just merged with a company in India. List what should be done by the CEO and explain how each item will establish successful communication.

Journal Ideas

1. Based on the information from the chapter, what do you think are the three biggest challenges an individual faces in intercultural communications?

2. If you were someone from a low-context culture doing business with a person living in a high-context culture, what are some of the ethical issues you might encounter?

Unit II

From

Neil A. Campbell
Jane B. Reece
Martha R. Taylor
Eric J. Simon

Biology:
Concepts & Connections
Fifth Edition

Chapter 21:
Nutrition and Digestion

An Introduction to Biology

Biology is defined as the science of life and of living organisms, including their structure, function, growth, origin, evolution, and distribution. This incorporates large structures such as the biosphere, which consists of all the environments on earth, down to the smallest, the organelle, which is a functional element of a cell. Biology is concerned with the impact that humans have on the natural world. There are many branches of biology such as anthropology, anatomy, botany, and zoology.

Introduction to biology courses are electives for most students, although most colleges require at least one physical science course accompanied by laboratory participation. Biology is a required course for those students seeking majors in pre-professional health and science-related careers. A degree in biology will prepare students to enter both research careers and applied careers in such fields as medicine, ecology, forestry and wildlife management, conservation, and oceanography.

Strategies for Reading Biology

When reading a biology textbook, it is necessary to define all new terms and pay close attention to all illustrations and figures. Since there will be many facts and details, it is often necessary to note the reasons and explanations that support the relationships of specific concepts. To visualize specific progressions, use a concept map or flow chart. The relationships between new concepts can be made clear by using hierarchical organizers, which show superordinate and subordinate relationships.

Getting Their Fill of Krill

WHALES ARE THE LARGEST ANIMALS in the world. Few other species, living or extinct, even approach their great size. The humpback whale, shown in the pictures on the facing page, is a medium-sized member of the whale clan. It can be 16 m long and weigh up to 65,000 kg (72 tons), about as much as 70 mid-size cars.

It takes an enormous amount of food to support a 72-ton animal. Humpback whales eat small fishes and crustaceans called krill, shown above. The painting on the next page shows a remarkable technique humpbacks often use to corral food organisms before gulping them in. Beginning about 20 m below the ocean surface, a humpback swims slowly in an upward spiral, blowing air bubbles as it goes. The rising bubbles form a cylindrical screen, or "bubble net." Krill and fish inside the bubble net swim away from the bubbles and become concentrated in the center of the cylinder. The whale then surges up through the center of the net with its mouth open, harvesting the catch in one giant gulp.

Humpback whales strain their food from seawater. Instead of teeth, these giants have an array of comblike plates called baleen on each side of their upper jaw. Notice the white baleen in the open mouth of the whale in the photograph on the facing page. To start feeding, a humpback whale opens its mouth, expands its throat, and takes a huge gulp of seawater. When its mouth closes, the baleen acts as a sieve: Water is forced back out through spaces in the baleen, trapping a mass of food in the mouth. The food is then swallowed whole, passing into the stomach, where digestion begins. The humpback's stomach can hold about half a ton of food at a time, and in a typical day, the animal's digestive system will process as much as 2 tons of krill and fish.

In about four months, a humpback whale eats and digests over 200 tons of foo

The humpback and most other large whales are endangered species, having been hunted almost to extinction for meat and whale oil by the 1960s. Today, most nations honor an international ban on whaling, and some species are showing signs of recovery. Humpbacks still roam the Atlantic and Pacific oceans. They feed in polar regions during summer months and migrate

Nutrition and Digestion

to warmer oceans to breed when temperatures begin to fall. The photograph on this page was taken during summer in the Pacific Northwest. Food is so abundant there that humpbacks harvest much more energy than they burn each day. Much of the excess is stored as a thick layer of fat, or blubber, just under their skin. After a summer of feasting, humpback whales leave Glacier Bay and head south to breeding and calving grounds off the Hawaiian Islands, some 6,000 km away. Living off body fat, they eat little, if at all, until they return to Alaskan waters eight months later.

In about four months, a humpback whale eats and digests over 200 tons of food and stores enough fat to keep its 72-ton body active for another eight months—a remarkable feat and a fitting introduction to this chapter on animal nutrition and digestion. ■ ■ ■

21.1 Animals ingest their food in a variety of ways

All animals eat other organisms—dead or alive, whole or by the piece. In general, animals fall into one of three dietary categories. **Herbivores** (from the Latin *herba,* green crop, and *vorus,* devouring), such as cattle, gorillas, snails, and sea urchins, eat mainly autotrophs (plants and algae). **Carnivores** (from the Latin *carne,* flesh), such as lions, hawks, spiders, and snakes, eat other animals. Animals that ingest *both* plants and animals are called **omnivores** (from the Latin *omnis,* all). Omnivores include crows, cockroaches, raccoons, and humans, who evolved as hunters, gatherers, and scavengers.

How do animals obtain and ingest their food? There are a variety of ways. **Suspension feeders** extract food particles suspended in the surrounding water. For example, the humpback whale described in the chapter introduction uses its baleen to sift krill and small fish from the water. Clams and oysters are also suspension feeders. A film of mucus on their gills traps tiny morsels suspended in the water, and beating cilia on the gills sweep the food along to the mouth. Tube worms (Figure 21.1A) filter food particles with their feathery tentacles.

Substrate feeders live in or on their food source and eat their way through it. Figure 21.1B shows a leaf miner caterpillar, the larva of a moth, eating its way through the soft green tissue inside an oak leaf. The dark spots are a trail of feces that the caterpillar leaves in its wake. Earthworms are also substrate feeders. They eat their way through the soil, digesting partially decayed organic material as they go. In doing so, they help aerate the soil, making it more suitable for plants.

Fluid feeders obtain food by sucking nutrient-rich fluids from a living host, either a plant or an animal. Aphids, for example, tap into the sugary sap in plants. Bloodsuckers, such as mosquitoes and ticks, pierce animals with needlelike mouthparts. The female mosquito in **Figure 21.1C** has just filled her abdomen with a meal of human blood. (Only female mosquitoes suck blood; males live on plant nectar.) In contrast to such parasitic fluid feeders, which harm their hosts, some fluid feeders actually benefit their hosts. For example, hummingbirds and bees move pollen between flowers as they fluid-feed on nectar.

Rather than filtering food from water, eating their way through a substrate, or sucking fluids, most animals are **bulk feeders**, meaning they ingest relatively large pieces of food. **Figure 21.1D** shows a great blue heron preparing to swallow its prey. A bulk feeder uses such diverse utensils as tentacles, pincers, claws, poisonous fangs, or jaws and teeth to kill its prey, to tear off pieces of meat or vegetation, or to take mouthfuls of animal or plant products.

Whatever the type of food or feeding mechanism, the processing of food involves four stages, as we see next.

? Blue whales, the largest animals ever to live, feed on krill. Blue whales are _____ feeders.

suspension ∎

Figure 21.1C
A fluid feeder
(mosquito)

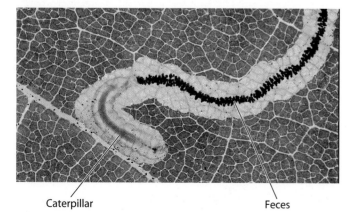

Figure 21.1B   A substrate feeder (caterpillar)

Caterpillar   Feces

Figure 21.1A   A suspension feeder (tube worm)

Figure 21.1D   A bulk feeder (great blue heron)

21.2 Overview: Food processing occurs in four stages

So far we have discussed what animals eat and how they feed. As shown in **Figure 21.2A**, ❶ **ingestion**, the act of eating, is only the first of four main stages of food processing. ❷ The second stage, **digestion**, is the breaking down of food into molecules small enough for the body to absorb. Digestion typically occurs in two phases. First, food may be mechanically broken into smaller pieces. In animals with teeth, the process of chewing or tearing breaks large chunks of food into smaller ones. The second phase of digestion is the chemical breakdown process called hydrolysis. Catalyzed by specific enzymes, hydrolysis breaks chemical bonds in food molecules by adding water to them (see Module 3.3).

Most of the organic matter in food consists of proteins, fats, and carbohydrates—all large polymers (multi-unit molecules made up of small units called monomers). Animals cannot use these materials directly for two reasons. First, as macromolecules, these polymers are too large to pass through plasma membranes and enter the cells. Second, an animal needs monomers to make the polymers of its own body. Most of the polymers in food (for instance, the proteins in beans) are different from those that make up an animal's body.

All organisms use the same monomers to make their polymers. For instance, cats, humans, and bean plants all make their proteins from the same 20 kinds of amino acids. Digestion in an animal breaks the macromolecules in food into their component monomers. As shown in **Figure 21.2B**, proteins are split into amino acids, polysaccharides and disaccharides are split into monosaccharides, nucleic acids are split into nucleotides, and fats are split into glycerol and fatty acids. The animal can then use these monomers to make the specific polymers it needs (see Modules 6.14 and 6.15).

The last two stages of food processing occur after digestion. ❸ In the third stage, **absorption**, the cells lining the digestive tract take up (absorb) the products of digestion—small molecules such as amino acids and simple sugars. From the digestive tract, these nutrients travel in the blood

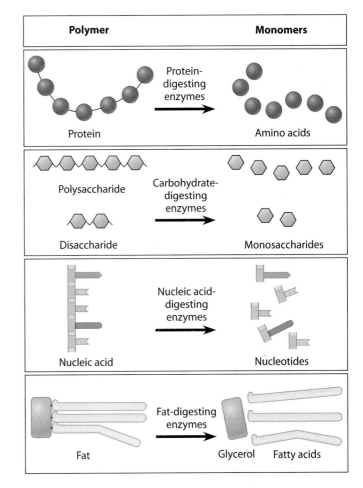

Polymer		Monomers

Figure 21.2B Chemical digestion: the breakdown of polymers to monomers

to body cells, where they are joined together to make the macromolecules of the cells or broken down further to provide energy. In an animal that eats much more than its body immediately uses, many of the nutrient molecules are converted to fat for storage. ❹ In the fourth and last stage of food processing, **elimination**, undigested material passes out of the digestive tract.

How can an animal digest food without digesting its own cells and tissues? After all, digestive enzymes hydrolyze the same biological materials (such as proteins, carbohydrates, and fats) that animals are made of—and it is obviously important to avoid digesting oneself! Animals avoid the risk of self-digestion by processing food in specialized compartments, as we discuss in the next module.

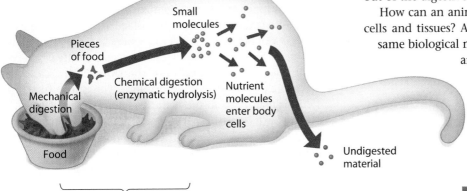

❶ Ingestion   ❷ Digestion   ❸ Absorption   ❹ Elimination

Figure 21.2A The four main stages of food processing

? What are the two main digestive processes?

■ Mechanical breakdown and chemical breakdown (enzymatic hydrolysis)

21.3 Digestion occurs in specialized compartments

Food vacuoles are the simplest digestive compartments. A cell engulfs food by phagocytosis, and the newly formed food vacuole fuses with a lysosome containing hydrolytic enzymes (see Module 4.10). Sponges (see Module 18.5) digest their food entirely in food vacuoles. In contrast, most animals have an internal compartment in which digestion occurs outside of cells, enabling an animal to devour much larger food than could be ingested by phagocytosis alone.

As we saw in Chapter 18, cnidarians and flatworms have a **gastrovascular cavity**, a digestive compartment with a single opening, the **mouth**. **Figure 21.3A** shows a hydra digesting a small crustacean called *Daphnia*. ❶ Gland cells lining the gastrovascular cavity secrete digestive enzymes that ❷ break down the soft tissues of the prey. ❸ Other cells engulf small food particles, which ❹ are broken down in food vacuoles. Undigested materials are expelled through the mouth.

Most animals have an **alimentary canal**, a digestive tube with two openings, a mouth and an anus. Because food moves in one direction, specialized regions of the tube can carry out digestion and absorption of nutrients in sequence.

Food entering the mouth usually passes into a **pharynx**, or throat. Depending on the species, the **esophagus** may channel food to a crop, gizzard, or stomach. A **crop** is a pouch-like organ in which food is softened and stored. **Stomachs** and **gizzards** may also store food temporarily, but they are more muscular and they churn and grind the food. Chemical digestion and nutrient absorption occur mainly in the **intestine**. Undigested materials are expelled through the **anus**.

Figure 21.3B illustrates three examples of alimentary canals. The digestive tract of an earthworm includes a muscular pharynx that sucks food in through the mouth. Food passes through the esophagus and is stored in the crop. The muscular gizzard, which contains small bits of sand and gravel, pulverizes the food. Digestion and absorption occur

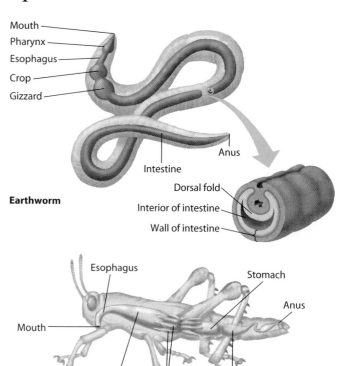

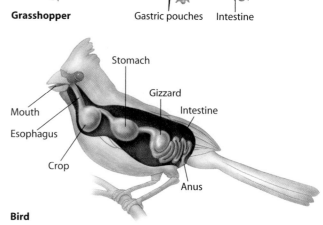

Figure 21.3B   Three examples of alimentary canals

in the intestine. As the enlargement shows, a dorsal fold of the intestinal wall increases the surface area for absorption.

A grasshopper also has a crop where food is stored and moistened. Most chemical digestion occurs in the stomach. Gastric pouches extending from the stomach increase the surface area for nutrient absorption. The short intestine functions mainly to absorb water and compact wastes.

Many birds have three separate chambers: a crop, a stomach, and a gravel-filled gizzard, in which food is pulverized. Chemical digestion and absorption occur in the intestine.

Next we look at the human digestive system.

?   What is an advantage of an alimentary canal, compared to a gastrovascular cavity?

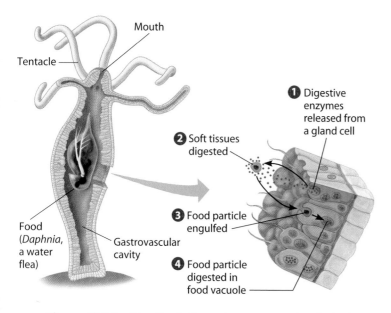

Figure 21.3A   Digestion in the gastrovascular cavity of a hydra

Specialized regions can carry out digestion and absorption sequentially. ■

21.4 The human digestive system consists of an alimentary canal and accessory glands

As an introduction to our own digestive system, **Figure 21.4** provides an overview of the human alimentary canal and the digestive glands associated with it. The main parts of the canal are the mouth, oral cavity, tongue, pharynx, esophagus, stomach, small intestine, large intestine, rectum, and anus. The digestive glands—the salivary glands, pancreas, and liver—are labeled in blue on the figure. They secrete digestive juices that enter the alimentary canal through ducts. Secretions from the liver are stored in the gallbladder before they are released into the intestine.

Once food is swallowed, muscles propel it through the alimentary canal by **peristalsis**, rhythmic waves of contraction of smooth muscles in the walls of the digestive tract (see Module 21.8). In only 5–10 seconds, food passes from the pharynx down the esophagus and into the stomach. A constriction at the base of the esophagus keeps food in the stomach.

A muscular ringlike valve, called the **pyloric sphincter**, regulates the passage of food out of the stomach and into the small intestine. The sphincter works like a drawstring, closing off the tube and keeping food in the stomach long enough for stomach acids and enzymes to begin digestion. The final steps of digestion and nutrient absorption occur in the small intestine over a period of 5–6 hours. Undigested material moves slowly through the large intestine (taking 12–24 hours), and feces are expelled through the anus.

In the next several modules, we follow a snack—an apple and some crackers and cheese—through the alimentary canal to see in more detail what happens to the food in each of the processing stations along the way.

? What is peristalsis, and what is its function in our digestive system?

■ Wavelike contractions of smooth muscles that move food along the alimentary canal

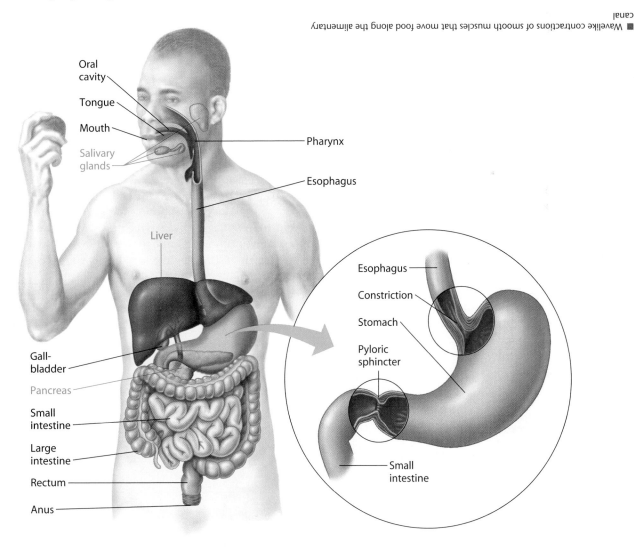

Figure 21.4 The human digestive tract

21.5 Digestion begins in the oral cavity

As you anticipate your apple, cheese, and crackers, your salivary glands may start delivering **saliva** through ducts to the oral cavity even before you take a bite. This is a response to the sight or smell (or even thought) of food. The presence of food in the oral cavity continues to stimulate salivation. In a typical day, your salivary glands secrete more than a liter of saliva.

Saliva contains several substances important in food processing. A slippery glycoprotein protects the soft lining of the mouth and lubricates food for easier swallowing. Buffers neutralize food acids, helping prevent tooth decay. Antibacterial agents kill many of the bacteria that enter the mouth with food. Saliva also contains salivary amylase, a digestive enzyme that begins hydrolyzing the starch in your cracker.

Mechanical and chemical digestion begin in the oral cavity. Chewing cuts, smashes, and grinds food, making it easier to swallow and exposing more food surface to digestive enzymes. As **Figure 21.5** shows, you have four kinds of teeth. Starting at the front on one side of the upper or lower jaw, there are two bladelike incisors. These you use for biting into your apple. Behind the incisors is a single pointed canine tooth. (Canine teeth are much bigger in carnivores, which use them to kill and rip apart prey.) Next come two premolars and three molars, which grind and crush the food. (The third molar, a "wisdom" tooth, does not appear in some people.)

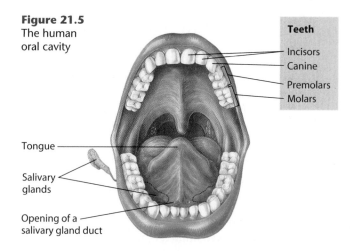

Figure 21.5
The human
oral cavity

Teeth
Incisors
Canine
Premolars
Molars

Tongue

Salivary
glands

Opening of a
salivary gland duct

Also prominent in the oral cavity is the tongue, a muscular organ covered with taste buds. Besides enabling you to taste your meal, the tongue manipulates food and helps shape it into a ball called a bolus. In swallowing, the tongue pushes the bolus to the back of the oral cavity and into the pharynx.

? Chewing functions in _____ digestion, and salivary amylase initiates the chemical digestion of _____.

■ mechanical . . . starch

21.6 The food and breathing passages both open into the pharynx

Openings into both the esophagus and the **trachea** (windpipe) are in the pharynx. Most of the time, as shown on the left in **Figure 21.6**, the esophageal opening is closed off by a sphincter (blue arrows), and air enters the trachea and proceeds to the lungs (black arrows). This situation changes when you start to swallow some of the apple you've just finished chewing. A bolus of food enters the pharynx, triggering the swallowing reflex (center drawing); the esophageal sphincter relaxes and allows the bolus to enter the esophagus (green arrow). At the same time, the larynx (voice box) moves upward and tips the epiglottis (a flap of cartilage and fibrous connective tissue) over the tracheal opening. In this position, the epiglottis prevents food from passing into the trachea. You can see this motion in the bobbing of your larynx (also called your Adam's apple) during swallowing. After the bolus enters the esophagus, the larynx moves downward, the epiglottis moves up again, and the breathing passage reopens (right drawing). The esophageal sphincter contracts above the bolus.

? What prevents food from going down the wrong tube?

■ The epiglottis tips down over the opening to the trachea during swallowing.

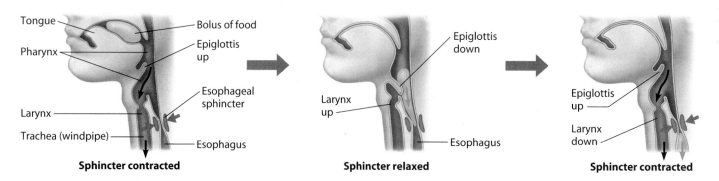

Tongue
Pharynx
Larynx
Trachea (windpipe)

Bolus of food
Epiglottis up
Esophageal sphincter
Esophagus

Sphincter contracted

Epiglottis down
Larynx up
Esophagus

Sphincter relaxed

Epiglottis up
Larynx down

Sphincter contracted

Figure 21.6 The swallowing reflex

21.7 The Heimlich maneuver can save lives

Sometimes our swallowing mechanism goes awry. A person may eat too quickly or fail to chew food thoroughly. Or an infant may swallow a toy or other object too big to pass through the esophagus. Such mishaps can lead to a blocked pharynx or trachea. Air cannot flow into the trachea, causing the person to choke. If breathing is not restored within minutes, brain damage or death may result.

To save someone who is choking, it is essential to dislodge any foreign objects in the throat and get air flowing. This quick assistance often comes through the use of the Heimlich maneuver. The procedure, invented by Dr. Henry Heimlich in the 1970s, allows people with little medical training to step in and aid a choking victim.

The maneuver is often performed on someone who is seated or standing up. Stand behind the victim and place your arms around the victim's waist. Make a fist with one hand, and place it against the victim's upper abdomen, well below the rib cage. Then place the other hand over the fist and press into the victim's abdomen with a quick upward thrust. When done correctly, the diaphragm is forcibly elevated, pushing air into the trachea. This procedure should be repeated until the lodged object is forced up and out of the victim's airway (Figure 21.7). The maneuver can also be performed on drowning victims to first clear the lungs of water before beginning CPR. And individuals can use their own fists or the back of a chair to force air upward and dislodge a foreign object from their own pharynx or trachea.

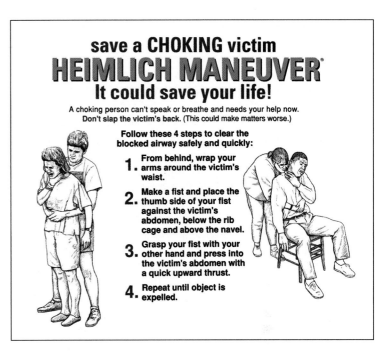

Figure 21.7 The Heimlich maneuver for helping choking victims

? If a piece of food is stuck in the pharynx, what effect could it have on nearby structures? (*Hint:* See Figure 21.6.)

■ The epiglottis may be tipped down, blocking the opening to the trachea.

21.8 The esophagus squeezes food along to the stomach by peristalsis

The esophagus is a muscular tube that conveys food boluses from the pharynx to the stomach. The muscles at the very top of the esophagus are under voluntary control; thus, the act of swallowing begins voluntarily. But then involuntary waves of contraction by smooth muscles in the rest of the esophagus take over. Figure 21.8 shows how waves of muscle contraction—peristalsis—squeeze a bolus toward the stomach. As food—such as your chewed up bite of apple—is swallowed, muscles above the bolus contract (blue arrows), pushing the bolus downward. At the same time, muscles around the bolus relax, allowing the passageway to open. Muscle contractions continue in waves until the bolus enters the stomach.

Waves of smooth muscle contraction also move materials through the small and large intestine. But first we explore what happens when your snack reaches the stomach.

? How does food get from the pharynx to the stomach of an astronaut in the weightless environment of a space station?

■ By peristalsis

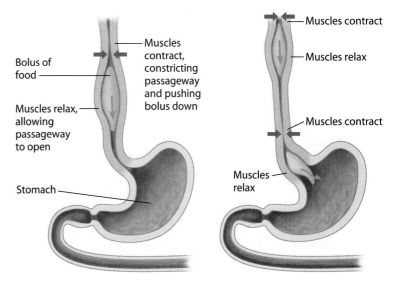

Figure 21.8 Peristalsis moving a food bolus down the esophagus

The stomach stores food and breaks it down with acid and enzymes

Having a stomach is the main reason we do not need to eat constantly. Our stomach is highly elastic and can stretch to accommodate about 2 liters (L) of food and drink, usually enough to satisfy our body's needs for many hours.

Some chemical digestion occurs in the stomach. The stomach secretes **gastric juice**, which is made up of mucus, enzymes, and strong acid. One function of the acid is to break apart the cells in food. The acid also kills most bacteria and other microbes that are swallowed with food.

The interior surface of the stomach wall is highly folded, and as both the micrograph and diagram in **Figure 21.9** show, it is dotted with pits leading down into tubular gastric glands. The gastric glands have three types of cells that secrete different components of the gastric juice. Mucous cells (dark pink) secrete mucus, which lubricates and protects the cells lining the stomach; parietal cells (yellow) secrete hydrochloric acid (HCl); and chief cells (tan) secrete pepsinogen, an inactive form of the enzyme pepsin.

The diagram on the far right of the figure indicates how pepsinogen, HCl, and pepsin interact in the stomach. ❶ Pepsinogen and HCl are secreted into the lumen (cavity) of the stomach. ❷ Next, the HCl converts pepsinogen to pepsin. ❸ Pepsin then activates more pepsinogen, starting a chain reaction. Pepsin begins the chemical digestion of proteins—those in your cheese snack, for instance. It splits the polypeptide chains of the proteins into smaller polypeptides. This action primes the proteins for further digestion, which will occur in the small intestine.

What prevents gastric juice from digesting away the stomach lining? Secreting pepsin in the inactive form of pepsinogen helps protect the cells of the gastric glands, and mucus helps protect the stomach lining from both pepsin and acid. Still, the epithelium is constantly eroded. Enough new cells are generated by mitosis to replace the stomach lining completely about every three days.

Cells in our gastric glands do not secrete gastric juice constantly. Their activity is regulated by a combination of nerve signals and hormones. When you see, smell, or taste food, a signal from your brain to your stomach stimulates your gastric glands to secrete gastric juice. Once you have food in your stomach, substances in the food stimulate cells in the stomach wall to release the hormone **gastrin** into the circulatory system. Gastrin circulates in the bloodstream, returning to the stomach wall. When it arrives there, it stimulates further secretion of gastric juice. As much as 3 L of gastric juice may be secreted a day. A negative-feedback mechanism like the one we described in Module 20.14 inhibits the secretion of gastric juice when the stomach contents become too acidic. The acid inhibits the release of gastrin, and with less gastrin in the blood, the gastric glands secrete less gastric juice.

About every 20 seconds, the stomach contents are mixed by the churning action of muscles in the stomach wall. You

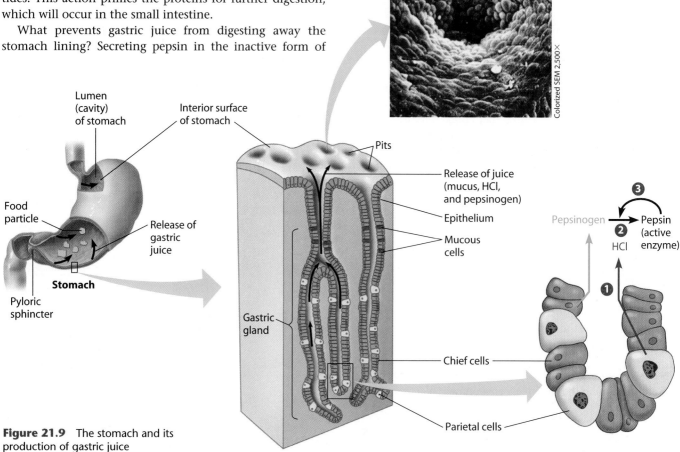

Figure 21.9 The stomach and its production of gastric juice

may feel hunger pangs when your empty stomach churns. (Other sensations of hunger result from appetite-controlling hormones that we will discuss in Module 21.22.) As a result of mixing and enzyme action, what begins in the stomach as a recently swallowed apple, cracker, and cheese snack becomes a nutrient-rich broth known as **acid chyme.**

The opening between the esophagus and the stomach is usually closed until a bolus arrives. Occasional backflow of acid chyme into the lower end of the esophagus causes the feeling we call heartburn (which should more accurately be called esophagus-burn). Some people suffer this backflow frequently and severely enough to harm the lining of the esophagus, a condition called GERD (gastroesophageal reflux disease).

Between the stomach and the small intestine, the pyloric sphincter helps regulate the passage of acid chyme from the stomach into the small intestine. With the acid chyme leaving the stomach only a squirt at a time, the stomach takes about 2–6 hours to empty after a meal. An acid chyme rich in fats stimulates the small intestine to release a hormone that slows the emptying of the stomach, providing more time for the digestion of fats in the intestine. Other hormones secreted by the small intestine influence the release of digestive juices from the pancreas and gallbladder.

We'll continue with the digestion of your snack in Module 21.11. But first, we'll consider the digestive problem of gastric ulcers.

? If you add pepsinogen to a test tube containing protein dissolved in distilled water, not much protein will be digested. What inorganic substance could you add to the tube to accelerate protein digestion? What effect will it have?

■ Hydrochloric acid or some other acid will convert inactive pepsinogen to active pepsin, which will begin the digestion of proteins.

21.10 Bacterial infections can cause ulcers

A stomachful of digestive juice laced with strong acid breaks apart the cells in our food, kills bacteria, and begins the digestion of proteins. At the same time, these chemicals, acidic enough to dissolve iron nails, can be harmful. A gel-like coat of mucus normally protects the stomach wall from the corrosive effect of digestive juice, but this is not foolproof protection. When it fails, open sores called **gastric ulcers** can develop in the stomach wall. The symptoms are usually a gnawing pain in the upper abdomen, which may occur a few hours after eating.

Gastric ulcers were formerly thought to result from the production of too much pepsin and/or acid or too little mucus. For years, the blame was put on factors that may cause these effects, such as aspirin, ibuprofen, smoking, alcohol, coffee, and stress. However, strong evidence now points to a spiral-shaped bacterium called *Helicobacter pylori* as the primary culprit (**Figure 21.10**). The low pH of the stomach kills most microbes, but not the acid-tolerant *H. pylori*. This bacterium burrows beneath the mucus and releases harmful chemicals. Growth of *H. pylori* seems to result in a localized loss of protective mucus and damage to the cells lining the stomach. Numerous white blood cells move into the stomach wall to fight the infection, and their presence is associated with mild inflammation of the stomach, called gastritis. Gastric ulcers develop when pepsin and hydrochloric acid destroy cells faster than the cells can regenerate. Eventually, the stomach wall may erode to the point that it actually has a hole in it. This hole can lead to life-threatening infection within the abdomen or internal bleeding. *H. pylori* is found in 70–90% of ulcer and gastritis sufferers. It is also found, however, in more than 33% of healthy people. Some studies link *H. pylori* to certain kinds of stomach cancer.

Gastric ulcers usually respond to a combination of antibiotics and bismuth (the active ingredient in Pepto-Bismol),

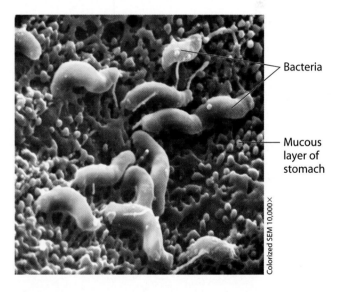

Bacteria

Mucous layer of stomach

Colorized SEM 10,000×

Figure 21.10 Ulcer-causing bacteria on the mucous layer of stomach

which eliminates the bacteria and promotes healing. Drugs that reduce stomach acidity may also help, and researchers are making progress toward developing a vaccine to prevent infection by *H. pylori*.

When digesting food leaves the stomach, it is accompanied by gastric juices, and so the first section of the small intestine—the duodenum—is also susceptible to ulcers, as is the esophagus in cases of severe GERD.

? In contrast to most microbes, the species that causes ulcers thrives in an environment with a very low _____.

pH ■

21.11 The small intestine is the major organ of chemical digestion and nutrient absorption

Returning to our journey through the digestive tract, what is the status of your snack as it passes out of the stomach into the small intestine? The food has been mechanically reduced to smaller pieces and mixed with juices; it now resembles a thick soup. Chemically, starch digestion began in the mouth, and protein breakdown began in the stomach. All other chemical digestion of the original macromolecules in the apple, cheese, and crackers occurs in the **small intestine.** Nutrients are also absorbed into the blood from the small intestine. With a length of over 6 m, the small intestine is the longest organ of the alimentary canal. (Its name is based not on its length but on its diameter, which is only about 2.5 cm; the large intestine is much shorter but has twice the diameter.)

Two large glandular organs, the pancreas and the liver, contribute to digestion in the small intestine (**Figure 21.11A**). The **pancreas** produces pancreatic juice, a mixture of digestive enzymes and an alkaline solution rich in bicarbonate. The alkaline solution neutralizes acid chyme as it enters the small intestine. The **liver** performs a wide variety of functions, including the production of bile. **Bile** contains bile salts that emulsify fats, making them more susceptible to attack by digestive enzymes. The **gallbladder** stores bile until it is needed in the small intestine. The first 25 cm or so of the small intestine is called the **duodenum.** This is where the acid chyme squirted from the stomach mixes with bile from the gallbladder, pancreatic juice from the pancreas, and digestive enzymes from gland cells in the intestinal wall itself.

Table 21.11 summarizes the processes of enzymatic digestion that occur in the small intestine. All four types of macromolecules (carbohydrates, proteins, nucleic acids, and fats) are digested. As we discuss the digestion of each, the table will help you keep track of the enzymes involved (shown in blue).

The digestion of carbohydrates that began in the oral cavity is completed in the small intestine. An enzyme called

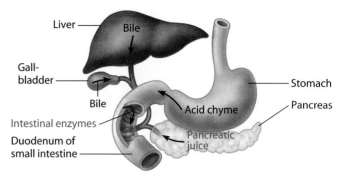

Figure 21.11A The small intestine and related digestive organs

pancreatic amylase hydrolyzes starch (a polysaccharide) into the disaccharide maltose. The enzyme maltase then splits maltose into the monosaccharide glucose. Maltase is one of a family of enzymes, each specific for the hydrolysis of a different disaccharide. Another enzyme, sucrase, hydrolyzes table sugar (sucrose), and lactase digests milk sugar (lactose, common in milk and cheese). Children generally have much more lactase than adults. Some adults lack lactase altogether, and ingesting milk products can give them cramps and diarrhea because they cannot digest the lactose (see the introduction to Chapter 3).

The small intestine also completes the digestion of proteins that was begun in the stomach. The pancreas and the duodenum secrete hydrolytic enzymes that completely dismantle polypeptides into amino acids. The enzymes trypsin and chymotrypsin break polypeptides into smaller polypeptides. Two other enzymes, aminopeptidase and carboxypeptidase, split off one amino acid at a time, working from both ends of a polypeptide. Another type of enzyme, dipeptidase, hydrolyzes fragments only two or three amino acids long.

TABLE 21.11 ENZYMATIC DIGESTION IN THE SMALL INTESTINE

Carbohydrates

Starch —Pancreatic amylase→ Maltose (and other disaccharides) —Maltase, sucrase, lactase, etc.→ Monosaccharides

Proteins

Polypeptides —Trypsin, chymotrypsin→ Smaller polypeptides —Aminopeptidase, carboxypeptidase, dipeptidase→ Amino acids

Nucleic acids

DNA and RNA —Nucleases→ Nucleotides —Other enzymes→ Nitrogenous bases, sugars, and phosphates

Fats

Fat globules —Bile salts→ Fat droplets (emulsified) —Lipase→ Fatty acids and glycerol

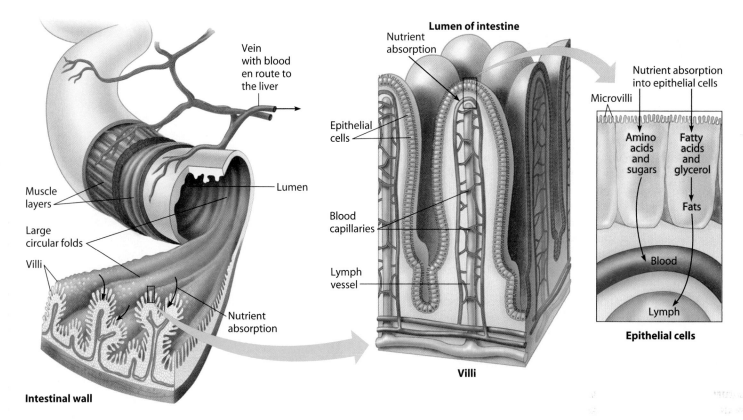

Figure 21.11B Structure of the small intestine

Working together, this enzyme team digests proteins much faster than any single enzyme could.

Yet another team of enzymes, the nucleases, hydrolyzes the nucleic acids in food. Nucleases from the pancreas split DNA and RNA (which are present in the cells of food items) into their component nucleotides. The nucleotides are then broken down into nitrogenous bases, sugars, and phosphates by other enzymes produced by the duodenal cells.

In contrast to starch and proteins, nearly all the fat in your cheese remains completely undigested until it reaches the duodenum. Hydrolysis of fats is a special problem because fats are insoluble in water. How is this problem solved? First, bile salts in bile cause fat globules to be physically broken up into smaller fat droplets, a process called emulsification. When there are many small droplets, a larger surface area of fat is exposed to lipase, an enzyme that breaks fat molecules down into fatty acids and glycerol.

By the time peristalsis has moved the mixture of chyme and digestive juices through the duodenum, chemical digestion of your meal is just about complete. The main function of the rest of the small intestine is the absorption of nutrients and water.

Structurally, the small intestine is well suited for its task of absorbing nutrients. Its lining has a huge surface area—roughly 300 m^2, about the size of a tennis court. As Figure 21.11B shows, the extensive surface area results from several kinds of folds and projections. Around the inner wall of the small intestine are large circular folds with numerous small, fingerlike projections called **villi** (singular, *villus*). Each of the epithelial cells lining a villus has many tiny surface projections, called **microvilli**. The microvilli extend into the lumen of the intestine and greatly increase the surface area across which nutrients are absorbed.

Some nutrients are absorbed by simple diffusion; other nutrients are pumped against concentration gradients into the epithelial cells. Notice that a small lymph vessel (yellow) and a network of capillaries (red, purple, and blue) penetrate the core of each villus. After fatty acids and glycerol are absorbed by an epithelial cell, these building blocks are recombined into fats that are then transported into the lymph vessel. Other absorbed nutrients, such as amino acids and sugars, pass out of the intestinal epithelium and then across the thin walls of the capillaries into the blood.

The capillaries that drain nutrients away from the villi converge into larger veins and eventually into a main vessel, the hepatic portal vein, that leads directly to the liver. The liver thus gets first access to nutrients absorbed from a meal. The liver converts many of the nutrients into new substances that the body needs. One of its main functions is to remove excess glucose from the blood and convert it to glycogen (a polysaccharide), which is stored in liver cells. From the liver, blood travels to the heart, which pumps the blood and the nutrients it contains to all parts of the body. The nutrients from your apple, cheese, and crackers are now on their way to being incorporated into your body.

Web/CD Activity 21A *Digestive System Function*

Web/CD Thinking as a Scientist *What Role Does Amylase Play in Digestion?*

? Amylase is to _____ as _____ is to DNA.

■ starch . . . nuclease

21.12 The large intestine reclaims water and compacts the feces

The **large intestine**, or **colon**, is about 1.5 m long and 5 cm in diameter. As the enlargement in **Figure 21.12** shows, it joins the small intestine at a T-shaped junction, where a sphincter controls the passage of unabsorbed food material out of the small intestine. One arm of the T is a blind pouch called the **cecum**. The **appendix**, a small, fingerlike extension of the cecum, contains a mass of white blood cells that make a minor contribution to immunity. Despite this role, the appendix itself is prone to infection (appendicitis). If this occurs, the appendix can be surgically removed without weakening the immune system.

The colon's main function is to absorb water from the alimentary canal. Altogether, about 7 L of fluid enters the lumen of the digestive tract each day as the solvent of the various digestive juices. About 90% of this water is absorbed back into the blood and tissue fluids, with the small intestine reclaiming most of it and the colon finishing the job. As the water is absorbed, the remains of the digested food become more solid as they are conveyed along the colon by peristalsis. These waste products of digestion, the **feces**, consist mainly of indigestible plant fibers (cellulose from your apple, for instance) and prokaryotes that normally live in the colon. Some of our colon bacteria, such as *E. coli,* produce important vitamins, including biotin, folic acid, several B vitamins, and vitamin K. These vitamins are absorbed into the bloodstream through the colon.

The terminal portion of the colon is the **rectum**, where the feces are stored until they can be eliminated. Strong contractions of the colon create the urge to defecate. Two rectal sphincters, one voluntary and the other involuntary, regulate the opening of the anus.

If the lining of the colon is irritated—by a viral or bacterial infection, for instance—the colon is less effective in re-

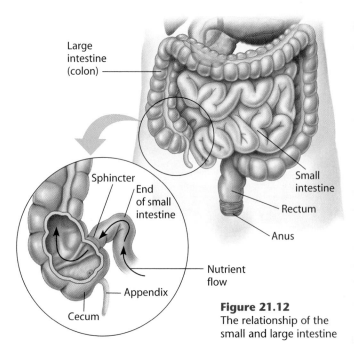

Figure 21.12
The relationship of the small and large intestine

claiming water, and diarrhea may result. The opposite problem, constipation, occurs when peristalsis moves the feces along too slowly; the colon reabsorbs too much water, and the feces become too compacted. Constipation often results from a diet that does not include enough plant fiber or from a lack of exercise.

? Explain why treatment of a chronic infection with antibiotics for an extended period of time may cause a vitamin K deficiency.

■ The antibiotics may kill the bacteria that synthesize vitamin K in the colon.

DIETS AND DIGESTIVE ADAPTATIONS

21.13 Adaptations of vertebrate digestive systems reflect diet

We have used our own alimentary canal to illustrate the basic plan of the vertebrate digestive system. However, vertebrate groups exhibit many variations on this plan. In each case, the structure and function of the animal's digestive system are adapted to the kind of food the animal eats.

The length of an animal's digestive tract tells us something about its diet. In general, herbivores and omnivores have longer alimentary canals, relative to their body size, than carnivores. A longer canal provides the extra time it takes to extract nutrients from vegetation, which is more difficult to digest than meat because of the cell walls in plant material. A longer canal also provides more surface area for absorbing nutrients, which are usually less concentrated in vegetation than in meat. A model case is the frog, which is carnivorous as an adult but mainly herbivorous as a tadpole, eating mostly

algae. A tadpole's intestine is long relative to its body size. When a tadpole transforms into an adult, the rest of its body grows more than its intestine, leaving the adult frog with an intestine that is shorter relative to its overall size.

In addition to a long alimentary canal, most herbivorous animals also have special chambers that house great numbers of microbes—bacteria and protists. The animals themselves cannot digest the cellulose in plants. The microbes break down the cellulose to simple sugars and other nutrients, which the animals then absorb directly or obtain by digesting the microbes.

Many herbivorous mammals—horses, elephants, rabbits and some rodents, for example—house cellulose-digesting microbes in the colon and in a large cecum, the pouch where the small and large intestines connect. Some of the nutrients cecum digest plant material, making it possible for the koala to get almost all its food and water from the leaves of eucalyptus trees.

Ruminant mammals, such as cattle, sheep, and deer, have a more elaborate system for cellulose digestion. The stomach of a ruminant has four chambers, as shown in **Figure 21.13B**. The arrows in this figure indicate the pathway of food. When a cow first chews and swallows a mouthful of grass, the food enters ❶ the rumen and then ❷ the reticulum (green arrows). Bacteria and protists in the rumen and reticulum immediately go to work on the cellulose-rich meal, and the cow helps by periodically regurgitating and rechewing her food (red arrows). This rumination, or "chewing the cud," softens and helps break down plant fibers, making them more accessible to digestion by the microbes.

As the blue arrows indicate, the cow swallows her cud into ❸ the omasum, where water is absorbed. The cud finally passes to ❹ the abomasum, where the cow's own enzymes complete digestion. Here, a cow obtains many of its nutrients by digesting the microbes along with the nutrients they produce. The microbes reproduce so rapidly that their numbers remain stable despite this constant loss. With its microbes and multistage food-processing system, a ruminant harvests more energy and nutrients from the cellulose in hay or grass than a nonruminant herbivore such as a horse or an elephant.

> **?** When a tadpole becomes an adult frog during metamorphosis, there is little growth of the intestine relative to the rest of the body. Thus, compared with the adult frog, a tadpole has a longer intestine relative to its body size. What does this suggest about the diets of these two stages in the frog's life history?

■ The tadpole is mainly herbivorous (eats mostly algae), while the adult frog is carnivorous (eats insects, for example).

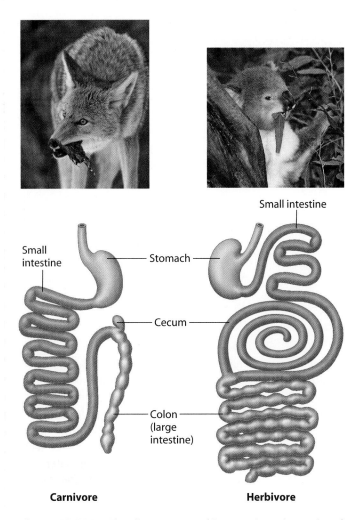

Figure 21.13A The alimentary canal in a carnivore (coyote) and an herbivore (koala)

produced by the microbes are absorbed in the cecum and colon. Most of the nutrients, however, are lost in the feces because they do not go through the small intestine, the main site of nutrient absorption. Rabbits and some rodents obtain these nutrients by eating some of their feces, thus passing the food through the alimentary canal a second time. The feces from the second round of digestion are more compact and are not reingested. Many desert rodents conserve water by eating their first round of feces.

Figure 21.13A compares the digestive tract of a carnivore, the coyote, with that of an herbivore, the koala. The koala is an Australian marsupial (see Module 18.21). These two mammals are about the same size, but the koala's intestine is much longer and includes the longest cecum (about 2 m) of any animal of its size. Bacteria in the

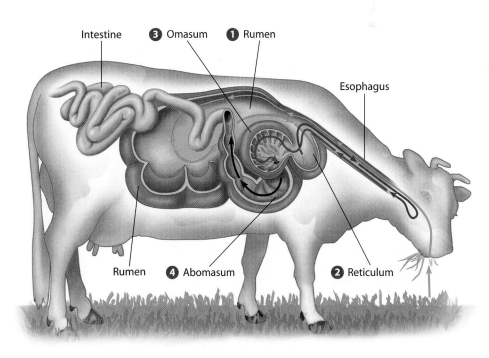

Figure 21.13B The digestive system of a ruminant mammal

CHAPTER 21 *Nutrition and Digestion* **51**

21.14 Overview: A healthy diet satisfies three needs

All animals—whether herbivores like cows, carnivores like cats, or omnivores like humans—have the same basic nutritional needs. All animals must obtain (1) fuel to power all body activities, (2) organic raw materials to make the animal's own molecules, and (3) essential nutrients, or substances the animal cannot make for itself from raw materials but must obtain from food, with "no assembly required."

We have seen that digestion breaks the organic polymers in food into monomers. Cells can then oxidize these monomers for energy or assemble them into their own polymers—the proteins, carbohydrates, lipids, and nucleic acids needed to build and maintain cell structure and function. Starting with the need for fuel and paying particular attention to humans, we discuss basic nutritional needs in the rest of this chapter.

? What is an "essential nutrient"?

■ A substance that an organism requires but cannot make

21.15 Chemical energy powers the body

Reading a book, walking to class, eating and digesting food, and every other activity your body performs require fuel in the form of chemical energy. Cellular metabolism produces the body's energy currency, ATP, by oxidizing organic molecules digested from food (see Module 6.12). Usually, cells use carbohydrates and fats as fuel sources. But when carbohydrates or fats are in short supply, cells will use proteins as an energy source. Fats are especially rich in energy: The oxidation of a gram of fat liberates more than twice the energy liberated from a gram of carbohydrate or protein. The energy content of food is measured in **kilocalories** (1 **kcal** = 1,000 calories). The calories listed on food labels or referred to elsewhere regarding nutrition are actually kilocalories and are written as *Calories* (with a capital C).

Cellular metabolism must continuously drive several processes for an animal to remain alive. These include cell maintenance, breathing, the beating of the heart, and, in birds and mammals, the maintenance of body temperature. The number of kilocalories (Calories) a resting animal requires to fuel these essential processes for a given time is called the **basal metabolic rate (BMR)**. The BMR for humans averages 1,300–1,500 kcal per day for adult females and about 1,600–1,800 kcal per day for adult males. This is about equivalent to the energy requirement of a 75-watt light bulb. But this is only a basal (base) rate—the amount of energy we "burn" lying motionless. Any activity, even working quietly at your desk, consumes kilocalories in addition to the BMR. The more strenuous the activity, the greater the energy demand. Table 21.15 gives you an idea of the amount of activity it takes for a 68-kg (150-lb) person to use up the kilocalories contained in several common foods.

What happens when we take in more kilocalories than we use up? Rather than discarding the extra energy, our cells store it in various forms. Our liver and muscles store energy in the form of glycogen, a polymer of glucose molecules. Most of us can store enough glycogen to supply about a day's worth of basal metabolism. Our cells also store excess energy as fat. This happens even if our diet contains little fat because the liver converts excess carbohydrates and proteins to fat. The average human's energy needs can be fueled by the oxidation of only 0.3 kg of fat per day. Most healthy people have enough stored fat to sustain them through several weeks of starvation. We discuss fat storage and its consequences in Module 21.22. But first we consider the essential nutrients that must be supplied in the diet.

? What is the basal metabolic rate?

■ The minimum number of kilocalories that a resting animal needs to maintain life's basic processes

TABLE 21.15 EXERCISE REQUIRED TO "BURN" THE CALORIES (KCAL) IN COMMON FOODS			
	Jogging	**Swimming**	**Walking**
Speed of exercise	9 min/mi	30 min/mi	20 min/mi
kcal "burned"/hour	700	540	160
Cheeseburger ($\frac{1}{4}$ lb) 560 kcal	48 min	1 hr, 2 min	3 hr, 30 min
Cheese pizza (1 slice) 450 kcal	38 min	50 min	2 hr, 49 min
Soft drink (12 oz) 173 kcal	15 min	19 min	65 min
Whole wheat bread (1 slice) 100 kcal	9 min	11 min	38 min

These data are for a person weighing 68 kg (150 lb).

21.16 An animal's diet must supply essential nutrients

Besides providing fuel and organic raw materials, an animal's diet must also supply **essential nutrients.** These are materials that must be obtained in preassembled form because the animal's cells cannot make them from *any* raw material. An individual whose diet is chronically deficient in calories is said to be *undernourished.* An individual whose diet is missing one or more essential nutrients is said to be *malnourished.* Because a diet of a single staple such as rice or corn can often provide sufficient calories, undernourishment is generally common only where drought, war, or some other crisis has severely disrupted the food supply. Another cause of undernourishment is anorexia nervosa, an eating disorder in which a person does not eat enough because of an intense fear of becoming fat. In human populations, malnutrition is much more common than undernutrition, and it is even possible for an overnourished (obese) individual to be malnourished. There are four classes of essential nutrients: essential fatty acids, essential amino acids, vitamins, and minerals.

Our cells make fats and other lipids by combining fatty acids with other molecules, such as glycerol (see Module 3.8). We can make most of the fatty acids we need. Those we cannot make, called **essential fatty acids,** we must obtain in our diet. One essential fatty acid, linoleic acid, is especially important because it is needed to make some of the phospholipids of cell membranes. Most diets furnish ample amounts of essential fatty acids, and deficiencies are rare.

Adult humans cannot make eight of the 20 kinds of amino acids needed to synthesize proteins. These eight, known as the **essential amino acids,** must be obtained from the diet. (Infants also require a ninth, histidine.) Because the body cannot store excess amino acids, a deficiency of a single essential amino acid limits the use of other amino acids, impairs protein synthesis, and can lead to protein deficiency, a serious type of malnutrition. This is the most common type of malnutrition among humans. The victims are usually children, who, if they survive infancy, are likely to be retarded mentally and underdeveloped physically.

The simplest way to get all the essential amino acids is to eat meat and animal by-products such as eggs, milk, and cheese. The proteins in these products are said to be "complete," meaning they provide all the essential amino acids in the proportions needed by the body. In contrast, most plant proteins are "incomplete," or deficient in one or more essential amino acids. In the next module, we discuss how vegetarians can obtain all the essential amino acids in their diet.

? What is the difference between undernutrition and malnutrition?

■ Undernutrition is a diet deficient in calories; malnutrition is a diet deficient in an essential nutrient.

CONNECTION

21.17 Vegetarians must be sure to obtain all eight essential amino acids

Vegetarian diets may range from avoiding meat to the vegan diet of avoiding animal products of any kind, including eggs, milk, and cheese. Is it possible for a person to be a vegetarian and obtain adequate nutrition? The answer is yes, but vegetarians have to know how to get all the essential nutrients.

People may become vegetarians by choice or, more commonly, because they simply cannot afford animal protein. Animal protein is more expensive to produce, and usually to buy, than plant protein, and most of the human population is primarily vegetarian. Nutritional problems can result when people have to rely on a single type of plant food—just corn, rice, or wheat, for instance. On such a limited diet, people are likely to become protein-deficient because they lack certain essential amino acids.

The key to being a healthy vegetarian is to eat a variety of plant foods that together supply sufficient quantities of all the essential amino acids. Simply by eating a combination of beans and corn, for example, vegetarians can get all the essential amino acids (**Figure 21.17**). Most societies have, by trial and error, developed balanced diets that prevent protein deficiency. The Mexican staple diet of corn tortillas and beans is one example.

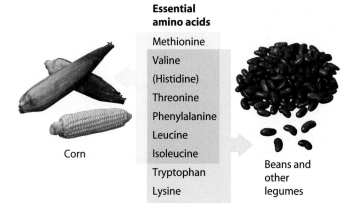

Essential amino acids

Methionine
Valine
(Histidine)
Threonine
Phenylalanine
Leucine
Isoleucine
Tryptophan
Lysine

Corn

Beans and other legumes

Figure 21.17 Essential amino acids from a vegetarian diet

? Look carefully at Figure 21.17. A diet consisting strictly of beans would probably result in a deficiency of the essential amino acid _____.

■ methionine

A healthy diet includes 13 vitamins

A **vitamin** is an organic nutrient that we must obtain from our diet, but is required in much smaller quantities than the essential amino acids. Most vitamins serve as coenzymes or parts of coenzymes; they have catalytic functions and are used over and over in metabolic reactions (see Module 5.7). Table 21.18 lists 13 essential vitamins and their major dietary sources. Though needed in only tiny amounts, vitamins are absolutely necessary, as you can see from the functions and symptoms of deficiencies listed in the table. Extreme excesses, however, can also be dangerous.

Water-soluble vitamins include the B complex and vitamin C. Fat-soluble vitamins include vitamins A, D, E, and K. In general, excess water-soluble vitamins will be eliminated in urine. Excessive amounts of fat-soluble vitamins, however, build up in body fat. Thus, overdoses may have toxic effects.

? Why are vitamins required in such small doses, compared with other essential organic nutrients?

■ Because vitamins generally have catalytic functions as coenzymes, and thus each vitamin molecule can repeat its function many times

TABLE 21.18 VITAMIN REQUIREMENTS OF HUMANS

Vitamin	Major Dietary Sources	Functions in the Body	Symptoms of Deficiency / Symptoms of Extreme Excess
Water-Soluble Vitamins			
Vitamin B-1 (thiamine)	Pork, legumes, peanuts, whole grains	Coenzyme used in removing CO_2 from organic compounds	Beriberi (nerve disorders, emaciation, anemia)
Vitamin B-2 (riboflavin)	Dairy products, meats, enriched grains, vegetables	Component of coenzyme FAD	Skin lesions such as cracks at corners of mouth
Niacin	Nuts, meats, grains	Component of coenzymes NAD⁺ and NADP⁺	Skin and gastrointestinal lesions, nervous disorders Liver damage
Vitamin B-6 (pyridoxine)	Meats, vegetables, whole grains	Coenzyme used in amino acid metabolism	Irritability, convulsions, muscular twitching, anemia Unstable gait, numb feet, poor coordination
Pantothenic acid	Most foods: meats, dairy products, whole grains, etc.	Component of coenzyme A	Fatigue, numbness, tingling of hands and feet
Folic acid (folacin)	Green vegetables, oranges, nuts, legumes, whole grains	Coenzyme in nucleic acid and amino acid metabolism; neural tube development in embryo	Anemia, gastrointestinal problems May mask deficiency of vitamin B-12
Vitamin B-12	Meats, eggs, dairy products	Coenzyme in nucleic acid metabolism; maturation of red blood cells	Anemia, nervous system disorders
Biotin	Legumes, other vegetables, meats	Coenzyme in synthesis of fat, glycogen, and amino acids	Scaly skin inflammation, neuromuscular disorders
Vitamin C (ascorbic acid)	Fruits and vegetables, especially citrus fruits, broccoli, cabbage, tomatoes, green peppers	Used in collagen synthesis (e.g., for bone, cartilage, gums); antioxidant; aids in detoxification; improves iron absorption	Scurvy (degeneration of skin, teeth, blood vessels), weakness, delayed wound healing, impaired immunity Gastrointestinal upset
Fat-Soluble Vitamins			
Vitamin A (retinol)	Dark green and orange vegetables and fruits, dairy products	Component of visual pigments; maintenance of epithelial tissues; antioxidant; helps prevent damage to cell membranes	Vision problems; dry, scaly skin Headache, irritability, vomiting, hair loss, blurred vision, liver and bone damage
Vitamin D	Dairy products, egg yolk (also made in human skin in presence of sunlight)	Aids in absorption and use of calcium and phosphorus; promotes bone growth	Rickets (bone deformities) in children; bone softening in adults Brain, cardiovascular, and kidney damage
Vitamin E (tocopherol)	Vegetable oils, nuts, seeds	Antioxidant; helps prevent damage to cell membranes	None well documented; possibly anemia
Vitamin K	Green vegetables, tea (also made by colon bacteria)	Important in blood clotting	Defective blood clotting Liver damage and anemia

Essential minerals are required for many body functions

Minerals are simple inorganic nutrients, usually required in small amounts. We must acquire the essential minerals listed in Table 21.19 from our diet; some of the major dietary sources are listed. The table also lists the functions and symptoms of deficiency for each mineral.

Along with other vertebrates, we humans require relatively large amounts of calcium and phosphorus to construct and maintain our skeleton. Too little calcium can result in the degenerative bone disease osteoporosis. Calcium is also necessary for the normal functioning of nerves and muscles, and phosphorus is an ingredient of ATP and nucleic acids. Iron is a component of hemoglobin, the oxygen-carrying protein of red blood cells, and of several electron carrier molecules that function in cellular respiration. Vertebrates need iodine to make the hormone thyroxine, which regulates metabolic rate. Many minerals are components of various enzymes.

Sodium, potassium, and chlorine are important in nerve function and help maintain the osmotic balance of cells. Most people ingest far more salt (sodium chloride) than they need. The average U.S. citizen eats enough salt to provide about 20 times the required amount of sodium. Ingesting too much sodium may be associated with high blood pressure.

? Which of the minerals listed in the table are involved with the formation or maintenance of teeth?

■ Calcium, phosphorus, and fluorine

TABLE 21.19 MINERAL REQUIREMENTS OF HUMANS

Mineral (chemical symbol)	Dietary Sources	Functions in the Body	Symptoms of Deficiency*
Calcium (Ca)	Dairy products, dark green vegetables, legumes	Bone and tooth formation, blood clotting, nerve and muscle function	Stunted growth, possibly loss of bone mass
Phosphorus (P)	Dairy products, meats, grains	Bone and tooth formation, acid-base balance, nucleotide synthesis	Weakness, loss of minerals from bone, calcium loss
Sulfur (S)	Proteins from many sources	Component of certain amino acids	Symptoms of protein deficiency
Potassium (K)	Meats, dairy products, many fruits and vegetables, grains	Acid-base balance, water balance, nerve function	Muscular weakness, paralysis, nausea, heart failure
Chlorine (Cl)	Table salt	Acid-base balance, water balance, nerve function, formation of gastric juice	Muscle cramps, reduced appetite
Sodium (Na)	Table salt	Acid-base balance, water balance, nerve function	Muscle cramps, reduced appetite
Magnesium (Mg)	Whole grains, green leafy vegetables	Component of certain enzymes	Nervous system disturbances
Iron (Fe)	Meats, eggs, legumes, whole grains, green leafy vegetables	Component of hemoglobin, of certain enzymes, and of electron carriers in energy metabolism	Iron-deficiency anemia, weakness, impaired immunity
Fluorine (F)	Fluoridated drinking water, tea, seafood	Maintenance of tooth (and probably bone) structure	Higher frequency of tooth decay
Zinc (Zn)	Meats, seafood, grains	Component of certain digestive enzymes and other proteins	Growth failure, scaly skin inflammation, reproductive failure, impaired immunity
Copper (Cu)	Seafood, nuts, legumes, organ meats	Component of enzymes in iron metabolism, electron transport	Anemia, bone and cardiovascular changes
Manganese (Mn)	Nuts, grains, vegetables, fruits, tea	Component of certain enzymes	Abnormal bone and cartilage
Iodine (I)	Seafood, dairy products, iodized salt	Component of thyroid hormones	Goiter (enlarged thyroid)
Cobalt (Co)	Meats, dairy products	Component of vitamin B-12	None, except as B-12 deficiency
Selenium (Se)	Seafood, meats, whole grains	Component of enzymes; functions in association with vitamin E	Muscle pain, maybe heart muscle deterioration
Chromium (Cr)	Brewer's yeast, liver, seafood, meats, some vegetables	Involved in glucose and energy metabolism	Impaired glucose metabolism
Molybdenum (Mo)	Legumes, grains, some vegetables	Component of certain enzymes	Disorder in excretion of nitrogen-containing compounds

*All of these minerals can be harmful when consumed in extreme excess.

21.20 Do you need to take vitamin and mineral supplements?

A healthy diet usually includes enough vitamins and minerals for most people and is considered the best source of these nutrition mainstays. Such diets meet the **Recommended Dietary Allowances (RDAs)**, minimum amounts of nutrients that are needed each day by healthy people, as determined by a national scientific panel. The subject of vitamin dosage, however, can cause heated scientific and popular debate. Some people argue that RDAs are set too low for some vitamins, and some of these people believe, probably mistakenly, that *massive* doses of vitamins confer health benefits. Research is far from complete, and debate continues, especially over optimal doses of vitamins C and E. Evidence indicates, however, that excessive amounts of some vitamins and minerals, such as vitamin A and iron, can definitely be harmful.

Vitamin and mineral supplements may be advisable for people who do not follow a healthy diet, who cannot consume certain foods, who are vegetarians, or who are dieting. Pregnant women and older people may have specific nutritional needs that require a supplement. However, unless recommended by a doctor, people should generally avoid megavitamins—supplements that far exceed daily recommended doses.

 What are RDAs?

■ Recommended Dietary Allowances: minimal daily amounts of nutrients determined to be required for health

21.21 What do food labels tell us?

Have you ever found yourself sitting at the breakfast table reading the label on a cereal box? What does it all mean?

The Food and Drug Administration (FDA) requires that various types of information be given on packaged-food labels, as shown in **Figure 21.21**. You'll find the ingredients listed in order from the greatest amount (by weight) to the least. There are also several kinds of "nutrition facts" found on food labels. First, a serving size of the food is defined according to standards set by the FDA. The energy content in "Calories" (that is, kilocalories) is listed per serving. Selected nutrients are also listed as amounts per serving and as percentages of a daily value. The daily values are based on a diet containing 2,000 kcal per day. For example, the 1.5 g of fat in a slice of this bread provides 2% of the daily fat allowance for a person needing 2,000 kcal per day.

Food labels emphasize nutrients believed to be associated with disease risks (fats, cholesterol, and sodium) and with a healthy diet (such as dietary fiber, protein, and certain vitamins and minerals). From the data shown, you can tell that each serving of this bread contains 19 g of total carbohydrate. Dietary fiber consists of indigestible complex carbohydrates, mainly cellulose. Subtracting 3 g of dietary fiber and 3 g of sugars (simple carbohydrates) from the 19 g of total carbohydrate tells you that each serving of this bread contains 13 g of digestible complex carbohydrate. This is chiefly starch.

To help consumers compare nutrient amounts in a particular food with their total daily needs, food labels also provide some general nutritional information. For example, the lower part of the label recommends less than 20 g of saturated fat and at least 25 g of dietary fiber for those following a 2,000-kcal daily diet.

Ingredients: whole wheat flour, water, high fructose corn syrup, wheat gluten, soybean or canola oil, molasses, yeast, salt, cultured whey, vinegar, soy flour, calcium sulfate (source of calcium).

Figure 21.21
Whole wheat bread label

Nutrition Facts

Serving Size 1 slice (43g)
Servings Per Container 16

Amount Per Serving

Calories 100   Calories from Fat 10

	% Daily Value*
Total Fat 1.5g	**2%**
Saturated Fat 0g	**0%**
Cholesterol 0mg	**0%**
Sodium 190mg	**8%**
Total Carbohydrate 19g	**6%**
Dietary Fiber 3g	**12%**
Sugars 3g	
Protein 4g	

Vitamin A 0%	•	Vitamin C 0%
Calcium 2%	•	Iron 4%
Thiamine 6%	•	Riboflavin 2%
Niacin 6%	•	Folic Acid 0%

* Percent Daily Values are based on a 2,000 calorie diet. Your daily values may be higher or lower depending on your calorie needs:

		Calories:	2,000	2,500
Total Fat	Less than		65g	80g
Sat. Fat	Less than		20g	25g
Cholesterol	Less than		300mg	300mg
Sodium	Less than		2,400mg	2,400mg
Total Carbohydrate			300g	375g
Dietary Fiber			25g	30g

Calories per gram:
Fat 9 • Carbohydrate 4 • Protein 4

 What percent of the daily requirements for the fat-soluble vitamins is provided by a slice of the bread in Figure 21.21? (*Hint*: Review Table 21.18.)

0% ■

21.22 Obesity is a human health problem

The World Health Organization now recognizes obesity as a major global health problem. The increased availability of fattening foods and large portions in many countries combined with more sedentary lifestyles puts excess weight on bodies. In the United States, the percentage of obese (very overweight) people has doubled to 30% in the past two decades, and another 35% are overweight. Weight problems often begin at a young age; 15% of children and adolescents in the United States are overweight.

Obesity contributes to a number of health problems, including the most common type of diabetes, cancer of the colon and breasts, and cardiovascular disease. Obesity is estimated to be a factor in 300,000 deaths per year in the United States.

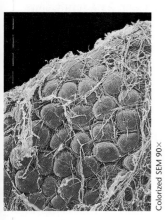

Figure 21.22A Human fat cells

Colorized SEM 90×

The obesity epidemic has stimulated an increase in scientific research on the causes and possible treatments for weight-control problems. Inheritance is one factor in obesity, which helps explain why certain people have to struggle so hard to control their weight, while others can eat and eat without gaining weight. Researchers have identified dozens of the genes that code for weight-regulating hormones. As researchers continue to study the signaling pathways that regulate both long-term and short-term appetite and the body's storage of fat, there is reason to be somewhat optimistic that obese people who have inherited defects in these weight-controlling mechanisms may someday be treated with a new generation of drugs. But so far, the diversity of defects in these complex systems has made it difficult to develop drugs that are effective and free from serious side effects.

The complexity of weight control in humans is evident from studies of the hormone leptin, one of the key long-term appetite regulators in mammals. Leptin is produced by adipose (fat) cells (**Figure 21.22A**). As adipose tissue increases, leptin levels in the blood rise, which normally cues the brain to suppress appetite. This is one of the feedback mechanisms that usually keep people from becoming obese in spite of access to an abundance of food. Conversely, loss of body fat decreases leptin levels, signaling the brain to increase appetite. Mice that inherit a defect in the gene for leptin become very obese (**Figure 21.22B**). Researchers found that they could treat these obese mice by injecting leptin.

The discovery of the leptin-deficiency mutation in mice made front-page news and initially generated much excitement because humans also have a leptin gene. And indeed, obese children who have inherited a mutant form of the leptin gene do lose weight after leptin treatments. However, relatively few obese people have such defects in leptin production. In fact, most obese humans have an abnormally high level of leptin, which, after all, is produced by adipose tissue. For some reason, the brain's satiety center does not respond to the high leptin levels in many obese people. One hypothesis is that in humans, perhaps in contrast to many other mammals, the function of the leptin system is to prevent weight loss, not protect against weight gain. Thus, the decline in leptin when body fat is lost stimulates appetite; but the high levels of leptin produced by large stores of body fat do not function to depress appetite. This physiological nuance may be a consequence of our evolutionary history.

Most of us crave foods that are fatty: fries, chips, burgers, cheese, and ice cream. Though fat hoarding can be a health liability today, it may actually have been advantageous in our evolutionary past. Only in the past few centuries have large numbers of people had access to a reliable supply of high-calorie food. Our ancestors on the African savanna were hunter-gatherers who probably survived mainly on seeds and other plant products, a diet only occasionally supplemented by hunting game or scavenging meat from animals killed by other predators. In such a feast-and-famine existence, natural selection may have favored those individuals with a physiology that induced them to gorge on rich, fatty foods on those rare occasions when such treats were available. Individuals with genes promoting the storage of fat during feasts may have been more likely than their thinner friends to survive famines. So perhaps our modern taste for fats, which contributes to the obesity epidemic, is partly an evolutionary vestige of our past, when food was less plentiful.

Next we explore some popular weight loss diets.

Figure 21.22B A mouse with a defect in a gene for leptin, an appetite-suppressing hormone (left); a normal mouse (right)

? What are two roles of the hormone leptin? Which of these roles does leptin appear not to play in obese humans?

■ A drop in leptin due to a loss of adipose tissue stimulates appetite; a high level of leptin, produced by increased body fat, depresses appetite. The second mechanism does not seem to function in some humans.

21.23 What are the health risks and benefits of fad diets?

As the numbers of people who are overweight or obese rise, so does interest in ways to shed body fat. The obesity epidemic has fueled explosive growth in the weight loss industry. Most of the trendy diets promoted by weight loss businesses claim to improve a person's health and appearance quickly and dramatically, and judging from the growing amounts of money flowing to these enterprises, dieters believe them. According to some estimates, the U.S. market for weight loss products and services, worth about $60 million in 1999, could reach more than $150 billion in 2007.

But the popularity of weight loss programs does not mean that all diet regimens are effective or medically sound. Weight loss can improve a person's health and, in a culture that values slender physiques, improve a person's self-image. But the health benefits and staying power of any diet are closely tied to how weight loss occurs. If a fad diet sheds pounds through unhealthy methods, any benefits may be short-lived, and long-term health problems may follow.

In recent years, many of the most popular—and controversial—weight loss schemes have focused on reduced intake of carbohydrates. Backers of these diets say that with fewer carbohydrates, the body must burn stored fat instead. Such diets dramatically restrict carbohydrate consumption, some allowing as little as 20 g of carbohydrates a day—less than 10% of the current RDA. Dieters on such plans are often told to replace carbohydrates with proteins and fats. People following "low-carb" diets often drop sugar, bread, fruits, and potatoes from their diets, swapping in cheese, nuts, and meat instead.

Some people have lost weight quickly on the regimen of a low-carbohydrate diet, and because of these success stories and the fatty foods the diet allows, the approach has surged in popularity. According to surveys, as many as one in five Americans have tried some type of low-carbohydrate diet. Americans spend as much as $15 billion a year on "low-carb" diet aids and foods. Although some studies have found these diets to be effective, others have found that they offer only short-lived benefits. Much of the initial weight reduction in

such a diet comes through water loss. Once the diet is stopped, the lost weight is quickly regained. The fatty foods encouraged in such diets may contribute to heart disease and kidney problems. Reductions in fruits and vegetables cut a person's intake of vitamins, minerals, and fiber, increasing the risk of diseases such as cancer. As a result, few doctors recommend low-carbohydrate diets as a healthy way to long-term weight loss.

Low-carbohydrate diets unseated low-fat diets, an earlier dieting trend with its own flood of low-fat (but often high-sugar) processed foods. Such low-fat regimens dramatically cut dietary fat, often reducing consumption of dairy products, meat, nuts, and oils. But a healthy body composition often requires a certain amount of fat. Low-fat diets often lack adequate amounts of fatty acids and protein, and may make it difficult for the body to absorb fat-soluble vitamins. A reasonable amount of fats and related lipids are essential components of the human body and seem to correlate with a healthy immune system.

Healthy women may have as much as 20–25% of their body weight in fat; for healthy men, the amount is typically 15–19%. Extremely thin people tend to have lower levels of vitamin A and beta-carotene in their blood, which may make them more susceptible to certain forms of cancer.

As the problems with fad diets reveal, the body requires a balance of nutrients for good health and long-term weight control. The best approach to weight control is a combination of exercise and a restricted but balanced diet that provides at least 1,200 kcal per day and adequate amounts of all essential nutrients (Table 21.23). A restricted, balanced diet, along with regular aerobic exercise, can trim the body gradually and keep extra fat off without harmful side effects.

? In what sense is maintaining a stable body weight a matter of caloric bookkeeping?

■ When we burn as many calories a day through BMR and activities as we take in with our food, a stable body weight will result.

TABLE 21.23 TYPES OF WEIGHT LOSS DIETS

Diet Type	Health Effects and Potential Problems
Extremely low-carbohydrate diets Less than 100 g of carbohydrates per day	Initial loss of weight is primarily water; problems may include fatigue and headaches; long-term adherence to diet may be associated with muscle loss
Extremely low-fat diets Less than 20% of kilocalories from fat	May be inadequate in essential fatty acids, protein, and certain minerals; may decrease absorption of fat-soluble vitamins; may result in irregular menstrual periods in women
Formula diets Based on formulated or packaged products; many are very low in kilocalories	If very low in kilocalories (less than 800 kcal per day), may result in loss of body protein and may cause dry skin, thinning hair, constipation, and salt imbalance
Balanced diet of 1,200 kcal or more	If carefully chosen, such a diet can meet all nutrient needs; weight loss is usually 1–2 pounds per week; dieter may become discouraged by slow progress

21.24 Diet can influence cardiovascular disease and cancer

Food influences far more than size and appearance. Diet also plays an important role in a person's risk of developing serious illnesses, including cardiovascular disease and cancer. **Figure 21.24** shows some of the risk factors associated with cardiovascular disease. Though certain factors are unavoidable, we can influence others through our behavior. Diet is an example of a behavioral factor that may affect cardiovascular health. For instance, a diet rich in saturated fats is linked to high blood cholesterol levels, which in turn may be linked to cardiovascular disease. Saturated fats are found in eggs, butter, lard, and most other animal products. Saturated fats are also found in artificially saturated ("hydrogenated") vegetable oils. The hydrogenation process, which solidifies vegetable oils, also produces a type of fatty acid called *trans* fats. These dangerous fats have also been linked to heart disease, and many doctors now recommend that people consume as few *trans* fats as possible. This requires careful reading of food ingredient labels, since hydrogenated oils are widely used in many processed foods, including crackers, store-bought cookies, and cereals. A food that contains hydrogenated or partially hydrogenated oils is likely to have *trans* fats.

Cholesterol is another factor in cardiovascular health. This molecule travels through the body in blood lipoproteins, which are particles made up of thousands of molecules of cholesterol and other lipids and one or more protein molecules (see Figure 5.20). High blood levels of a family of lipoproteins called **low-density lipoproteins (LDLs)** generally correlate with a tendency to develop blocked blood vessels, high blood pressure, and consequent heart attacks. In contrast to LDLs, cholesterol carriers called **high-density lipoproteins (HDLs)** may decrease the risk of vessel blockage, perhaps because some HDLs convey blood cholesterol to the liver, where it is broken down. Many researchers believe that reducing LDLs while maintaining or increasing HDLs lowers the risk of cardiovascular disease. Exercise tends to increase HDL levels, while smoking lowers them.

A diet high in saturated fats tends to increase LDL levels. *Trans* fats tend not only to increase LDL levels, but also to lower HDL levels, a two-pronged attack on cardiovascular

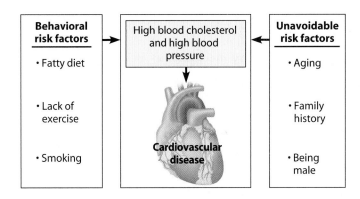

Figure 21.24 Risk factors associated with cardiovascular disease

health. By contrast, eating mainly unsaturated fats, such as fish oil and most liquid vegetable oils (including corn, soybean, and olive oils), tends to lower LDL levels and raise HDL levels. These oils are also important sources of vitamin E, whose antioxidant effect may help prevent blood vessel blockage.

As discussed in Module 11.20, diet also seems to be involved in some forms of cancer. Some research suggests a link between diets heavy in fats or carbohydrates and the incidence of breast cancer. The incidence of colon cancer and prostate cancer may be linked to a diet rich in saturated fat or red meat. Other foods may help fight cancer. For example, some fruits and other plant-based foods are rich in antioxidants, chemicals that help protect cells from damaging molecules known as free radicals. Antioxidants may help prevent cancer, although this link is still debated by scientists.

The relationship between foods and cancer is complex, and much remains to be learned. The American Cancer Society suggests that following the dietary guidelines listed in **Table 21.24**, in combination with physical activity, can help lower cancer risk. The ACS's main recommendation is to "eat a variety of healthful foods, with an emphasis on plant sources."

■   ■   ■

In this chapter, we have seen that a balanced diet supplies enough raw materials to make all the macromolecules we need, the proper amounts of prefabricated essential nutrients, and enough kilocalories to satisfy our energy needs. Energy remains a theme in Chapter 22, as we look at how the body obtains the oxygen it needs to harvest energy from food molecules.

? If you are trying to minimize the damaging effects of blood cholesterol on your cardiovascular system, your goal is to increase/decrease (*choose one*) your LDLs and increase/decrease (*choose one*) your HDLs.

■ decrease . . . increase

TABLE 21.24 DIETARY GUIDELINES FOR REDUCING CANCER RISK

Eat 5 or more servings of a variety of fruits and vegetables daily.

Choose whole grain rice, bread, pasta, and cereals.

Limit consumption of red meats, especially those high in fat.

To avoid possible carcinogens, minimize consumption of cured and smoked foods, such as hot dogs, salami, and bacon. Avoid moldy foods. Avoid charred foods.

If you drink alcoholic beverages, limit yourself to a maximum of one or two drinks a day (a drink = 12 oz beer, 5 oz wine, 1.5 oz 80% distilled spirits).

CHAPTER REVIEW

Reviewing the Concepts

Obtaining and Processing Food (Introduction–21.3)

Animal feeding mechanisms include suspension, substrate, fluid, and bulk feeding. Animals may be herbivores, carnivores, or omnivores **(Introduction–21.1)**.

Food processing includes four stages: ingestion, digestion, absorption, and elimination **(21.2)**.

Digestive compartments may be food vacuoles (sponges), a gastrovascular cavity (cnidarians and flatworms), or, in most animals, an alimentary canal running from mouth to anus with specialized regions **(21.3)**.

Human Digestive System (21.4–21.12)

The human digestive system consists of an alimentary canal and accessory glands. The rhythmic muscle contractions of peristalsis squeeze food along the alimentary canal. The pyloric sphincter regulates passage of food from the stomach to the small intestine **(21.4)**.

Oral cavity. The teeth break up food, saliva moistens it, and salivary enzymes begin the hydrolysis of starch. The tongue pushes the bolus of food into the pharynx **(21.5)**.

Pharynx and esophagus. The swallowing reflex moves food from the pharynx into the esophagus, while keeping it out of the trachea. The Heimlich maneuver can dislodge food from the pharynx or trachea during choking **(21.6–21.7)**. Peristalsis in the esophagus moves food into the stomach **(21.8)**.

The stomach stores food and mixes it with acidic gastric juice. Pepsin in gastric juice begins the hydrolysis of protein **(21.9)**. Bacterial infections in the stomach and duodenum are associated with ulcers **(21.10)**.

 **The small intestine** is the site of most digestion and absorption. Alkaline pancreatic juice neutralizes the acid chyme, and its enzymes digest food polymers. Bile, made in the liver and stored in the gallbladder, emulsifies fat for attack by enzymes. Enzymes from cells of the intestine complete the digestion of many nutrients. Folds of the intestinal lining and tiny, fingerlike villi (with microscopic microvilli) increase the absorptive surface. Nutrients pass across the epithelium and into the blood, which flows to the liver, where nutrients are processed and stored **(21.11)**.

The large intestine, or colon, reabsorbs water from undigested material. Feces are stored in the rectum **(21.12)**.

Diets and Digestive Adaptations (21.13)

Dietary adaptations of herbivores include longer alimentary canals and cellulose-digesting microbes housed in special chambers. Ruminants such as cows process food with the aid of microbes in four chambers **(21.13)**.

Nutrition (21.14–21.24)

A healthy diet provides fuel for activities, raw materials for biosynthesis, and essential nutrients **(21.14)**. The basal metabolic rate (BMR) is the energy a resting animal requires each day. Excess energy is stored as glycogen or fat **(21.15)**.

Essential nutrients are those that an animal must obtain from its diet. The eight essential amino acids can be obtained from animal protein or from the proper combination of plant foods **(21.16–21.17)**.

Vitamins and minerals are essential in the human diet. Most vitamins function as coenzymes **(21.18)**. Minerals are inorganic nutrients that play a variety of roles **(21.19)**. Supplements ensure a sufficient quantity of vitamins and nutrients; megadoses may be dangerous **(21.20)**. Food labels provide important nutritional information **(21.21)**.

Obesity is a serious health problem, caused by lack of exercise and abundance of fattening foods, and may partly stem from an evolutionary advantage of fat hoarding **(21.22)**.

Weight loss diets may help individuals lose weight but may have health risks. A healthy diet may reduce the risk of cardiovascular disease and cancer **(21.23–21.24)**.

Connecting the Concepts

1. Label the parts of the human digestive system below and indicate the functions of these organs and glands.

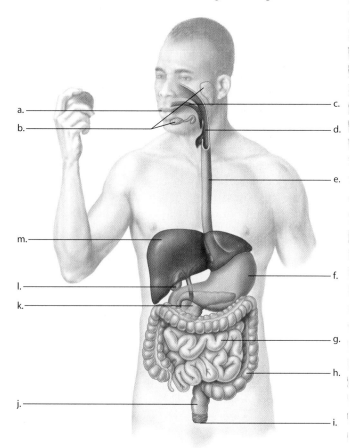

a.

b.

c.

d.

e.

m.

l.

k.

f.

g.

h.

j.

i.

2. Complete the following map summarizing the nutritional needs of animals that are met by a healthy diet.

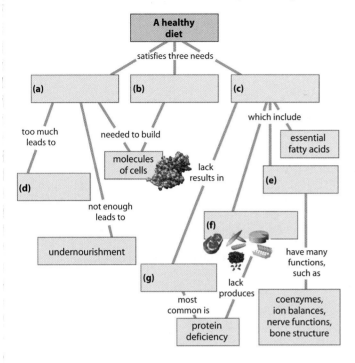

Testing Your Knowledge

Multiple Choice

3. Earthworms, which are substrate feeders,
   a. feed mostly on mineral substrates.
   b. filter small organisms from the soil.
   c. are bulk feeders.
   d. are herbivores that eat autotrophs.
   e. eat their way through the soil, feeding on partially decayed organic matter.

4. The energy content of fats
   a. is released by bile salts.
   b. may be lost unless an herbivore eats some of its feces.
   c. is more than two times that of carbohydrates or proteins.
   d. can reverse the effects of malnutrition.
   e. Both c and d are correct.

5. Which of the following statements is false?
   a. The average human has enough stored fat to supply calories for several weeks.
   b. An increase in leptin levels leads to an increase in appetite and weight gain.
   c. The interconversion of glucose and glycogen takes place in the liver.
   d. After glycogen stores are filled, excessive calories are stored as fat, regardless of their original food source.
   e. Carbohydrates and fats are preferentially used as fuel before proteins are used.

6. Which of the following is mismatched with its function?
   a. most B vitamins—coenzymes
   b. vitamin E—antioxidant
   c. vitamin K—blood clotting
   d. iron—component of thyroid hormones
   e. phosphorus—bone formation, nucleotide synthesis

7. Why do many vegetarians combine different protein sources or eat some eggs or milk products?
   a. to make sure they obtain sufficient calories
   b. to provide sufficient vitamins
   c. to make sure they ingest all essential fatty acids
   d. to make their diet more interesting
   e. to provide all essential amino acids at the same time

Describing, Comparing, and Explaining

8. A peanut butter and jelly sandwich contains carbohydrates, proteins, and fats. Describe what happens to the sandwich when you eat it. Discuss ingestion, digestion, absorption, and elimination.

Applying the Concepts

9. How might our craving for fatty foods, which is helping to fuel the obesity crisis, have evolved through natural selection?

10. Use this Nutrition Facts label to answer these questions:
    a. What percentage of the total Calories in this product is from fat?
    b. Is this product a good source of vitamin A and calcium? Explain.
    c. Each gram of fat supplies 9 Calories. Based on the grams of saturated fat and its % Daily Value, calculate the upper limit of saturated fat (in grams and Calories) that an individual on a 2,000-Calorie/day diet should consume.

Nutrition Facts

Serving Size 1/2 Cup (83g)
Servings Per Container 8

Amount Per Serving

Calories 190 Calories from Fat 110

	% Daily Value*
Total Fat 12g	**18%**
Saturated Fat 8g	**40%**
Cholesterol 45mg	**15%**
Sodium 75mg	**3%**
Total Carbohydrate 18g	**6%**
Dietary Fiber 0g	**0%**
Sugars 17g	
Protein 3g	

Vitamin A 10%	•	Vitamin C 8%
Calcium 10%	•	Iron 0%

*Percent Daily Values (DV) are based on a 2,000 calorie diet.

11. The media report numerous claims and counterclaims about the benefits and dangers of certain foods, dietary supplements, and diets. Have you modified your eating habits on the basis of nutritional information disseminated by the media? Why or why not? How should one evaluate whether such nutritional claims are valid?

12. It is estimated that 10% of Americans don't get enough to eat on a regular basis. Worldwide, at least 840 million people go to bed hungry most nights, and millions of people have starved to death in recent decades. In some cases, war, poor crop yields, and disease epidemics strip people of food. Many also blame global food distribution systems, saying it is not inadequate food production but unequal food distribution that causes food shortages. What responsibility do nations have for feeding their citizens? For feeding the people of other countries? What do you think you can do to lessen world hunger?

Answers to all questions can be found in Appendix 3.
For study help and Activities, go to campbellbiology.com or the student CD-ROM.

Testing Your Understanding—Unit II

Biology: Concepts & Connections,
Chapter 21: Nutrition and Digestion

 Pages 38–44
CHECKING YOUR COMPREHENSION

Choose the best answer for each of the following questions.

1. The introductory section of the chapter that focuses on whales suggests that
   a. whales are the largest animals in the world.
   b. ingesting nutrients is a complex process.
   c. digestion is very challenging for most mammals.
   d. the diet of a whale is not sufficient to ensure proper nourishment.

2. Which statement is not true concerning animal ingestion?
   a. Substrate feeders sustain life on their food source as they eat it.
   b. Bulk feeders primarily consume hefty portions of fare at one time.
   c. Suspension feeders are able to feed on land and in the water.
   d. Fluid feeders obtain their food from live vegetation and animals.

3. By examining Figure 21.2B, one can learn that
   a. enzymes separate during chemical digestion.
   b. polymers are too large to pass through plasma membranes.
   c. nucleic acid-digesting enzymes act differently than all other enzymes.
   d. monomers become polymers after the breakdown of diminutive proteins.

Identify the following statements as true or false.

4. The four states of food processing are interchangeable.

5. Saliva is comprised of many different substances that aid food processing.

6. The digestive glands are comprised of the salivary glands, pancreas, and gall bladder.

Answer the following questions.

7. Explain the similarities and differences between herbivores, carnivores, and omnivores.

8. Describe the activity portrayed in Figure 21.2A.

9. Compare the alimentary canal of the bird to the alimentary canal of the grasshopper.

Define each term as it is used in the chapter.

10. trachea

11. gastrovascular cavity

12. peristalsis

13. alimentary canal

14. crop

Discussion and Critical Thinking Questions

1. List the different items you eat in a typical lunch. Analyze the purpose of the four types of teeth in your mouth and describe in detail which ones would be involved in eating which items.

2. Some illustrations in this section are photographs while others are graphic representations of specific organs. How does the composition of the visuals in this section affect their usefulness? Choose one of each type and explain its benefits and detriments.

Pages 45–52
CHECKING YOUR COMPREHENSION

Choose the best answer for each of the following questions.

1. Which of the following statements best describes the purpose of the Heimlich maneuver?
   a. To elevate the diaphragm and contract the esophagus during peristalsis.
   b. To stand behind a choking person and expel an object from their stomach.
   c. To clear the throat of a foreign object or rid the lungs of excess water.
   d. To release acid and enzymes from the stomach to eject alien matter.

2. The primary function of Figure 21.11B is to
   a. illustrate in detail the configuration of the small intestines.
   b. illustrate the process of chemical digestion in the small intestines.
   c. compare and contrast the intestinal walls to the lumen of the intestines.
   d. explain the process of nutrient absorption into epithelial cells.

3. Which of the following information would not be useful when examining the adaptation of an animal's digestive system?
   a. The length of the animal's digestive tract.
   b. The complexity of an animal's system for cellulose digestion.
   c. The type of food the animal eats.
   d. The duration of the animal's rumination.

Identify the following statements as true or false.

4. Digestive acids can cause gastric ulcers.

5. In the absence of peristalsis, food would reach the stomach with the use of gravity.

6. Omnivores have different basic nutritional needs than herbivores and carnivores.

Answer the following questions.

7. List the components of gastric juice.

8. Explain how polypeptides are transformed into amino acids in the small intestines.

9. Identify the main function of the colon.

Define each term as it is used in the chapter.

10. gastrin

11. acid chyme

12. bile

13. appendix

14. duodenum

Discussion and Critical Thinking Questions

1. Which two figures in this section of the text were most useful to your understanding of the various organs and their functions? Explain what made them superior to the other graphics in the section.

2. Using the information in this section, explain what types of foods the body has a hard time digesting.

3. Evaluate Table 21.15. What is the main point of the table, and what is the most important information revealed that is crucial to a person's dietary choices and exercise regime?

Pages 53–59
CHECKING YOUR COMPREHENSION

Choose the best answer for each of the following questions.

1. Which of the following vitamins yield extreme results when deficient in a person's body?
   a. Vitamin D, niacin, and biotin
   b. Biotin, vitamin E, and vitamin K
   c. Niacin, vitamin C, and folic acid
   d. Pantothenic acid, ascorbic acid, and vitamin B-6

2. Which of the following facts is not given regarding obesity?
   a. Scientists found that obesity is genetic.
   b. Research indicates that obesity results from malfunctioning digestion.
   c. Fattening food and sedimentary lifestyles contribute to obesity.
   d. Craving fatty foods can be traced back through evolution.

3. What information cannot be found in Figure 21.21?
   a. The ingredients of the product.
   b. The serving size of the product.
   c. The shelf life of the product.
   d. The general nutritional information of the product.

Identify the following statements as true or false.

4. The text infers that there are different types of vegetarian diets.

5. Leptin levels are directly related to the ability to depress appetite.

6. Low-carbohydrate diets have been found to have only short-lived benefits.

Answer the following questions.

7. Explain the difference between being undernourished and malnourished.

8. List the eight essential amino acids.

9. Identify the differences between vitamins and minerals.

Discussion and Critical Thinking Questions

1. What are the two main reasons that "Dietary Sources" are included in Table 21.19?

2. Explain the importance of the research conducted with mice regarding obesity. What can we learn from this research, and what other research do you think would be beneficial?

3. What information about cholesterol is important to take into consideration when making decisions about behavioral risk factors of cardiovascular disease and cancer?

Chapter Review
END OF CHAPTER ANALYSIS

1. Which of the following would be the best strategy regarding the Chapter Review prior to reading the chapter?
   a. Skim it prior to reading the chapter to preview the information.
   b. Answer all of the questions to see if you really need to read the chapter.
   c. Answer only the "Applying the Concepts" questions prior to reading the chapter.
   d. Don't look at any of it until after reading the chapter.

2. After reading the chapter, you should be able to answer all of the following questions except which one?
   a. What occurs in the small intestines during digestion?
   b. What essential information is included on food labels?
   c. Why do ruminant mammals have elaborate systems of digestion?
   d. What are the symptoms of mineral and vitamin deficiencies?

3. The chapter employs all of the following techniques for making the material easier to read except
   a. marginal annotations.
   b. graphic elements.
   c. boldface type.
   d. chapter outline.

Group Projects

1. Survey ten people about their favorite foods. Using information in the chapter regarding nutrients, diets, and cholesterol, rank the ten foods from most healthy to least healthy.

2. Many people in today's society are cognizant of the health dangers of certain kinds of diets but continue to practice fad dieting. What advice would you give someone who relies on formula diets? What advice would you give someone who relies on extremely low-fat diets?

Journal Ideas

1. In your journal write down everything you eat for seven days. Using the information in Table 21.18 and Table 21.19, evaluate your ingestion of the vitamins and minerals needed to ensure a healthy diet and maintain optimum body functions. What vitamins and minerals is your diet lacking, and what should you eat to increase their presence in your body?

2. Using the information presented in the chapter, imagine you are a piece of food, and trace your movement through digestion from the time you are introduced into the oral cavity.

Unit III

From

Margaret K. Lial
Stanley A. Salzman
Diana L. Hestwood

Basic College Mathematics

Seventh Edition

Chapter 10:
Statistics

An Introduction to Statistics

Statistics is the branch of mathematics that deals with the collection, analysis, and presentation of data. Statistical science is used in a variety of academic disciplines such as economics, psychology, biology, medicine, sociology, anthropology, astronomy, physics, chemistry, geology, engineering, computer science, business, and government.

Statistics is a higher-level math course that is required for students who plan to study in the mathematical fields. Many college students enroll in statistics courses to fulfill higher-level mathematic requirements. There is a demand for qualified statisticians in many career fields such as actuarial, meteorology, educational testing and measurement, biostatistics, statistical computing, financial engineering, medicine, pharmaceutical research, risk assessment, and environmental science.

Strategies for Reading Statistics

When reading a statistics textbook, it is important to read the introduction, summaries, section headings, and diagrams. It is necessary to look at the problems at the end of the chapter to understand the expectations. Take note of new terms and formulas. Solving problems is the most important part of learning mathematics, so be sure to carefully read through the problems and draw appropriate diagrams.

Statistics

The old saying, "A picture is worth a thousand words" was never more true than when applied to the understanding of data. As an information society, we are constantly being bombarded with facts and numbers. The ability to understand and interpret the many types of information and the many ways it is presented has become essential. For example, if you own or manage a business, you need to understand and interpret the sales history of the business and the performance of employees to make wise managerial decisions. (See **Section 10.2,** Exercises 25–32 and 35–42, and **Section 10.3,** Exercises 29–36.)

10.1 Circle Graphs

OBJECTIVES

1 Read and understand a circle graph.
2 Use a circle graph.
3 Draw a circle graph.

1 Use the circle graph to answer each question.

(a) The greatest number of hours is spent in which activity?

(b) How many more hours are spent working than studying?

(c) Find the total number of hours spent studying, working, and attending classes.

2 Use the circle graph to find each ratio. Write the ratios as fractions in lowest terms.

(a) Hours spent driving to whole day

(b) Hours spent sleeping to whole day

(c) Hours spent attending class and studying to whole day

(d) Hours spent driving and working to whole day

The word *statistics* originally came from words that mean *state numbers.* State numbers refer to numerical information, or *data,* gathered by the government such as the number of births, deaths, or marriages in a population. Today, the word *statistics* has a much broader application; data from the fields of economics, social science, and business can all be organized and studied under the branch of mathematics called *statistics.*

OBJECTIVE 1 **Read and understand a circle graph.** It can be hard to understand a large collection of data. The graphs described in this section can be used to help you make sense of such data. The **circle graph** is used to show how a total amount is divided into parts. The circle graph below shows you how 24 hours in the life of a college student are divided among different activities.

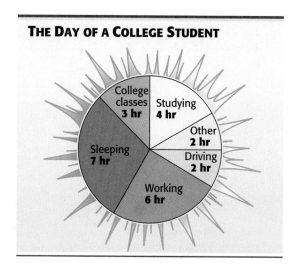

THE DAY OF A COLLEGE STUDENT

College classes 3 hr | Studying 4 hr | Other 2 hr | Driving 2 hr | Working 6 hr | Sleeping 7 hr

> **Work Problem 1 at the Side.**

OBJECTIVE 2 **Use a circle graph.** The above circle graph uses pie-shaped pieces called *sectors* to show the amount of time spent on each activity (the total must be 24 hours); a circle graph can therefore be used to compare the time spent on one activity to the total number of hours in the day.

EXAMPLE 1 **Using a Circle Graph**

Find the ratio of time spent in college classes to the total number of hours in a day. Write the ratio as a fraction in lowest terms. (See **Section 5.1.**)

The circle graph shows that 3 of the 24 hours in a day are spent in class. The ratio of class time to the hours in a day is shown below.

$$\frac{3 \text{ hours (college classes)}}{24 \text{ hours (whole day)}} = \frac{3 \text{ hours}}{24 \text{ hours}} = \frac{3 \div 3}{24 \div 3} = \frac{1}{8} \leftarrow \text{Lowest terms}$$

> **Work Problem 2 at the Side.**

The circle graph above can also be used to find the ratio of the time spent on one activity to the time spent on any other activity.

ANSWERS
1. (a) sleeping (b) 2 hr (c) 13 hr
2. (a) $\frac{1}{12}$ (b) $\frac{7}{24}$ (c) $\frac{7}{24}$ (d) $\frac{1}{3}$

EXAMPLE 2 **Finding a Ratio from a Circle Graph**

Use the circle graph on a student's day to find the ratio of study time to class time. Write the ratio as a fraction in lowest terms.

The circle graph shows 4 hours spent studying and 3 hours spent in class. The ratio of study time to class time is shown below.

$$\frac{4 \text{ hours (study)}}{3 \text{ hours (class)}} = \frac{4 \text{ hours}}{3 \text{ hours}} = \frac{4}{3}$$

Work Problem 3 at the Side. ▶▶▶

A circle graph often shows data as percents. For example, suppose that the yearly vending machine snack food sales in the United States were $36 billion. The circle graph below shows how sales were divided among various types of snack foods. The entire circle represents $36 billion in sales. Each sector represents the sales of one snack item as a percent of the total sales (the total must be 100%).

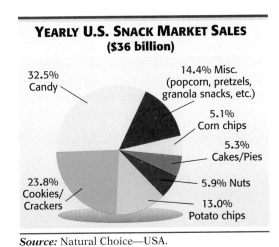

YEARLY U.S. SNACK MARKET SALES
($36 billion)

32.5% Candy

14.4% Misc. (popcorn, pretzels, granola snacks, etc.)

5.1% Corn chips

5.3% Cakes/Pies

5.9% Nuts

13.0% Potato chips

23.8% Cookies/ Crackers

Source: Natural Choice—USA.

EXAMPLE 3 **Calculating an Amount Using a Circle Graph**

Use the circle graph above on vending machine snack sales to find the amount spent on candy for the year.

Recall the percent equation.

part = percent • whole

The total sales are $36 billion, so the whole is $36 billion. The percent is 32.5, or as a decimal, 0.325. Find the part.

$$\begin{array}{ccc} \text{part} = & \text{percent} & \cdot & \text{whole} \\ \downarrow & \downarrow & & \downarrow \end{array}$$

$$x = 0.325 \cdot 36 \text{ billion}$$

$$x = 11.7 \text{ billion}$$

The amount spent on candy was $11.7 billion or $11,700,000,000.

Work Problem 4 at the Side. ▶▶▶

3 Use the circle graph on a student's day to find the following ratios. Write the ratios as fractions in lowest terms.

(a) Hours spent in class to hours spent studying

(b) Hours spent working to hours spent sleeping

(c) Hours spent driving to hours spent working

(d) Hours spent in class to hours spent for "Other"

4 Use the circle graph on vending machine snack sales to find the following.

(a) The amount spent on corn chips

(b) The amount spent on miscellaneous (popcorn, pretzels, granola snacks, etc.)

(c) The amount spent on cakes/pies

(d) The amount spent on cookies/crackers

ANSWERS

3. (a) $\frac{3}{4}$ (b) $\frac{6}{7}$ (c) $\frac{1}{3}$ (d) $\frac{3}{2}$

4. (a) $1.836 billion or $1,836,000,000
   (b) $5.184 billion or $5,184,000,000
   (c) $1.908 billion or $1,908,000,000
   (d) $8.568 billion or $8,568,000,000

OBJECTIVE 3 Draw a circle graph. The coordinator of the Fair Oaks Youth Soccer League organizes teams in five age groups. She places the players in various age groups as follows.

Age Group	Percent of Total
Under 8 years	20%
Ages 8–9	15%
Ages 10–11	25%
Ages 12–13	25%
Ages 14–15	15%
Total	100%

You can show these percents by using a circle graph. A circle has 360 degrees (written 360°). The 360° represents the entire league, or 100% of the soccer players.

EXAMPLE 4 Drawing a Circle Graph

Using the data on *age groups,* find the number of degrees in the sector that would represent the "Under 8" group, and begin constructing a circle graph.

Recall that a complete circle has 360° (see **Section 8.1**). Because the "Under 8" group makes up 20% of the total number of players, the number of degrees needed for the "Under 8" sector of the circle graph is 20% of 360°.

$$(360°)(20\%) = (360°)(0.2) = 72°$$

Use a tool called a **protractor** to make a circle graph. First, using a straightedge, draw a line from the center of a circle to the left edge. Place the hole in the protractor over the center of the circle, making sure that 0 on the protractor lines up with the line that was drawn. Find 72° and make a mark as shown in the illustration. Then remove the protractor and use the straightedge to draw a line from the center of the circle to the 72° mark at the edge of the circle. This sector is 72° and represents the "Under 8" group.

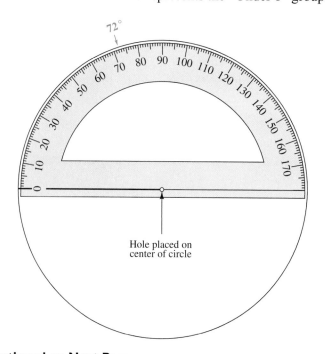

Hole placed on center of circle

Continued on Next Page

To draw the "Ages 8–9" sector, begin by finding the number of degrees in the sector.

$$(360°)(15\%) = (360°)(0.15) = 54°$$

Again, place the hole of the protractor over the center of the circle, but this time align 0 on the second line that was drawn. Make a mark at 54° and draw a line as before. This sector is 54° and represents the "Ages 8–9" group.

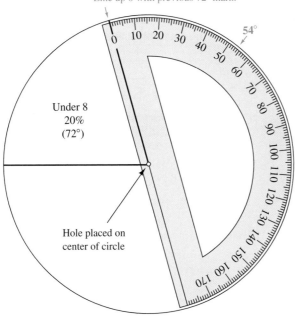

Line up 0 with previous 72° mark.

CAUTION

You must be certain that the hole in the protractor is placed over the exact center of the circle each time you measure the size of a sector.

Work Problem 5 at the Side. ▶▶▶

Use this circle for Problem 5 at the side.

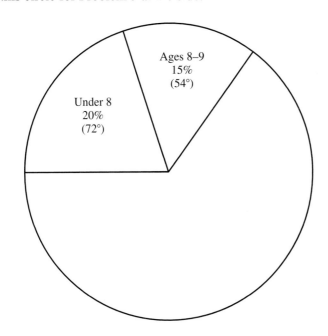

⑤ Using the information on the soccer age groups in the table, find the number of degrees needed for each sector and complete the circle graph at the bottom left.

(a) Ages 10–11

(b) Ages 12–13

(c) Ages 14–15

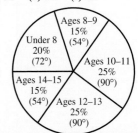

Real-Data Applications

Just in Time

Antique clocks usually chime either on the hour or both on the hour and the half hour. The mechanism that controls the chimes is a set of gears called the count plate and hammer wheel, and a lever called the count hook.

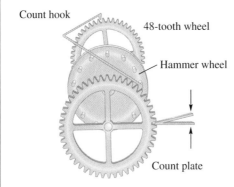

Count hook

48-tooth wheel

Hammer wheel

Count plate

Hour-Striking Clocks

1. If a clock chimes only on the hour, what will be the total number of chimes in a 12-hour period? (*Hint:* For example, it will chime 6 times at 6:00.)

    $1 + 2 + \cdots + 12 = 78$ chimes

2. If the count plate has one gear tooth for each chime, what fractional part of the count plate is one tooth?

    $$\frac{1}{78}$$

3. How many degrees correspond to one gear tooth? **4.62° (rounded) or $4\frac{8}{13}°$**

4. The mechanism designed to move the count plate has two wheels. The hammer wheel has 13 pins, which is combined with a wheel with 48 teeth and a pinion that fits 8 teeth. That gives a 6:1 ratio. What is significant about the combination of 13 and 6 that causes the count plate to move one gear tooth?

    $13 \times 6 = 78$, so the gear advances $\frac{1}{78}$ of the circle.

Hour- and Half-Hour-Striking Clocks

5. If a clock chimes on the hour and also one time on each half hour, what will be the total number of chimes in a 12-hour period? **$78 + 12 = 90$ chimes**

6. If the count plate has one tooth for each chime, what fractional part of the count plate makes one tooth? **$\frac{1}{90}$**

7. How many degrees correspond to one gear tooth? **4°**

8. If the count plate has a diameter of 2 in., what is the circumference of the count plate, rounded to the nearest hundredth? What is the width of each gear tooth, rounded to the nearest hundredth? (*Note:* Use $\pi \approx 3.14$.) **$C \approx 6.28$ in.; width of gear tooth ≈ 0.07 in.**

10.1 Exercises

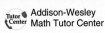
This circle graph shows the cost of adding an art studio to an existing home. Use this circle graph to answer Exercises 1–6. Write ratios as fractions in lowest terms. See Examples 1 and 2.

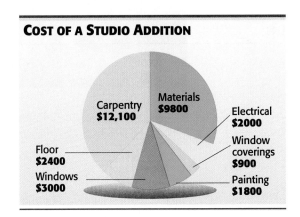

COST OF A STUDIO ADDITION

Carpentry $12,100
Materials $9800
Electrical $2000
Window coverings $900
Floor $2400
Windows $3000
Painting $1800

1. Find the total cost of adding the art studio

   $32,000

2. What is the largest single expense in adding the studio?

   carpentry

3. Find the ratio of the cost of materials to the total remodeling cost.

   $$\frac{9800}{32,000} = \frac{49}{160}$$

4. Find the ratio of the cost of painting to the total remodeling cost.

   $$\frac{1800}{32,000} = \frac{9}{160}$$

5. Find the ratio of the cost of carpentry to the cost of window coverings.

   $$\frac{12,100}{900} = \frac{121}{9}$$

6. Find the ratio of the cost of windows to the cost of the floor.

   $$\frac{3000}{2400} = \frac{5}{4}$$

This circle graph, adapted from USA Today, *shows the number of people in a survey who gave various reasons for eating dinner at restaurants. Use this circle graph to answer Exercises 7–14. Write ratios as fractions in lowest terms. See Examples 1 and 2.*

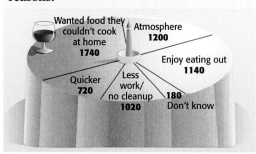

ON THE TOWN
When asked in a survey why they ate dinner in restaurants, a group of people gave these reasons.

Wanted food they couldn't cook at home **1740**

Atmosphere **1200**

Enjoy eating out **1140**

Quicker **720**

Less work/no cleanup **1020**

180 Don't know

Source: Market Facts for Tyson Foods.

7. Which reason was given by the least number of people?

Don't know

8. Which reason was given by the second-highest number of people?

Atmosphere

9. Those who said dining out is "Quicker" to total people in the survey

$$\frac{720}{6000} = \frac{3}{25}$$

10. Those who said "Enjoy eating out" to the total people in the survey

$$\frac{1140}{6000} = \frac{19}{100}$$

11. Those who said "Less work/no cleanup" to those who said "Atmosphere"

$$\frac{1020}{1200} = \frac{17}{20}$$

12. Those who said "Don't know" to those who said "Quicker"

$$\frac{180}{720} = \frac{1}{4}$$

13. Those who said "Wanted food they couldn't cook at home" to those who said "Less work/no cleanup"

$$\frac{1740}{1020} = \frac{29}{17}$$

14. Those who said "Atmosphere" to those who said "Enjoy eating out"

$$\frac{1200}{1140} = \frac{20}{19}$$

This circle graph shows the favorite hot dog toppings in the United States. Each topping is expressed as a percent of the 3200 people in the survey. Use the graph to find the number of people in the survey who favored each of the toppings in Exercises 15–20.

15. Onions

160 people

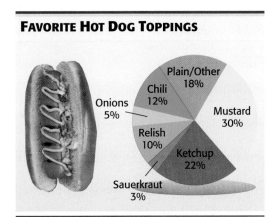

FAVORITE HOT DOG TOPPINGS

Plain/Other 18%
Chili 12%
Onions 5%
Mustard 30%
Relish 10%
Ketchup 22%
Sauerkraut 3%

Source: National Hot Dog and Sausage Council.

16. Ketchup

704 people

17. Sauerkraut

96 people

18. Relish

320 people

19. Mustard

960 people

20. Chili

384 people

The National Academy of Sciences recommends that adults get 1000 mg of calcium daily, or about three 8-ounce glasses of milk. The circle graph, adapted from USA Today, *shows the daily consumption of milk products by adults. If 5540 adults were surveyed in this study, find the number of people giving each response in Exercises 21–26. Round to the nearest whole number. See Example 3.*

21. Consume none or very few milk products

1219 people (rounded)

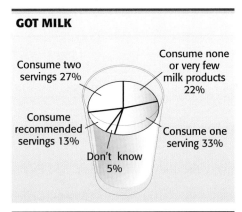

GOT MILK

Consume two servings 27%
Consume none or very few milk products 22%
Consume recommended servings 13%
Consume one serving 33%
Don't know 5%

Source: Market Facts for Milk Mustache Mobile 100-City Cruise for Calcium.

22. Consume recommended servings

720 people (rounded)

23. Consume one serving

1828 people (rounded)

24. Consume two servings

1496 people (rounded)

25. Don't know

277 people

26. Consume less than the recommended servings (Do not include those who don't know.)

4543 people (rounded)

27. Describe the procedure for determining how large each sector must be to represent each of the items in a circle graph.

   First find the percent of the total that is to be represented by each item. Next, multiply the percent by 360° to find the size of each sector. Finally, use a protractor to draw each sector.

28. A protractor is the tool used to draw a circle graph. Give a brief explanation of what the protractor does and how you would use it to measure and draw each sector in the circle graph.

   A protractor is used to measure the number of degrees in a sector. First, you must draw a line from the center of the circle to the left edge. Next, place the hole of the protractor over the center of the circle, making sure that the 0 on the protractor is on the line. Finally, make a mark at the desired number of degrees. This gives you the size of the sector.

During one semester Kara Diano spent $5460 for school expenses as shown in the following chart. Find all numbers missing from the chart.

Item	Dollar Amount	Percent of Total	Degrees of a Circle
29. Rent	$1365	25%	**90°**
30. Food	$1092	**20%**	72°
31. Clothing	$546	**10%**	**36°**
32. Books	$546	10%	**36°**
33. Tuition	$819	15%	**54°**
34. Savings	$273	**5%**	**18°**
35. Entertainment	$819	**15%**	54°

36. Draw a circle graph by using the above information. See Example 4.

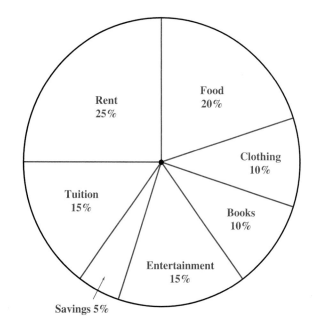

37. White Water Rafting Company divides its annual sales into five categories as follows.

Category	Annual Sales
Adventure classes	$12,500
Grocery and provision sales	$40,000
Equipment rentals	$60,000
Rafting tours	$50,000
Equipment sales	$37,500

(a) Find the total sales for the year.

$200,000

(b) Find the number of degrees in a circle graph for each item.

22.5°; 72°; 108°; 90°; 67.5°

(c) Make a circle graph showing this information.

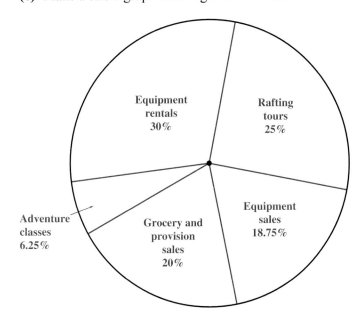

38. A book publisher had 25% of total sales in mysteries, 10% in biographies, 15% in cookbooks, 15% in romance novels, 20% in science, and the rest in business books.

(a) Find the number of degrees in a circle graph for each type of book.

90°; 36°; 54°; 54°; 72°; 54°

(b) Draw a circle graph.

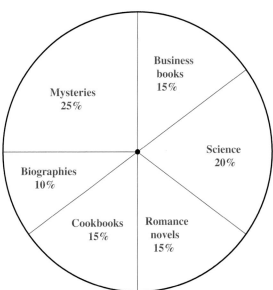

39. The Pathfinder Research Group asked 4488 Americans how they fall asleep, and the results are shown in the figure on the right.

(a) Use this information to complete the chart and draw a circle graph. Round to the nearest whole percent and to the nearest degree.

Sleeping Position	Number of Americans	Percent of Total	Number of Degrees
Side	2464	55% (rounded)	198°
Not sure	220	5% (rounded)	18°
Stomach	536	12% (rounded)	43° (rounded)
Varies	520	12% (rounded)	43° (rounded)
Back	748	17% (rounded)	61° (rounded)

(b) Add up the percents. Is the total 100%? Explain why or why not.

No. The total is 101% due to rounding.

(c) Add up the degrees. Is the total 360°? Explain why or why not.

No. The total is 363° due to rounding.

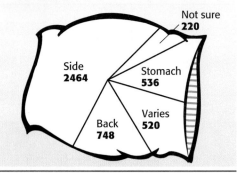

SET TO SLEEP

Number of Americans surveyed who fall asleep on their:

Not sure 220

Side 2464

Stomach 536

Varies 520

Back 748

Source: Pathfinder Research Group.

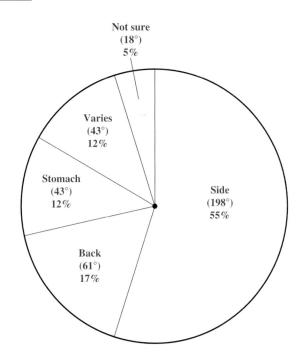

10.2 Bar Graphs and Line Graphs

OBJECTIVE 1 Read and understand a bar graph.   Bar graphs are useful when showing comparisons. For example, the bar graph below compares the number of college graduates who continued taking advanced courses in their major field during each of 5 years.

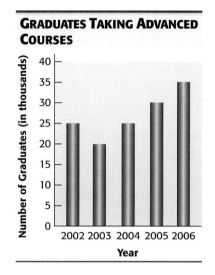

GRADUATES TAKING ADVANCED COURSES

EXAMPLE 1 Using a Bar Graph

How many college graduates took advanced classes in their major field in 2004?

The bar for 2004 rises to 25. Notice the label along the left side of the graph that says "Number of Graduates (in thousands)." The phrase *in thousands* means you have to multiply 25 by 1000 to get 25,000. So, 25,000 (not 25) graduates took advanced classes in their major field in 2004.

Work Problem 1 at the Side.))))

OBJECTIVE 2 Read and understand a double-bar graph.   A double-bar graph can be used to compare two sets of data. The graph below shows the number of DSL (digital subscriber line) installations each quarter for two different years.

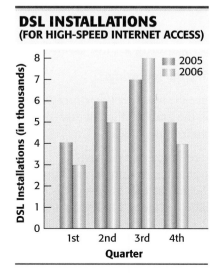

DSL INSTALLATIONS
(FOR HIGH-SPEED INTERNET ACCESS)

2005
2006

Read and understand

1 a bar graph;

2 a double-bar graph;

3 a line graph;

4 a comparison line graph.

---

1 Use the bar graph at the left to find the number of college graduates who took advanced classes in their major field in each of these years.

(a) 2002

(b) 2003

(c) 2005

(d) 2006

ANSWERS
1. (a) 25,000 graduates
   (b) 20,000 graduates
   (c) 30,000 graduates
   (d) 35,000 graduates

2 Use the double-bar graph to find the number of DSL installations in 2005 and 2006 for each quarter.

(a) 1st quarter

(b) 3rd quarter

(c) 4th quarter

(d) Find the greatest number of installations. Identify the quarter and the year in which they occurred.

EXAMPLE 2 **Reading a Double-Bar Graph**

Use the double-bar graph on the previous page to find the following.

(a) The number of DSL installations in the second quarter of 2005
There are two bars for the second quarter. The color code in the upper right-hand corner of the graph tells you that the **red bars** represent 2005. So the **red bar** on the *left* is for the 2nd quarter of 2005. It rises to 6. Multiply 6 by 1000 because the label on the left side of the graph says *in thousands*. So there were 6000 DSL installations for the second quarter in 2005.

(b) The number of DSL installations in the second quarter of 2006
The green bar for the second quarter rises to 5 and 5 times 1000 is 5000. So, in the second quarter of 2006, there were 5000 DSL installations.

> **CAUTION**
> Use a ruler or straightedge to line up the top of the bar with the number on the left side of the graph.

◀◀◀ Work Problem 2 at the Side.

---

3 Use the line graph at the right to find the number of trout stocked in each month.

(a) June

(b) May

(c) April

(d) July

OBJECTIVE **3** **Read and understand a line graph.** A **line graph** is often useful for showing a trend. The line graph below shows the number of trout stocked along the Feather River over a 5-month period. Each dot indicates the number of trout stocked during the month directly below that dot.

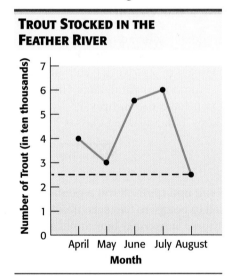

TROUT STOCKED IN THE FEATHER RIVER

EXAMPLE 3 **Understanding a Line Graph**

Use the line graph to find the following.

(a) In which month were the least number of trout stocked?
The lowest point on the graph is the dot directly over August, so the least number of trout were stocked in August.

(b) How many trout were stocked in August?
Use a ruler or straightedge to line up the August dot with the numbers along the left edge of the graph. The August dot is halfway between the 2 and the 3. Notice that the label on the left side says *in ten thousands*. So August is halfway between $(2 \cdot 10,000)$ and $(3 \cdot 10,000)$. It is halfway between 20,000 and 30,000. That means 25,000 trout were stocked in August.

◀◀◀ Work Problem 3 at the Side.

OBJECTIVE 4 Read and understand a comparison line graph. Two sets of data can also be compared by drawing two line graphs together as a **comparison line graph.** For example, the line graph below compares the number of minivans and the number of sport-utility vehicles (SUVs) sold during each of 5 years.

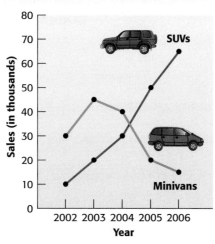

RIDING HIGH
SALES OF MINIVANS COMPARED TO SUVs

4 Use the comparison line graph at the left to find the following.

(a) The number of minivans sold in 2002, 2004, 2005, and 2006.

(b) The number of SUVs sold in 2002, 2003, 2004, and 2005

EXAMPLE 4 Interpreting a Comparison Line Graph

Use the comparison line graph above to find the following.

(a) The number of minivans sold in 2003
    Find the dot on the blue line above 2003. Use a ruler or straightedge to line up the dot with the numbers along the left edge. The dot is halfway between 40 and 50, which is 45. Then, 45 times 1000 is 45,000 minivans sold in 2003.

(b) The number of SUVs sold in 2006
    The red line on the graph shows that 65,000 SUVs were sold in 2006.

(c) The first full year in which the number of SUVs sold was greater than the number of minivans sold

> **NOTE**
> Both the double-bar graph and the comparison line graph are used to compare two or more sets of data.

Work Problem 4 at the Side. ▶▶▶

Grocery Shopping

1. The graph at the right is a double-bar graph. What is it about? Write a brief paragraph describing the general purpose of the graph.

A comparison is made between the strategies used by men and women while grocery shopping. The purpose of the survey might be for general interest, or to gain information to help grocery stores decide how to spend advertising money.

2. Which two strategies do women use most often?

Check ads for specials; Mail/newspaper coupons

3. Which two strategies do men use most often?

Stock up on bargains; Stick to list

4. Which two strategies show the greatest difference in use between the men and women surveyed?

Check ads for specials; Mail/newspaper coupons

5. Which two strategies show the least difference? **Buy store brands; Stock up on bargains**

6. The sum of the percents for the women's responses and the men's responses do not add to 100%. Why? **Although the graph does not say, the people surveyed apparently could choose more than one strategy.**

7. Is it possible to decide how many of the people in the survey use *none* of the strategies listed? Why? **No, because "none of these" was not a choice, and those polled apparently could choose more than one strategy.**

8. Sometimes people "jump to conclusions" without enough evidence. Which of these conclusions are appropriate, based on the information in the graph?

   (a) Men and women use a variety of saving strategies when grocery shopping. **reasonable**
   (b) Men spend more for groceries than women. **reasonable**
   (c) Men eat more groceries than women. **unreasonable**
   (d) Women are better grocery shoppers than men. **unreasonable**
   (e) There are some differences in the grocery shopping strategies used by men and women.
   reasonable

9. Conduct a survey of your class members. Find out how many of them regularly use each of the saving strategies shown in the graph. Complete the table below. **Answers will vary.**

10. Make a double-bar graph showing your survey data. How is your data similar to the graph shown above? How is it different? **Answers will vary.**

GENDER BUYS

On average, each person spends $32 weekly on groceries. Men average $35 and women $32. Saving strategies include:

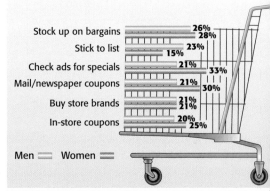

Men ▭ Women ▭

Source: Food Marketing Institute.

Teaching notes for this activity are provided in the *Printed Test Bank and Instructor's Resource Guide.*

Strategy	Number of Women Using Strategy	Percent of Women Using Strategy	Number of Men Using Strategy	Percent of Men Using Strategy
Stock up on bargains				
Stick to list				
Check ads for specials				
Mail/newspaper coupons				
Buy store brands				
In-store coupons				
Total				

10.2 Exercises

| **FOR EXTRA HELP** | 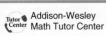 Addison-Wesley Math Tutor Center | 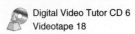 MathXL | Digital Video Tutor CD 6 Videotape 18 | 📖 Student's Solutions Manual | *MyMathLab* MyMathLab | 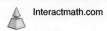 Interactmath.com |

The American Farm Bureau Federation reports that the average adult in the United States will work 40 *days (rounded to the nearest day) to earn enough to pay the annual household food bill. This was found by multiplying the average percent of household income spent on food by 365 (the number of days in a year). This bar graph shows the percent of income spent in various countries of the world. Use this graph to answer Exercises 1–6. See Example 1.*

TAKING A BITE OUT OF HOUSEHOLD INCOME

The average American adult will work 40 days each year to earn enough to pay the household food bill. Percent of household income spent on food in:

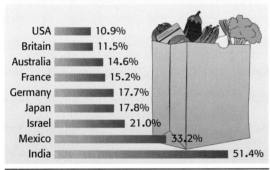

USA 10.9%
Britain 11.5%
Australia 14.6%
France 15.2%
Germany 17.7%
Japan 17.8%
Israel 21.0%
Mexico 33.2%
India 51.4%

Source: American Farm Bureau Federation.

1. In which country is the highest percent of income spent on food? What percent is this?

   India; 51.4%

2. In which country is the lowest percent of income spent on food? What percent is this?

   USA; 10.9%

3. List all countries in the graph in which less than 15% of household income is spent, on average, for food.

   USA, Britain, and Australia

4. List all countries in the graph in which more than 20% of household income is spent, on average, for food.

   Israel, Mexico, and India

5. How many days each year will the average adult have to work to earn enough to pay for food in Mexico? Round to the nearest day.

   121 days (rounded)

6. How many days each year will the average adult have to work to earn enough to pay for food in Israel? Round to the nearest day.

   77 days (rounded)

This double-bar graph shows the number of workers who were unemployed in a city during the first six months of 2005 and 2006. Use this graph to answer Exercises 7–12. See Example 2.

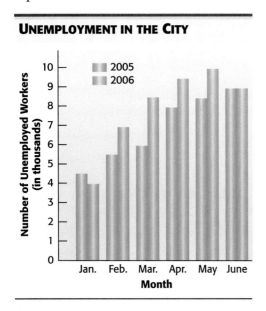

7. In which month in 2006 were the greatest number of workers unemployed? What was the total number unemployed in that month?

   May; 10,000 unemployed

8. How many workers were unemployed in January of 2005?

   4500 workers

9. How many more workers were unemployed in February of 2006 than in February of 2005?

   1500 workers

10. How many fewer workers were unemployed in March of 2005 than in March of 2006?

    2500 workers

11. Find the increase in the number of unemployed workers from February 2005 to April 2006.

    4000 workers

12. Find the increase in the number of unemployed workers from January 2006 to June 2006.

    5000 workers

This double-bar graph shows sales of super unleaded and supreme unleaded gasoline at a service station for each of 5 years. Use this graph to answer Exercises 13–18. See Example 2.

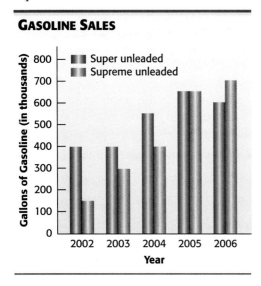

13. How many gallons of supreme unleaded gasoline were sold in 2002?

    150,000 gal

14. How many gallons of super unleaded gasoline were sold in 2005?

    650,000 gal

15. In which year did the greatest difference in sales between super unleaded and supreme unleaded gasoline occur? Find the difference.

    2002; 250,000 gal

16. In which year did the sales of supreme unleaded gasoline surpass the sales of super unleaded gasoline?

    2006

17. Find the increase in supreme unleaded gasoline sales from 2002 to 2006.

    550,000 gal

18. Find the increase in super unleaded gasoline sales from 2002 to 2006.

    200,000 gal

This line graph shows how the personal computer (PC) has evolved over the two decades of its existence. What began as a technician's dream is now a common tool of business and home life. Use this line graph to answer Exercises 19–24. See Example 3.

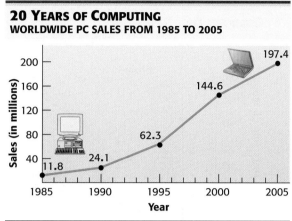

20 YEARS OF COMPUTING
WORLDWIDE PC SALES FROM 1985 TO 2005

Source: Gartner Dataquest.

19. Find the number of PCs shipped in 1990.

24.1 million or 24,100,000 PCs

20. What was the number of PCs shipped in 1995?

62.3 million or 62,300,000 PCs

21. Find the increase in the number of PCs shipped in 2005 from the number shipped in 1995.

135.1 million or 135,100,000 PCs

22. How many more PCs were shipped in 2000 than in 1990?   **120.5 million or 120,500,000 PCs**

23. Give two possible explanations for the increase in the number of PCs shipped.

Answers will vary. Some possibilities are: Greater demand as a result of lower price; more uses and applications for the owner, improved technology.

24. Give two possible conditions that could result in a decrease in PC shipments in the future.

Answers will vary. Some possibilities are: Fewer people will want a computer because they already own one, new technology will replace the computer with something better.

This comparison line graph shows the number of compact discs (CDs) sold by two different chain stores during each of 5 years. Use this graph to find the annual number of CDs sold in each year shown in Exercises 25–30. See Example 4.

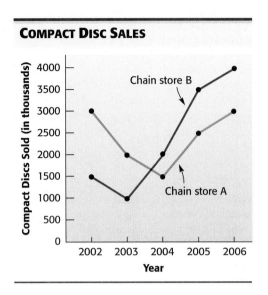

COMPACT DISC SALES

25. Chain store A in 2006   **3,000,000 CDs**

26. Chain store A in 2005   **2,500,000 CDs**

27. Chain store A in 2004   **1,500,000 CDs**

28. Chain store B in 2006   **4,000,000 CDs**

29. Chain store B in 2005   **3,500,000 CDs**

30. Chain store B in 2004   **2,000,000 CDs**

31. Looking at the comparison line graph above, which store would you like to own? Explain why. Based on the graph, what amount of sales would you predict for your store in 2007?

Probably store B with greater sales. Predicted sales might be 4,500,000 CDs to 5,000,000 CDs in 2007.

32. In the comparison line graph above, store B used to have lower sales than store A. What might have happened to cause this change? Give two possible explanations.

Some possible answers are that store B may have started to: do more advertising; keep longer store hours; give better training to their staff; employ more help; give better service than store A.

🖉 **33.** Explain in your own words why a bar graph or a line graph (not a double-bar graph or comparison line graph) can be used to show only one set of data.

A single bar or a single line must be used for each set of data. To show multiple sets of data, multiple sets of bars or lines must be used.

🖉 **34.** The double-bar graph and the comparison line graph are both useful for comparing two sets of data. Explain how this works and give your own example.

You would use a set of bars or a set of lines for each set of data. One example is the number of miles driven by two salespeople over a 3-year period.

This comparison line graph shows the sales and profits of Tacos-to-Go for each of 4 years. Use the graph to answer Exercises 35–42. See Example 4.

35. Total sales in 2006 **$40,000**

36. Total sales in 2005 **$30,000**

37. Total sales in 2004 **$25,000**

38. Profit in 2006 **$15,000**

39. Profit in 2005 **$5000**

40. Profit in 2004 **$5000**

🖉 **41.** Give two possible explanations for the decrease in sales from 2003 to 2004 and two possible explanations for the increase in sales from 2004 to 2006.

Answers will vary. Some possibilities are that the decrease in sales may have resulted from poor service or greater competition. The increase in sales may have been a result of more advertising or better service.

🖉 **42.** Based on the graph, what conclusion can you make about the relationship between sales and profits?

As sales increase or decrease, so do profits.

RELATING CONCEPTS (EXERCISES 43–48) For Individual or Group Work

This newspaper clipping, adapted from USA Today, *shows some statistics regarding LifeSavers. Use this information to* **work Exercises 43–48 in order.**

ROLL WITH IT

Sweet-toothed fans recently voted to change three of the original flavors. The new five-flavor roll will include cherry, watermelon, pineapple, raspberry, and blackberry. The orange, lemon, and lime flavors have been replaced.

LifeSavers by the numbers:

Year first flavor invented: **1912 (Pep-O-Mint)**

Year five-flavor roll invented: **1935**

Total number of flavors today: **25**

Number of candies per roll: **14**

LifeSavers produced daily: **3 million**

Pounds of sugar used per day: **250,000**

Number of miniature rolls given out at Halloween: **88 million**

43. The first LifeSaver flavor was Pep-O-Mint. How long after the Pep-O-Mint LifeSaver was invented was the five-flavor roll invented?

    23 yr

44. In addition to the five flavors, how many more flavors of LifeSavers are there?

    20 additional flavors

45. Find the number of rolls of LifeSavers produced daily. Round to the nearest whole number.

    214,286 rolls each day (rounded)

46. Use your answer from Exercise 45 to find the amount of sugar in one roll of LifeSavers. Round to the nearest hundredth of a pound.

    1.17 lb (rounded)

47. Check your work in Exercise 46. Is the answer reasonable? Explain why or why not.

    The weight of one roll of LifeSavers is much less than 1.17 lb. The answer is "correct" using the information given, but some of the data given must not be accurate.

48. Name three possible causes of errors in statistics.

    Answers will vary. Possible answers are: Misprints or typographical errors; careless reporting of data; math errors.

10.3 Frequency Distributions and Histograms

The owner of Towne Insurance Agency has kept track of her personal phone sales call activity over the past 50 weeks. The number of sales calls made for each of the weeks is given below. Read down the columns, beginning with the left column, for successive weeks of the year.

75	65	40	50	45	30	30	35	45	25
75	70	60	55	30	25	44	30	35	30
75	70	50	30	50	20	30	30	20	25
60	62	45	45	48	40	35	25	20	25
75	45	50	40	35	40	40	30	27	40

OBJECTIVES

1 Understand a frequency distribution.
2 Arrange data in class intervals.
3 Read and understand a histogram.

OBJECTIVE 1 Understand a frequency distribution. A long list of numbers can be confusing. You can make the data easier to read by putting it in a special type of table called a **frequency distribution.**

EXAMPLE 1 Preparing a Frequency Distribution

Using the data above, construct a table that shows each possible number of sales calls. Then go through the original data and place a *tally* mark (I) in the tally column next to each corresponding value. Total the tally marks and place the totals in the third column. The result is a frequency distribution table.

Number of Sales Calls	Tally	Frequency	Number of Sales Calls	Tally	Frequency
20	III	3	48	I	1
25	THI	5	50	IIII	4
27	I	1	55	I	1
30	THI IIII	9	60	II	2
35	IIII	4	62	I	1
40	THI I	6	65	I	1
44	I	1	70	II	2
45	THI	5	75	IIII	4

Work Problem 1 at the Side. ▶▶▶

OBJECTIVE 2 Arrange data in class intervals. The frequency distribution given in Example 1 above contains a great deal of information—perhaps too much to digest. It can be simplified by combining the number of sales calls into groups, forming the class intervals shown below.

GROUPED DATA

Class Intervals (Number of Sales Calls)	Class Frequency (Number of Weeks)
20–29	9
30–39	13
40–49	13
50–59	5
60–69	4
70–79	6

1 Use the frequency distribution table at the left to find the following.

(a) The least number of sales calls made in a week

(b) The most common number of sales calls made in a week

(c) The number of weeks in which 35 calls were made

(d) The number of weeks in which 45 calls were made

ANSWERS
1. (a) 20 calls (b) 30 calls
   (c) 4 weeks (d) 5 weeks

2 Use the grouped data for the insurance agency on the previous page to answer each question.

(a) During how many weeks were fewer than 50 calls made?

(b) During how many weeks were 50 or more calls made?

NOTE
The number of class intervals in the left column of the grouped data table is arbitrary. Grouped data usually has between 5 and 15 class intervals.

EXAMPLE 2 Analyzing a Frequency Distribution

Use the grouped data for the insurance agency (on the preceding page) to answer the following questions.

(a) During how many weeks were fewer than 30 calls made?
The first class in the grouped data table (20–29) is the number of weeks during which fewer than 30 calls were made. Therefore, the owner made fewer than 30 calls during 9 weeks out of the 50 weeks shown.

(b) During how many weeks were 40 or more calls made?
The last four classes in the grouped data table are the number of weeks during which 40 or more calls were made.

$$13 + 5 + 4 + 6 = 28 \text{ weeks}$$

Work Problem 2 at the Side.

OBJECTIVE **3** **Read and understand a histogram.** The results in the grouped data table have been used to draw the special bar graph below, which is called a **histogram.** In a histogram, the width of each bar represents a range of numbers (*class interval*). The height of each bar in a histogram gives the *class frequency,* that is, the number of occurrences in each class interval.

3 Use the histogram at the right to answer each question.

(a) During how many weeks were fewer than 60 calls made?

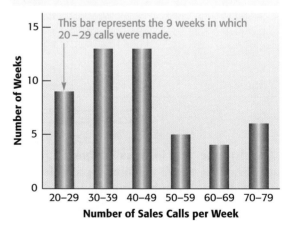

SALES CALL DATA FOR THE PAST 50 WEEKS (GROUPED DATA)

This bar represents the 9 weeks in which 20–29 calls were made.

Number of Weeks

Number of Sales Calls per Week

(b) During how many weeks were 60 or more calls made?

EXAMPLE 3 Using a Histogram

Use the histogram to find the number of weeks in which fewer than 40 calls were made.
Because 20–29 calls were made during 9 of the weeks and 30–39 calls were made during 13 of the weeks, the number of weeks in which fewer than 40 calls were made is $9 + 13 = 22$ weeks.

ANSWERS
2. (a) 35 weeks   (b) 15 weeks
3. (a) 40 weeks   (b) 10 weeks

Work Problem 3 at the Side.

10.3 Exercises

The Quilters Club of America recorded the ages of its members and used the results to construct this histogram. Use the histogram to answer Exercises 1–6. See Example 3.

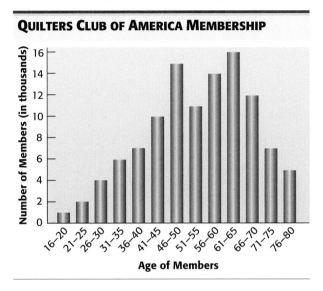

QUILTERS CLUB OF AMERICA MEMBERSHIP

Number of Members (in thousands) vs. Age of Members

1. The greatest number of members are in which age group? How many members are in that group?

61–65 years; 16,000 members

2. The least number of members are in which age group? How many members are in that group?

16–20 years; 1000 members

3. Find the number of members 35 years of age and under.

13,000 members

4. Find the number of members ages 61 to 80.

40,000 members

5. How many members are 41 to 60 years of age?

50,000 members

6. How many members are 46 to 55 years of age?

26,000 members

This histogram shows the annual earnings for the part-time employees of Wally World Amusement Park. Use this histogram to answer Exercises 7–12. See Example 3.

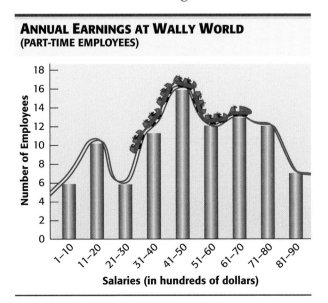

ANNUAL EARNINGS AT WALLY WORLD (PART-TIME EMPLOYEES)

Number of Employees vs. Salaries (in hundreds of dollars)

7. The greatest number of employees are in which earnings group? How many are in that group?

$4100 to $5000; 16 employees

8. The fewest number of employees are in which earnings groups? How many are in each group?

$100 to $1000, 6 employees; $2100 to $3000, 6 employees

9. Find the number of employees who earn $3100 to $4000.

11 employees

10. Find the number of employees who earn $1100 to $2000.

10 employees

11. How many employees earn $5000 or less?

49 employees

12. How many employees earn $6100 or more?

32 employees

13. Describe class interval and class frequency. How are they used when preparing a histogram?

Class intervals are the result of combining data into groupings. Class frequency is the number of data items that fit in each class interval. These are used to group data and to have multiple responses (frequency) in a class interval—this makes the data easier to interpret.

14. What might be a problem of using two few or too many class intervals?

If too few class intervals were used, the class frequencies would be high and any differences in the data might not be observable. If too many class intervals were used, interpretation might become impossible because class frequencies would be very low or nonexistent.

This list shows the number of new accounts opened annually by the employees of the Schools Credit Union. Use it to complete the table. See Example 1.

186	191	144	198	147	158	174
193	142	155	174	162	151	178
145	151	199	182	147	195	146

	Class Intervals (Number of New Accounts)	Tally	Class Frequency (Number of Employees)
15.	140–149	ЖІ I	6
16.	150–159	IIII	4
17.	160–169	I	I
18.	170–179	III	3
19.	180–189	II	2
20.	190–199	ЖІ	5

As part of a new college-assistance program, the manager of Zapp Software asked her 30 employees how many college credits each had completed. Use her list of responses to complete the following table. See Examples 1–3.

74	133	0	127	20	30
103	27	158	118	138	121
149	132	64	141	130	76
42	50	95	56	65	104
4	140	12	88	119	64

	Class Intervals (Number of Credits)	**Tally**	**Class Frequency (Number of Employees)**
21.	0–24	IIII	4
22.	25–49	III	3
23.	50–74	IIII I	6
24.	75–99	III	3
25.	100–124	IIII	5
26.	125–149	IIII III	8
27.	150–174	I	1

28. Construct a histogram by using the data in Exercises 21–27.

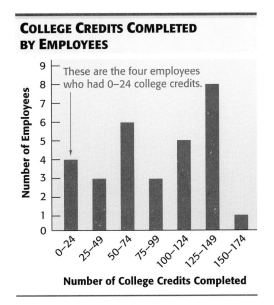

COLLEGE CREDITS COMPLETED BY EMPLOYEES

These are the four employees who had 0–24 college credits.

Number of Employees

Number of College Credits Completed

Century 21 All Professional Realty has 80 salespeople spread over its five offices. The number of homes sold by each of these salespeople during the past year is shown below. Use these numbers to complete the following table. See Example 1.

9	33	14	8	17	10	25	11	4	16	3	9	5	7	14	18
15	24	19	30	16	31	21	20	30	2	6	6	27	17	3	32
3	8	5	11	15	26	7	18	29	10	7	3	12	9	25	15
11	6	10	4	2	35	10	25	5	19	34	2	4	14	11	28
8	13	25	15	23	26	12	4	22	12	21	12	22	10	18	21

	Class Intervals (New Homes Sold)	**Tally**	**Class Frequency (Number of Salespeople)**
29.	1–5	̶J̶H̶T ̶J̶H̶T IIII	14
30.	6–10	̶J̶H̶T ̶J̶H̶T ̶J̶H̶T II	17
31.	11–15	̶J̶H̶T ̶J̶H̶T ̶J̶H̶T I	16
32.	16–20	̶J̶H̶T ̶J̶H̶T	10
33.	21–25	̶J̶H̶T ̶J̶H̶T I	11
34.	26–30	̶J̶H̶T II	7
35.	31–35	̶J̶H̶T	5

36. Make a histogram showing the results from Exercises 29–35.

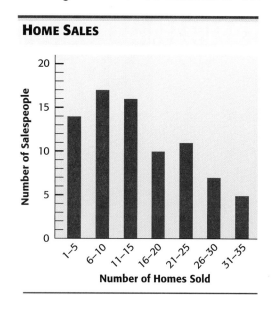

10.4 Mean, Median, and Mode

Businesses, governments, colleges, and others working with lists of numbers are often faced with the problem of analyzing a mass of raw data. The measures discussed in this section are helpful for such analyses.

O B J E C T I V E S

1 Find the mean of a list of numbers.

2 Find a weighted mean.

3 Find the median.

4 Find the mode.

OBJECTIVE 1 Find the mean of a list of numbers.   When analyzing data, one of the first things to look for is a *measure of central tendency*—a single number that we can use to represent the entire list of numbers. One such measure is the *average* or **mean.** The mean can be found with the following formula.

1 Tanya has test scores of 96, 98, 84, 88, 82, and 92. Find her mean (average) score.

Finding the Mean (Average)

$$\text{mean} = \frac{\text{sum of all values}}{\text{number of values}}$$

EXAMPLE 1 Finding the Mean

David had test scores of 84, 90, 95, 98, and 88. Find the mean (average) of these scores.

Use the formula for finding the mean. Add up all the test scores and then divide by the number of tests.

$$\text{mean} = \frac{84 + 90 + 95 + 98 + 88}{5} \quad \begin{array}{l}\leftarrow \text{Sum of test scores} \\ \leftarrow \text{Number of tests}\end{array}$$

$$\text{mean} = \frac{455}{5} \quad \text{Divide.}$$

$$\text{mean} = 91$$

David has a mean score of 91.

2 Find the mean for each list of numbers. Round to the nearest cent if necessary.

(a) Monthly gasoline expenses of $50.28, $85.16, $110.50, $78, $120.70, $58.64, $73.80, $86.24, $67.85, $96.56, $138.65, $48.90

> **Work Problem 1 at the Side.** ❯❯❯

EXAMPLE 2 Applying the Average or Mean

Milk sales at a local 7-Eleven for each of the days last week were

$$\$86, \$103, \$118, \$117, \$126, \$158, \text{ and } \$149$$

For the local 7-Eleven, find the mean (rounded to the nearest cent) as shown below.

$$\text{mean} = \frac{\$86 + \$103 + \$118 + \$117 + \$126 + \$158 + \$149}{7}$$

$$\text{mean} = \frac{\$857}{7}$$

$$\text{mean} \approx \$122.43$$

The mean daily sales amount for milk was $122.43.

(b) A list of the sales for one year at eight different office supply stores: $749,820; $765,480; $643,744; $824,222; $485,886; $668,178; $702,294; $525,800

> **Work Problem 2 at the Side.** ❯❯❯

ANSWERS

1. 90

2. **(a)** $\dfrac{\$1015.28}{12} \approx \$84.61$ (rounded)

   (b) $\dfrac{\$5,365,424}{8} = \$670,678$

③ The numbers below show the amount that Heather Hall spent for lottery tickets and the number of days that she spent that amount. Find the weighted mean.

Value	Frequency
$ 2	4
$ 4	6
$ 6	5
$ 8	6
$10	12
$12	5
$14	8
$16	4

OBJECTIVE ② Find a weighted mean. Some items in a list might appear more than once. In this case, we find a **weighted mean,** in which each value is "weighted" by multiplying it by the number of times it occurs.

EXAMPLE 3 Understanding the Weighted Mean

The following table shows the amount of contribution and the number of times (frequency) the amount was given to a food pantry. Find the weighted mean.

Contribution Value	Frequency	
$ 3	4 ←	4 people each contributed $3
$ 5	2	
$ 7	1	
$ 8	5	
$ 9	3	
$10	2	
$12	1	
$13	2	

The same amount was given by more than one person: for example, $5 was given twice and $8 was given five times. Other amounts, such as $12, were given once. To find the mean, multiply each contribution value by its frequency. Then add the products. Next, add the numbers in the *frequency* column to find the total number of values.

Value	Frequency	Product
$ 3	4	(3 • 4) = $12
$ 5	2	(5 • 2) = $10
$ 7	1	(7 • 1) = $ 7
$ 8	5	(8 • 5) = $40
$ 9	3	(9 • 3) = $27
$10	2	(10 • 2) = $20
$12	1	(12 • 1) = $12
$13	2	(13 • 2) = $26
Totals	20	$154

Finally, divide the totals.

$$\text{mean} = \frac{\$154}{20} = \$7.70$$

The mean contribution to the food pantry was $7.70.

◀◀◀ Work Problem 3 at the Side.

A common use of the weighted mean is to find a student's *grade point average* (GPA), as shown by the next example.

EXAMPLE 4 **Applying the Weighted Mean**

Find the grade point average for a student earning the following grades. Assume A = 4, B = 3, C = 2, D = 1, and F = 0. The number of credits determines how many times the grade is counted (the frequency).

Course	Credits	Grade	Credits · Grade
Mathematics	4	A (= 4)	4 · 4 = 16
Speech	3	C (= 2)	3 · 2 = 6
English	3	B (= 3)	3 · 3 = 9
Computer science	2	A (= 4)	2 · 4 = 8
Art history	2	D (= 1)	2 · 1 = 2
Totals	14		41

It is common to round grade point averages to the nearest hundredth. So the grade point average for this student is rounded to 2.93.

$$\text{GPA} = \frac{41}{14} \approx 2.93$$

> **Work Problem 4 at the Side.** ▶▶▶

OBJECTIVE ③ Find the median. Because it can be affected by extremely high or low numbers, the mean is often a poor indicator of central tendency for a list of numbers. In cases like this, another measure of central tendency, called the *median,* can be used. The **median** divides a group of numbers in half; half the numbers lie above the median, and half lie below the median.

Find the median by listing the numbers *in order* from *smallest* to *largest.* If the list contains an *odd* number of items, the median is the *middle number.*

EXAMPLE 5 **Finding the Median**

Find the median for the following list of prices for women's T-shirts.

$9, $23, $15, $8, $18, $12, $24

First arrange the numbers in numerical order from smallest to largest.

Smallest → 8, 9, 12, 15, 18, 23, 24 ← Largest

Next, find the middle number in the list.

8, 9, 12, 15, 18, 23, 24

Three are below.   Middle number.   Three are above.

The median price is $15.

> **Work Problem 5 at the Side.** ▶▶▶

④ Find the grade point average (GPA) for Greg Barnes, who earned the following grades last semester. Round to the nearest hundredth.

Course	Credits	Grade
Mathematics	3	A (= 4)
P.E.	1	C (= 2)
English	3	C (= 2)
Keyboarding	2	B (= 3)
Recreation	4	B (= 3)

⑤ Find the median for the following weights of bagged groceries.

14 lb, 18 lb, 10 lb, 17 lb, 15 lb, 19 lb, 20 lb

ANSWERS
4. GPA ≈ 2.92
5. 17 lb (the middle number when the numbers are arranged from smallest to largest)

6 Find the median for the following list of measurements.

125 m, 87 m, 96 m, 108 m, 136 m, 74 m

If a list contains an *even* number of items, there is no single middle number. In this case, the median is defined as the mean (average) of the *middle two* numbers.

EXAMPLE 6 Finding the Median for an Even Number of Items

Find the median for the following list of ages.

74, 7, 15, 13, 25, 28, 47, 59, 32, 68

First arrange the numbers in numerical order from smallest to largest. Then find the middle two numbers.

Smallest → 7, 13, 15, 25, 28, 32, 47, 59, 68, 74 ← Largest

Middle two numbers

The median age is the mean of the two middle numbers.

$$\text{median} = \frac{28 + 32}{2} = \frac{60}{2} = 30 \text{ years}$$

> Work Problem 6 at the Side.

7 Find the mode for each list of numbers.

(a) Ages of summer work applicants (in years): 19, 18, 22, 20, 18

OBJECTIVE 4 Find the mode. The last important statistical measure is the **mode,** the number that occurs *most often* in a list of numbers. For example, if the test scores for 10 students were

↓ ↓ ↓
74, 81, 39, 74, 82, 80, 100, 92, 74, and 85,

then the mode is 74. Three students earned a score of 74, so 74 appears more times on the list than any other score. (It is not necessary to place the numbers in numerical order when looking for the mode.)

A list can have two modes; such a list is sometimes called **bimodal.** If no number occurs more frequently than any other number in a list, the list has *no mode.*

(b) Total points on a screening exam: 312, 219, 782, 312, 219, 426

EXAMPLE 7 Finding the Mode

Find the mode for each list of numbers.

(a) 51, 32, 49, 73, 49, 90
The number 49 occurs more often than any other number; therefore, 49 is the mode.

(b) 482, 485, 483, 485, 487, 487, 489
Because both 485 and 487 occur twice, each is a mode. This list is *bimodal.*

(c) Monthly commissions of sales people: $1706, $1289, $1653, $1892, $1301, $1782

(c) $10,708; $11,519; $10,972; $12,546; $13,905; $12,182
No number occurs more than once. This list has *no mode.*

> Work Problem 7 at the Side.

Measures of Central Tendency

The **mean** is the sum of all the values divided by the number of values. It is the mathematical average.

6. $\frac{96 + 108}{2} = \frac{204}{2} = 102$ m

7. **(a)** 18 yr
   (b) bimodal, 219 points and 312 points (this list has two modes)
   (c) no mode (no number occurs more than once)

The **median** is the middle number in a group of values that are listed from smallest to largest. It divides a group of numbers in half.

The **mode** is the value that occurs most often in a group of values.

10.4 Exercises

| FOR EXTRA HELP | Tutor Center Addison-Wesley Math Tutor Center | 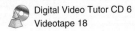 MathXL | Digital Video Tutor CD 6 Videotape 18 | Student's Solutions Manual | *MyMathLab* MyMathLab | 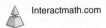 Interactmath.com |

Find the mean for each list of numbers. Round answers to the nearest tenth if necessary. See Example 1.

1. Shopping center ages (in years) of 6, 22, 15, 2, 8, 13

   11 yr

2. Minutes of cell phone use each day: 53, 77, 38, 29, 46, 48, 52

   49 minutes

3. Inches of rain per month of 3.1, 1.5, 2.8, 0.8, 4.1

   2.5 in. of rain (rounded)

4. Algebra quiz scores of 32, 26, 30, 19, 51, 46, 38, 39

   35.1 (rounded)

5. Annual salaries of $38,500; $39,720; $42,183; $21,982; $43,250

   $37,127

6. Numbers of people attending baseball games: 27,500; 18,250; 17,357; 14,298; 33,110

   22,103 people

Solve each application problem. See Example 2.

7. The Athletic Shoe Store sold shoes at the following prices: $75.52, $36.15, $58.24, $21.86, $47.68, $106.57, $82.72, $52.14, $28.60, $72.92. Find the average (mean) shoe sales amount.

   $58.24

8. In one evening, a waitress collected the following checks from her dinner customers: $30.10, $42.80, $91.60, $51.20, $88.30, $21.90, $43.70, $51.20. Find the average (mean) dinner check amount.

   $52.60

Find the weighted mean. Round answers to the nearest tenth. See Example 3.

9.

Customers Each Hour	Frequency
8	2
11	12
15	5
26	1

12.5 customers (rounded)

10.

Deliveries Each Week	Frequency
4	1
8	3
16	5
20	1

12.8 deliveries

11.

Fish per Boat	Frequency
12	4
13	2
15	5
19	3
22	1
23	5

17.2 fish (rounded)

12.

Patients per Clinic	Frequency
25	1
26	2
29	5
30	4
32	3
33	5

30.2 patients (rounded)

Solve each application problem. See Example 4.

13. The table below shows the face value (policy amount) of life insurance policies sold and the number of policies sold for each amount by the New World Life Company during one week. Find the weighted mean amount for the policies sold.

Policy Amount	Number of Policies Sold
$ 10,000	6
$ 20,000	24
$ 25,000	12
$ 30,000	8
$ 50,000	5
$100,000	3
$250,000	2

$35,500

14. Detroit Metro-Sales Company prepared the following table showing the gasoline mileage obtained by each of the cars in their automobile fleet. Find the weighted mean to determine the miles per gallon for the fleet of cars.

Miles per Gallon	Number of Autos
15	5
20	6
24	10
30	14
32	5
35	6
40	4

27.7 miles per gallon

Find the median for each list of numbers. See Example 5.

15. Number of books loaned: 125, 100, 150, 135, 114, 172

130 books

16. Number of hits for a World Wide Web site (in thousands): 140, 85, 122, 114, 98

114,000 hits

17. Calories in fast-food menu items: 501, 412, 521, 515, 298, 621, 346, 528

508 calories

18. Number of cars in the parking lot each day: 520, 523, 513, 1283, 338, 509, 290, 420

511 cars

Find the mode or modes for each list of numbers. See Example 7.

19. Porosity of soil samples: 21%, 18%, 21%, 28%, 22%, 21%, 25%

21%

20. Low daily temperatures: 21, 32, 46, 32, 49, 32, 49

32

21. Ages of residents (in years) at Leisure Village: 74, 68, 68, 68, 75, 75, 74, 74, 70

68 and 74 yr

22. Number of pages read: 86, 84, 79, 75, 88, 66, 72, 85, 71

no mode

23. When can the mean be a poor measure of central tendency? What might you do in such a situation?

When the data contains a few very low or a few very high values, the mean will give a poor indication of the average. Consider using the median or mode instead.

24. What is the purpose of the weighted mean? Give an example of where it is used.

When the same value occurs more than once, the value must be multiplied by the number of times it occurs (weighted). A good example of using the weighted mean is when finding grade point averages. It must be used because you have several *credits* with the same *grade value*.

25. When is the median a better measure of central tendency than the mean to describe a set of data? Make up a list of numbers to illustrate your explanation. Calculate both the mean and the median.

The median is a better measure of central tendency when the list contains one or more extreme values. Find the mean and the median of the following home values: $182,000; $164,000; $191,000; $115,000; $982,000.
mean home value = $326,800;
median home value = $182,000

26. Suppose you own a hat shop and can order a certain hat in only one size. You look at last year's sales to decide on the size to order. Should you find the mean, median, or mode for these sales? Explain your answer.

The size to order is the mode. The mode is the size most worn by customers and it would be wise to order most hats in this size.

Find the grade point average for students earning the following grades. Assume A = 4, B = 3, C = 2, D = 1, *and* F = 0. *Round answers to the nearest hundredth.*

27.

Credits	Grade
4	B
2	A
5	C
1	F
3	B

2.60

28.

Credits	Grade
3	A
3	B
4	B
3	C
3	C

2.81 (rounded)

29.

Credits	Grade
2	A
3	C
4	A
1	C
4	B

3.14 (rounded)

30.

Credits	Grade
3	A
2	A
5	B
4	A
1	A

3.67 (rounded)

RELATING CONCEPTS (EXERCISES 31–40)   For Individual or Group Work

*Gluco Industries manufactures and sells glucose monitors and other diabetes-related products. The number of sales calls made over an 8-week period by two sales representatives, Scott Samuels and Rob Stricker, is shown below. Use this information to **work Exercises 31–40 in order.***

	Number of Calls	
Week	**Samuels**	**Stricker**
1	39	21
2	15	22
3	40	20
4	22	23
5	13	19
6	22	24
7	17	25
8	8	22

31. Find the total number of sales calls made by each of the sales representatives.

176 sales calls

32. Find the mean number of sales calls made by Samuels and by Stricker.

mean Samuels: 22; mean Stricker: 22

33. Find the median number of sales calls made by Samuels and by Stricker.

median Samuels: 19.5; median Stricker: 22

34. Find the mode for the number of sales calls for each of the sales representatives.

mode Samuels: 22; mode Stricker: 22

35. How do the mean, median, and mode for the two sales representatives compare?

The mean and mode are identical for both sales representatives and the medians are close.

36. Explain how the number of weekly sales calls made by each of the sales representatives compare to each other.

The number of weekly sales calls made by Samuels varies greatly from week to week while the number of weekly sales calls made by Stricker remains fairly constant.

*To show the variation or spread of the number of sales calls made by each of the sales representatives requires some **measure of the dispersion,** or spread of the numbers around the mean. A common measure of the dispersion is the **range.** The range is the difference between the largest value and the smallest value in the set of numbers.*

37. Find the range for the number of sales calls made by Samuels.

range = 40 − 8 = 32

38. Find the range for the number of sales calls made by Stricker.

range = 25 − 19 = 6

39. Is the performance data for these two sales representatives sufficient to accurately determine which is the best? What else might you want to know?

No, not with any certainty. What else might you want to know? There probably are additional questions that need to be answered before a determination could be made, such as the dollar amount of sales, number of repeat customers, and so on.

40. List three possible explanations for the wide variation (range) in the number of sales calls for Samuels.

Answers will vary. Some possible answers are: He works hard one week, then takes it easy the next week; the characteristics of the sales territories vary greatly; illness or personal problems may be affecting performance.

Chapter 10

10.1	**circle graph**	A circle graph shows how a total amount is divided into parts or sectors. It is based on percents of 360°.
	protractor	A protractor is a device (usually in the shape of a half-circle) used to measure the number of degrees in angles or parts of a circle.
10.2	**bar graph**	A bar graph uses bars of various heights or lengths to show quantity or frequency.
	double-bar graph	A double-bar graph compares two sets of data by showing two sets of bars.
	line graph	A line graph uses dots connected by lines to show trends.
	comparison line graph	A comparison line graph shows how two sets of data relate to each other by showing a line graph for each item.
10.3	**frequency distribution**	A frequency distribution is a table that includes a column showing each possible number in the data collected. The original data is then entered in another column using a tally mark for each corresponding value. The tally marks are totaled and the totals are placed in a third column.
	histogram	A histogram is a bar graph in which the width of each bar represents a range of numbers (class interval) and the height represents the quantity or frequency of items that fall within the interval.
10.4	**mean**	The mean is the sum of all the values divided by the number of values. It is often called the *average*.
	weighted mean	The weighted mean is a mean calculated so that each value is multiplied by its frequency.
	median	The median is the middle number in a group of values that are listed from smallest to largest. It divides a group of values in half. If there are an even number of values, the median is the mean (average) of the two middle values.
	mode	The mode is the value that occurs most often in a group of values.
	bimodal	A list of numbers is bimodal when it has two modes. The two values occur the same number of times.
	dispersion	The dispersion is the variation or spread of the numbers around the mean.
	range	The range is a common measure of the dispersion of numbers. It is the difference between the largest value and the smallest value in the set of numbers.

NEW FORMULAS

Mean or average: mean $= \dfrac{\text{sum of all values}}{\text{number of values}}$

TEST YOUR WORD POWER

See how well you have learned the vocabulary in this chapter. Answers follow the Quick Review.

1. A **circle graph**
   A. uses bars of various heights to show quantity or frequency
   B. shows how a total amount is divided into parts or sectors
   C. uses dots connected by lines to show trends
   D. uses bars of various widths to represent a range of numbers.

2. A **bar graph**
   A. uses bars of various heights to show quantity or frequency
   B. shows how a total amount is divided into parts or sectors
   C. uses dots connected by lines to show trends
   D. uses bars of various widths to represent a range of numbers.

3. A **histogram** is a graph in which
   A. tally marks are used to record original data
   B. two sets of data are compared using two sets of bars
   C. dots are connected by lines to show trends
   D. the width of each bar represents a range of numbers and the height represents the frequency of items within that range.

4. A **protractor** is a device used to
   A. construct a histogram
   B. calculate measures of central tendency
   C. measure the number of degrees in angles or parts of a circle
   D. compare two sets of data.

5. The **mean** is
   A. calculated so that each value is multiplied by its frequency
   B. the sum of all values divided by the number of values
   C. the middle number in a group of values that are listed from smallest to largest
   D. the value that occurs most often in a group of values.

6. The **mode** is
   A. calculated so that each value is multiplied by its frequency
   B. the sum of all values divided by the number of values
   C. the middle number in a group of values that are listed from smallest to largest
   D. the value that occurs most often in a group of values.

Concepts	*Examples*

10.1 *Constructing a Circle Graph*

Step 1   Determine the percent of the total for each item.

Step 2   Find the number of degrees out of 360° that each percent represents.

Step 3   Use a protractor to measure the number of degrees for each item in the circle.

Construct a circle graph for the following table, which lists expenses for a business trip.

Item	Amount
Transportation	$200
Lodging	$300
Food	$250
Entertainment	$150
Other	$100
Total	$1000

Item	Amount	Percent of Total	Sector Size
Transportation	$200	$\frac{\$200}{\$1000} = \frac{1}{5} = 20\%$ so $360° \cdot 20\%$ $= 360 \cdot 0.20$	$= 72°$
Lodging	$300	$\frac{\$300}{\$1000} = \frac{3}{10} = 30\%$ so $360° \cdot 30\%$ $= 360 \cdot 0.30$	$= 108°$
Food	$250	$\frac{\$250}{\$1000} = \frac{1}{4} = 25\%$ so $360° \cdot 25\%$ $= 360 \cdot 0.25$	$= 90°$
Entertainment	$150	$\frac{\$150}{\$1000} = \frac{3}{20} = 15\%$ so $360° \cdot 15\%$ $= 360 \cdot 0.15$	$= 54°$
Other	$100	$\frac{\$100}{\$1000} = \frac{1}{10} = 10\%$ so $360° \cdot 10\%$ $= 360 \cdot 0.10$	$= 36°$

BUSINESS TRIP EXPENSES

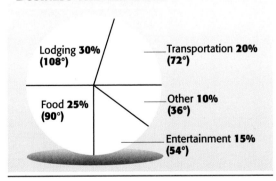

Lodging **30%** (108°)

Transportation **20%** (72°)

Food **25%** (90°)

Other **10%** (36°)

Entertainment **15%** (54°)

Concepts

10.2 *Reading a Bar Graph*

The height of the bar is used to show the quantity or frequency (number) in a specific category. Use a ruler or straightedge to line up the top of each bar with the numbers on the left side of the graph.

10.2 *Reading a Line Graph*

A dot is used to show the number or quantity in a specific class. The dots are connected with lines. This kind of graph is used to show a trend.

Examples

Use the bar graph below to determine the number of students who earned each letter grade.

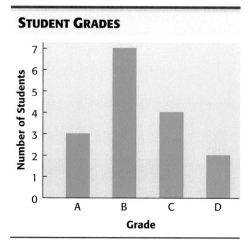

Grade	Number of Students
A	3
B	7
C	4
D	2

The line graph below shows the annual sales for the Fabric Supply Center for each of 4 years.

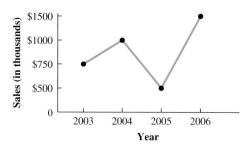

Find the sales in each year.

Year	Total Sales
2003	$750 • 1000 = $ 750,000
2004	$1000 • 1000 = $1,000,000
2005	$500 • 1000 = $ 500,000
2006	$1500 • 1000 = $1,500,000

Concepts

10.3 *Preparing a Frequency Distribution and a Histogram from Raw Data*

Step 1 Construct a table listing each value, and the number of times this value occurs.

Step 2 Divide the data into groups, categories, or classes.

Step 3 Draw bars representing these groups to make a histogram.

Examples

Draw a histogram for the following list of student quiz scores.

12	15	15	14
13	20	10	12
11	9	10	12
17	20	16	17
14	18	19	13

Quiz Score	Tally	Frequency	
9	I	1	1st
10	II	2	class
11	I	1	interval
12	III	3	2nd
13	II	2	class
14	II	2	interval
15	II	2	3rd
16	I	1	class
17	II	2	interval
18	I	1	4th
19	I	1	class
20	II	2	interval

Class Interval (Quiz Scores)	Frequency (Number of Students)
9–11	4
12–14	7
15–17	5
18–20	4

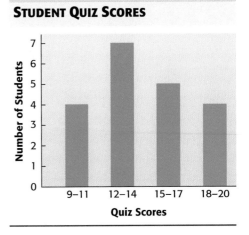

STUDENT QUIZ SCORES

Concepts

10.4 *Finding the Mean (Average) of a Set of Numbers*
Step 1   Add all values to obtain a total.
Step 2   Divide the total by the number of values.

$$\text{mean (average)} = \frac{\text{sum of all values}}{\text{number of values}}$$

10.4 *Finding the Weighted Mean*
Step 1   Multiply frequency by value.
Step 2   Add all the products from Step 1.
Step 3   Divide the sum in Step 2 by the total number of pieces of data.

Examples

The test scores for Keith Zagorin in his algebra course were as follows:

80	92	92	94
76	88	84	93

Find Keith's mean (average) test score to the nearest tenth.

$$\text{mean} = \frac{80 + 92 + 92 + 94 + 76 + 88 + 84 + 93}{8}$$

$$= \frac{699}{8} \approx 87.4$$

Keith's mean test score is approximately 87.4.

This table shows the distribution of the number of school-age children in a survey of 30 families.

Number of School-Age Children	Frequency (Number of Families)
0	12
1	6
2	7
3	3
4	2
Total of 30 families	

Find the mean number of school-age children per family. Round to the nearest hundredth.

Value	Frequency	Product	
0	12	$(0 \cdot 12) =$	0
1	6	$(1 \cdot 6) =$	6
2	7	$(2 \cdot 7) =$	14
3	3	$(3 \cdot 3) =$	9
4	2	$(4 \cdot 2) =$	8
Totals	30		37

$$\text{mean} = \frac{37}{30} \approx 1.23$$

The mean number of school-age children per family is approximately 1.23.

Concepts

10.4 *Finding the Median of a Set of Numbers*

Step 1 Arrange the data from smallest to largest.

Step 2 Select the middle value, or, if there is an even number of values, find the average of the two middle values.

10.4 *Finding the Mode of a Set of Values*

Find the value that appears most often in the list of values. If no value appears more than once, there is no mode. If two different values appear the same number of times, the list is bimodal.

Examples

Find the median for Keith Zagorin's test scores from the previous page.

The data arranged from smallest to largest is as follows:

$$76 \quad 80 \quad 84 \quad \underbrace{88 \quad 92}_{\text{Middle values}} \quad 92 \quad 93 \quad 94$$

The middle two values are 88 and 92. The average of these two values is

$$\frac{88 + 92}{2} = 90$$

Keith's median test score is 90.

Find the mode for Keith's test scores shown above.

The most frequently occurring score is 92 (it occurs twice). Therefore, the mode is 92.

ANSWERS TO TEST YOUR WORD POWER

1. (B) *Example:*

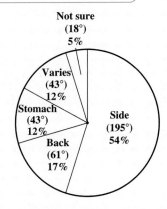

2. (A) *Example:*

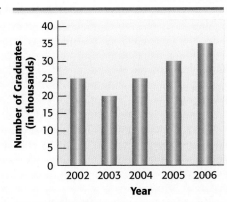

3. (D) *Example:*

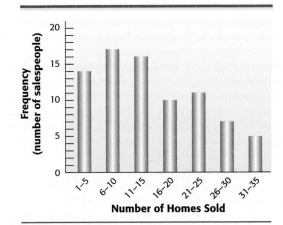

4. (C) *Example:*

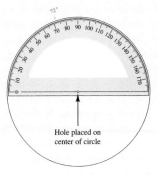

Hole placed on center of circle

5. (B) *Example:* The mean of the values $5, $9, $7, $5, $2, and $8, is

$$\frac{\$5 + \$9 + \$7 + \$5 + \$2 + \$8}{6} = \frac{\$36}{6} = \$6.$$

6. (D) *Example:* The mode of the values $5, $9, $7, $5, $2, and $8 is $5 because $5 appears twice in the list.

Real-Data Applications

Surfing the Net

1. Look at the "Source" information at the bottom of the graph. How were the numbers in the graph obtained? **500 regular users of the Internet were polled by NUKE InterNETWORK.**

2. A researcher seeks information about members of a *population*. The individuals who are polled must be representative of the *population*. Describe the population that was targeted by this survey. **regular users of the Internet**

3. How many people in the poll said they cut back on television viewing to find time to use the Internet? **260 people**

4. Find the number of people in the poll who cut back on each of the other activities listed in the graph. **Video/computer games, 180 people; Sleeping, 90 people; Reading, 60 people; Seeing friends, 60 people; Work/school, 55 people; Other, 50 people; Exercising, 15 people**

5. Add up all the responses to the poll from Problems 3 and 4. Why is the total more than the 500 people that were in the poll? **770 total responses; Each could choose more than one category.**

6. Suppose you took a similar poll of 100 students at your school. Would you expect the results to be similar to those shown in the graph? Why or why not? **No. A group of 100 students probably would include some who do not surf the Internet and therefore would not choose any of the answers.**

7. Suppose you first asked students if they regularly used the Internet, and then took a similar poll of 100 of those students. Would you expect the results to be similar to those shown in the graph? Why or why not? **Yes. Those students are probably representative of the graph's population.**

8. Conduct a survey of your class members. First find out if they regularly use the Internet. Ask those who regularly use the Internet which of the activities they cut back on to have more surfing time. Each person polled can select more than one activity.

    (a) How many students are in your class poll?

    (b) Complete the table using the responses from those who regularly use the Internet.

CAUGHT IN THE NET

Web users have cut back on the following activities to get more online time:

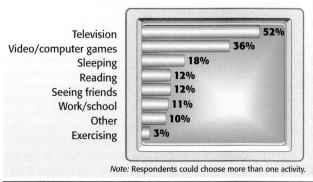

Note: Respondents could choose more than one activity.

Source: NUKE InterNETWORK poll of 500 regular users.

Activity	Number Who Cut Back on the Activity	Percent Who Cut Back on the Activity
Television		
Video/computer games		
Sleeping		
Reading		
Seeing friends		
Work/school		
Other		
Exercising		

9. Make a bar graph showing your survey data. How is your data similar to the graph shown above? How is it different? **Answers will vary.**

Teaching notes for this activity are provided in the *Printed Test Bank and Instructor's Resource Guide*

Chapter **10**

REVIEW EXERCISES

[10.1]

1. This circle graph shows the cost of a family vacation. What is the largest single expense of the vacation? How much is that item?   **lodging; $560**

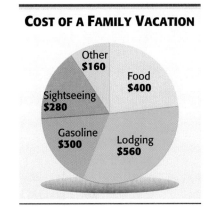

COST OF A FAMILY VACATION

Using the circle graph in Exercise 1, find each ratio. Write the ratios as fractions in lowest terms.

2. Cost of the food to the total cost of the vacation

$$\frac{400}{1700} = \frac{4}{17}$$

3. Cost of gasoline to the total cost of the vacation

$$\frac{300}{1700} = \frac{3}{17}$$

4. Cost of sightseeing to the total cost of the vacation

$$\frac{280}{1700} = \frac{14}{85}$$

5. Cost of gasoline to the cost of the Other category

$$\frac{300}{160} = \frac{15}{8}$$

6. Cost of the lodging to the cost of the food

$$\frac{560}{400} = \frac{7}{5}$$

[10.2] *This bar graph shows recent trends in employee bene-fits. It includes the most frequently offered "work perks" and the percent of the responding companies offering them. The survey was conducted on-line and included 4800 companies ranging in size from 2 to 5000 employees. Use this graph to find the number of companies offering each work perk listed in Exercises 7–10 and to answer Exercises 11 and 12. (Source: Work Perks Survey, Ceridian Employer Services, www.ces.ceridian.com)*

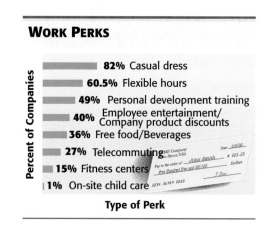

WORK PERKS

Percent of Companies
- **82%** Casual dress
- **60.5%** Flexible hours
- **49%** Personal development training
- **40%** Employee entertainment/ Company product discounts
- **36%** Free food/Beverages
- **27%** Telecommuting
- **15%** Fitness centers
- **1%** On-site child care

Type of Perk

7. Casual dress

3936 companies

8. Free food/Beverages

1728 companies

9. Fitness centers

720 companies

10. Flexible hours

2904 companies

11. Which two work perks do companies offer least often? Give one possible explanation why these work perks are not offered.

On-site child care and Fitness centers Answers will vary. Perhaps employers feel that they are not needed or would not be used. Or it may be that they would be too expensive for the benefit derived.

12. Which two work perks do companies offer most often? Give one possible explanation why these work perks are so popular.

Flexible hours and Casual dress Answers will vary. Perhaps employees request them and appreciate them. Or, it may be that neither of them cost the employer anything to offer.

This double-bar graph shows the number of acre-feet of water in Lake Natoma for each of the first six months of 2005 and 2006. Use this graph to answer Exercises 13–18.

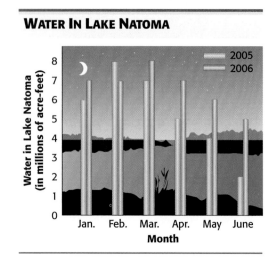

WATER IN LAKE NATOMA

Water in Lake Natoma (in millions of acre-feet)

□ 2005
□ 2006

Month: Jan. Feb. Mar. Apr. May June

13. During which month in 2006 was the greatest amount of water in the lake? How much was there?

March; 8,000,000 acre-feet

14. During which month in 2005 was the least amount of water in the lake? How much was there?

June; 2,000,000 acre-feet

15. How many acre-feet of water were in the lake in June of 2006?

5,000,000 acre-feet

16. How many acre-feet of water were in the lake in May of 2005?

4,000,000 acre-feet

17. Find the decrease in the amount of water in the lake from March 2005 to June 2005.

5,000,000 acre-feet

18. Find the decrease in the amount of water in the lake from April 2006 to June 2006.

2,000,000 acre-feet

This comparison line graph shows the annual floor-covering sales of two different home improvement centers during each of 5 years. Use this graph to find the amount of annual floor-covering sales in each year shown in Exercises 19–22 and to answer Exercises 23 and 24.

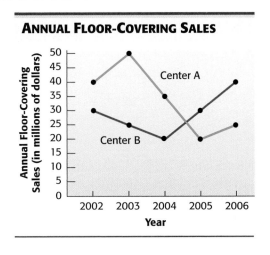

19. Center A in 2003

$50,000,000

20. Center A in 2005

$20,000,000

21. Center B in 2004

$20,000,000

22. Center B in 2006

$40,000,000

23. What trend do you see in center A's sales from 2003 to 2006? Why might this have happened?

The floor-covering sales decreased for 2 years and then moved up slightly. Answers will vary. Perhaps there is less new construction, remodeling, and home improvement in the area near center A, or better product selection and service have reversed the decline in sales.

24. What trend do you see in center B's sales starting in 2004? Why might this have happened?

The floor-covering sales are increasing. Answers will vary. Perhaps new construction and home remodeling have increased in the area near center B, or greater advertising has attracted more customers.

[10.4] *Find the mean for each list of numbers. Round answers to the nearest tenth if necessary.*

25. Digital cameras sold: 18, 12, 15, 24, 9, 42, 54, 87, 21, 3

28.5 digital cameras

26. Number of harassment complaints filed: 31, 9, 8, 22, 46, 51, 48, 42, 53, 42

35.2 complaints

Find the weighted mean for each list. Round to the nearest tenth if necessary.

27.

Dollar Value	Frequency
$42	3
$47	7
$53	2
$55	3
$59	5

$51.05

28.

Total Points	Frequency
243	1
247	3
251	5
255	7
263	4
271	2
279	2

257.3 points (rounded)

Find the median for each list of numbers.

29. The number of accident forms filed: 43, 37, 13, 68, 54, 75, 28, 35, 39

39 forms

30. Commissions of $576, $578, $542, $151, $559, $565, $525, $590

$562

Find the mode or modes for each list of numbers.

31. Running shoes priced at $79, $56, $110, $79, $72, $86, $79

$79

32. Boat launchings: 18, 25, 63, 32, 28, 37, 32, 26, 18

18 and 32 launchings (bimodal)

MIXED REVIEW EXERCISES

The Broadway Hair Salon spent $22,400 to open a new shop. This amount was spent as shown below. Find all the missing numbers in Exercises 33–37.

Item	Dollar Amount	Percent of Total	Degrees of Circle
33. Plumbing and electrical changes	$2240	10%	36°
34. Work stations	$7840	35%	126°
35. Small appliances	$4480	20%	72°
36. Interior decoration	$5600	25%	90°
37. Supplies	$2240	10%	36°

38. Draw a circle graph using the information in Exercises 33–37.

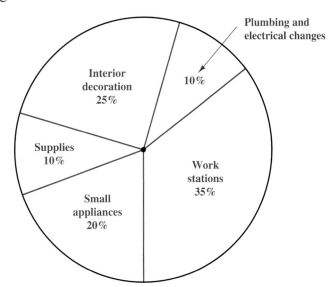

Find the mean for each list of numbers. Round answers to the nearest tenth if necessary.

39. Number of volunteers for the project: 48, 72, 52, 148, 180

100 volunteers

40. Number of flu vaccinations in a day: 122, 135, 146, 159, 128, 147, 168, 139, 158

144.7 vaccinations (rounded)

Find the mode or modes for each list of numbers.

41. Job applicants meeting the qualifications: 48, 43, 46, 47, 48, 48, 43

48 applicants

42. Number of two-bedroom apartments in each building: 26, 31, 31, 37, 43, 51, 31, 43, 43

31 and 43 two-bedroom apartments (bimodal)

Find the median for each list of numbers.

43. Hours worked: 4.7, 3.2, 2.9, 5.3, 7.1, 8.2, 9.4, 1.0

5.0 hr

44. Number of e-mails each day: 35, 51, 9, 2, 17, 12, 46, 23, 3, 19, 39, 27

21 e-mails

Here are the scores of 40 students on a computer science exam. Complete the table.

78	89	36	59	78	99	92	86
73	78	85	57	99	95	82	76
63	93	53	76	92	79	72	62
74	81	77	76	59	84	76	94
58	37	76	54	80	30	45	38

	Class Intervals (Scores)	**Tally**	**Class Frequency (Number of Students)**
45.	30–39	IIII	4
46.	40–49	I	1
47.	50–59	JHH I	6
48.	60–69	II	2
49.	70–79	JHH JHH III	13
50.	80–89	JHH II	7
51.	90–99	JHH II	7

52. Construct a histogram by using the data in Exercises 45–51.

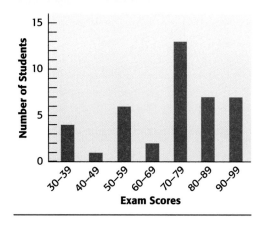

COMPUTER SCIENCE EXAM SCORES

Find each weighted mean. Round answers to the nearest tenth if necessary.

53.

Test Score	Frequency
46	4
54	10
62	8
70	12
78	10

64.5 (rounded)

54.

Units Sold	Frequency
104	6
112	14
115	21
119	13
123	22
127	6
132	9

118.8 units (rounded)

Chapter **10**

TEST

This circle graph shows the advertising budget for Lakeland Amusement Park. Find the dollar amount budgeted for each category. The total advertising budget of Lakeland Amusement Park is $2,800,000.

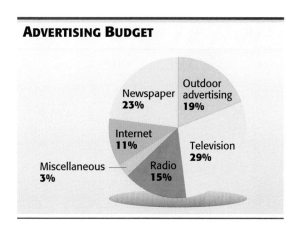

ADVERTISING BUDGET

Newspaper 23% · Outdoor advertising 19% · Internet 11% · Television 29% · Miscellaneous 3% · Radio 15%

1. Newspaper

1. $644,000

2. Outdoor advertising

2. $532,000

3. Television

3. $812,000

4. Radio

4. $420,000

5. Miscellaneous

5. $84,000

6. Internet

6. $308,000

During a one-year period, Whitings Oak Furniture Sales had the following expenses. Find all numbers missing from the chart.

Item	Dollar Amount	Percent of Total	Degrees of a Circle
7. Salaries	$144,000	30%	___
8. Delivery expense	$48,000	10%	___
9. Advertising	$96,000	20%	___
10. Rent	$144,000	30%	___
11. Other	$48,000	___	36°

7. <u>108°</u>

8. <u>36°</u>

9. <u>72°</u>

10. <u>108°</u>

11. <u>10%</u>

12.

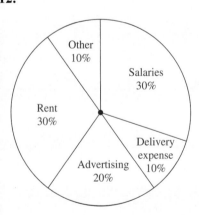

12. Draw a circle graph using the information in Problems 7–11.

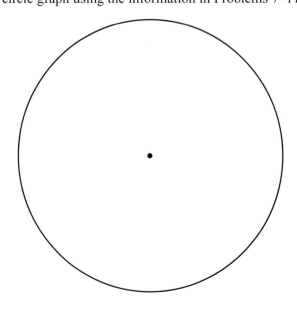

Here are the profits for each of the past 20 weeks from Alan's Snack Bar vending machines. Complete the table.

$142 $137 $125 $132 $147 $129 $151 $172 $175 $129

$159 $148 $173 $160 $152 $174 $169 $163 $149 $173

Profit	Number of Weeks
13. $120–129	————
14. $130–139	————
15. $140–149	————
16. $150–159	————
17. $160–169	————
18. $170–179	————

13. <u>3</u>

14. <u>2</u>

15. <u>4</u>

16. <u>3</u>

17. <u>3</u>

18. <u>5</u>

19. Use the information in Problems 13–18 to draw a histogram.

19. See histogram at left.

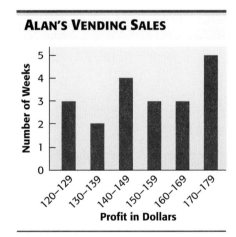

ALAN'S VENDING SALES

Find the mean for each list of numbers. Round answers to the nearest tenth if necessary.

20. Number of miles run each week while training: 52, 61, 68, 69, 73, 75, 79, 84, 91, 98

20. <u>75 mi</u>

21. Weight in pounds for the largest bass caught in the lake: 11, 14, 12, 14, 20, 16, 17, 18

21. <u>15.3 lb (rounded)</u>

22. Airplane speeds in miles per hour: 458, 432, 496, 491, 500, 508, 512, 396, 492, 504

22. <u>478.9 mph</u>

Credits	Grade		
3	A	3 · 4 =	12
2	C	2 · 2 =	4
4	B	4 · 3 =	12
9			28

23. $28 ÷ 9 ≈ 3.11$

✎ **23.** Explain why a weighted mean must be used to determine a student's grade point average. Calculate your own grade point average for last semester or quarter. If you are a new student, make up a grade point average problem of your own and solve it. Round to the nearest hundredth.

The weighted mean must be used because different classes are worth different numbers of credits. GPA problems will vary; one possibility is shown at the left.

8, 17, 23, 32, 64

24. ⤒ Median

✎ **24.** Explain in your own words the procedure for finding the median when there are an odd number of values in a list. Make up a problem with a list of five numbers and solve for the median.

Arrange the values in order, from smallest to largest. When there is an odd number of values in a list, the median is the middle value. Students' problems will vary; one possibility is shown at the left.

Find the weighted mean for the following. Round answers to the nearest tenth if necessary.

25. 25.5

25.

Cost	Frequency
12	5
20	6
22	8
28	4
38	6
48	2

26. 173.7 (rounded)

26.

Value	Frequency
150	15
160	17
170	21
180	28
190	19
200	7

Find the median for each list of numbers.

27. 31.5 degrees

27. Lowest daily temperatures in degrees Fahrenheit: 32, 41, 28, 28, 37, 35, 16, 31

28. 10.0 meters

28. The length of steel beams in meters: 7.6, 11.4, 6.2, 12.5, 31.7, 22.8, 9.1, 10.0, 9.5

Find the mode or modes for each list of numbers.

29. 52 milliliters

29. Blood sample amounts in milliliters: 72, 46, 52, 37, 28, 18, 52, 61

30. 103 and 104 degrees

30. Hot tub temperatures in degrees Fahrenheit of 96, 104, 103, 104, 103, 104, 91, 74, 103

Testing Your Understanding—Unit III

Basic College Mathematics,
Chapter 10: Statistics

Pages 71–82
CHECKING YOUR COMPREHENSION

Identify the following statements as true or false.

1. A circle graph always shows data as percents.

2. The percent equation used to determine an amount for a circle graph is part = percent × whole.

3. A circle has 380 degrees.

4. The On the Town survey indicates that the number one reason for eating dinner in restaurants was because the respondents wanted food they couldn't eat at home.

Choose the best answer for each of the following questions.

5. The Yearly U.S. Snack Market Sales graph indicates the second most popular snack food is
   a. misc. (popcorn, pretzels, granola snacks, etc.).
   b. corn chips.
   c. cookies/crackers.
   d. potato chips.

6. In Example 4, what two age groups had the most members?
   a. Under 8 years and Ages 8–9
   b. Ages 10–11 and Ages 12–13
   c. Ages 10–11 and Ages 8–9
   d. Ages 8–9 and Ages 14–15

7. On a circle graph the categories are expressed in
   a. numbers.
   b. sales.
   c. words.
   d. sectors.

Answer each of the following questions.

8. What was the source of the data for the Favorite Hot Dog Toppings graph?

9. What must you do to ensure the protractor correctly measures the size of the sector?

10. What is the purpose of a circle graph?

Define each term as it is used in the chapter.

11. statistics

12. circle graph

13. protractor

Discussion and Critical Thinking Questions

1. What does the author infer by using the phrase "a picture is worth a thousand words"?

2. Give three different examples of how a circle graph might be used?

3. Survey your classmates regarding their favorite ice cream flavor. Construct a circle graph of the responses.

Pages 83–92
CHECKING YOUR COMPREHENSION

Identify the following statements as true or false.

1. The double-bar graph and comparison line graph are used for comparing two sets of data.

2. The Tacos-to-Go Annual Sales line graph indicates that both sales and profits decreased between 2005 and 2006.

3. Line graphs are produced by connecting dots.

Choose the best answer for each of the following questions.

4. The primary purpose of the Taking a Bite Out of Household Income graph in the text is
   a. to show the percentage of household income spent on food around the world.
   b. to report that it takes the average adult in the U.S. 40 days to pay the annual food bill.
   c. to demonstrate how to interpret a bar graph.
   d. to indicate which country spends the highest percentage of their income on food.

5. The text suggests that when completing a line graph, which of the following should be used?
   a. ruler
   b. protractor
   c. bars
   d. calculator

6. Which of the following graphs would be most useful for reporting the number of sales of HDTV televisions in both 2005 and 2006?
   a. comparison line graph
   b. bar graph
   c. line graph
   d. double-bar graph

Answer each of the following questions.

7. According to the text, when are bar graphs most useful?

8. Explain what the comparison line graph in Objective 4 illustrates.

9. Discuss the differences between line and bar graphs.

Define each term as it is used in the chapter.

10. bar graph

11. double-bar graph

12. line graph

13. comparison line graph

Discussion and Critical Thinking Questions

1. Give an example of when a comparison line graph might be used.

2. What information would be needed to create a double-bar chart comparing sales of peppermint and five-flavor LifeSavers over the past 10 years?

3. Explain why you think bar or line graphs are used instead of raw data.

 Pages 93–124
CHECKING YOUR COMPREHENSION

Identify the following statements as true or false.

1. A mean is not a measure of central tendency.

2. The median can be affected by extremely high or low numbers.

3. It is necessary to place numbers in numerical order when determining the mode.

Choose the best answer for each of the following questions.

4. The primary purpose of preparing a frequency distribution is to
   a. make data easier to read.
   b. put data in class intervals.
   c. tally the frequency of values.
   d. put data in a table.

5. To show the variation in a spread of numbers, which measure would be used?
   a. measure of central tendency
   b. mode
   c. weighted mean
   d. measure of dispersion

6. Find the mode in the following list of numbers: 34, 82, 60, 33, 82, 12, 98, 78, 12, 82, 33.
   a. 33
   b. 82
   c. 12
   d. both a and c

Answer each of the following questions.

7. What example does the text give of a common use of the weighted mean?

8. Can a list have no mode? Explain why or why not.

9. In what instance is there no median?

Define each term as it is used in the chapter.

10. frequency distribution

11. histogram

12. mean

13. weighted mean

14. median

15. mode

16. bimodal

17. dispersion

18. range

Discussion and Critical Thinking Questions

1. What information is needed when determining the mean age of freshman students?

2. Give an example of when a histogram would be useful to show a frequency distribution.

3. Survey the class members regarding how many miles they travel from home to school. Calculate the mean, median, and mode.

 Chapter Review
END OF CHAPTER ANALYSIS

Choose the best answer for each of the following questions.

1. After reading the chapter, you should be able to answer all of the following except
   a. What is the purpose of a pie chart?
   b. How do you determine the range?
   c. What are the differences between bar and line charts?
   d. How do you determine an analysis of variance?

2. The author utilizes which of the following to assist readers to actually apply the statistical concepts?
   a. highlighting
   b. exercises
   c. marginal notations
   d. chapter objectives

3. What was the purpose of the Relating Concepts exercises in the chapter?
   a. to tie concepts together with problem-solving skills
   b. to emphasize important points
   c. to provide an explanation of how mathematics are used in the real world
   d. to help avoid common problems

Group Projects

1. Choose any of the statistical concepts outlined in the chapter and explain how it could be used in a presentation by the chairman of a computer company to show stockholders the earnings for the past year.

2. You have been asked to teach a brief lesson on statistics. Develop a summary of the key concepts in the chapter.

Journal Ideas

1. Based on what you learned from the chapter, give three examples of how statistics are used and give one example of how you encounter statistics in your life.

2. In what ways do you think statistics could be misused or misinterpreted?

Unit IV

From

Palmira Brummett
Robert R. Edgar
Neil J. Hackett
George F. Jewsbury
Barbara Molony

Civilization Past & Present

Eleventh Edition
Volume I

Chapter 16:
Global Encounters

An Introduction to World History

World history examines history in terms of the development and growth of global civilization. This field addresses history from social, economic, political, and religious accounts to better understand and appreciate a global perspective. World historians look for similarities and differences among cultures to better understand the human experience.

World history is a requirement for most college students since it provides a fuller understanding of other civilizations around the world. There are career opportunities for historians in government services, law, teaching, business, advertising, broadcasting, and historical services.

Strategies for Reading World History

When reading a world history textbook, it is important not to be distracted by facts and dates. What is important is to understand why events happened and how they relate to other historical events. Readings on history generally give more information than needed, so try to ask yourself during key passages: What is the point of this section of the text? It is important to take time to scan material and then revisit the text to delve deeper into passages. Also, history is interpretive, so keep in mind that although the information has been well researched and documented, it is subject to differing accounts of interpretation.

Global Encounters

Europe and the New World
Economy, 1400–1650

During the fifteenth century, European nations began a process of exploration, conquest, and trade, affecting almost all areas of the world. Their activities were mirrored in other parts of the world as Asian and Arab states took the lead in expanding their trading networks and their connections with each other. The processes were furthered by improved navigational technology and the resulting expansion of trade that encouraged long sea voyages by Arabs, Japanese, and Chinese. Likewise, sea power, rather than land-based armies, was the key to Europe's becoming a significant force in various parts of the world, especially the Americas and Africa.

European endeavors overseas were obviously related—both as cause and as effect—to trends set in motion as Europe emerged from the medieval era. The Crusades and the Renaissance stimulated European curiosity; the Reformation produced thousands of zealous missionaries seeking converts in foreign lands and refugees searching for religious freedom; and the monarchs of emerging sovereign states sought revenues, first by trading in the Indian Ocean and later by exploiting new worlds. Perhaps the most permeating influence was the rise of European capitalism, with its monetary values, profit-seeking motivations, investment institutions, and consistent impulses toward economic expansion. Some historians have labeled this whole economic transformation the Commercial Revolution. Others have used the phrase to refer to the shift in trade routes from the Mediterranean to the Atlantic. Interpreted either way, the Commercial Revolution and its accompanying European expansion helped usher in a modern era, largely at the expense of Africans and Amerindians.

Europe's Commercial Revolution developed in two quite distinct phases. The first phase involved Portugal and Spain; the second phase, after 1600, was led by the Netherlands, England, and to some extent France. The second fostered a maritime imperialism based more on trade and finance than the more directly exploitative systems of the first phase.

1300

1394–1460 Prince Henry the Navigator

1400

1400s Iberian navigators develop new naval technology; Spain and Portugal stake claims in Asia, Africa, and the Americas; Atlantic slave trade begins

1492 Christopher Columbus reaches San Salvador

1498 Vasco da Gama rounds Cape of Good Hope, reaches India

1500

1513 Vasco de Balboa reaches Pacific Ocean

1519 Hernando Cortés arrives in Mexico, defeats Aztecs

1520 Ferdinand Magellan rounds South America

1600

c. 1600 Second phase of European overseas expansion begins

1609 Henry Hudson establishes Dutch claims in North America; English East India Company chartered

1620 Pilgrims land at Plymouth

THE IBERIAN GOLDEN AGE

■ *What motivated the Portuguese and Spanish to develop global commercial networks?*

Portugal and Spain, the two Iberian states, launched the new era in competition with each other, although neither was able to maintain initial advantages over the long term. Portugal lacked the manpower and resources required by an empire spread over three continents. Spain wasted its new wealth in waging continuous wars while neglecting to develop its own economy. In 1503 Portuguese pepper cost only one-fifth as much as pepper coming through Venice and the eastern Mediterranean. Within decades, gold and silver from the New World poured into Spain. Iberian bullion and exotic commodities, flowing into northern banks and markets, provided a major stimulus to European capitalism. This early European impact abroad also generated great cultural diffusion, promoting an intercontinental spread of peoples, plants, animals, and knowledge that the world had never seen before. But it also destroyed Amerindian states and weakened societies in Africa.

Conditions Favoring Iberian Expansion

A number of conditions invited Iberian maritime expansion in the fifteenth century. Muslim control over the eastern caravan routes, particularly after the

Portuguese and Spanish Exploration and Expansion

1470–1541	Francisco Pizarro
1474–1566	Bartolomé de Las Casas
1479	Treaty of Alcacovas
1494	Treaty of Tordesillas
1509–1515	Alfonso de Albuquerque serves as eastern viceroy of Portugal
1510–1554	Francisco de Coronado
1510	Portuguese acquire Goa, in India
1531	Pizarro defeats Incas in Peru
c. 1550	Spanish introduce plantation system to Brazil
1565	St. Augustine founded; first European colony in North America

Turks took Constantinople in 1453, brought rising prices in Europe. At the same time, the sprawling Islamic world lacked both unity and intimidating sea power, and China, after 1440, had abandoned its extensive naval forays into the Indian Ocean. Because Muslim and Italian rivals prevented the Iberian states from tapping into the spice trade in the eastern Mediterranean and the gold trade in West Africa, Portugal and Spain sought alternative sea routes to the East, where their centuries-old struggle with Muslims in the Mediterranean might be continued on the ocean shores of sub-Saharan Africa and Asia.

During the 1400s, Iberian navigators became proficient in new naval technology and tactics. They adopted the compass (which came from China through the Middle East), the **astrolabe,** and the triangular **lateen sail** that gave their ships the ability to take advantage of winds coming from oblique angles and cut weeks off longer voyages. They also learned to tack against the wind, thus partly freeing them from hugging the coast on long voyages. This skill was important because prevailing winds and ocean currents made it impossible for Portuguese sailors to go farther south than Cape Bojador (bo-hyah-DOR) and still return home. In 1434, a Portuguese seafarer learned that it was possible to sail west toward the Canary Islands and catch trade winds that allowed ships to proceed home. This discovery opened up a new era of exploration.

The Iberians, especially the Portuguese, were also skilled cartographers and chartmakers. But their main advantages lay with their ships and naval guns. The stormy Atlantic required broad bows, deep keels, and complex square rigging for driving and maneuvering fighting ships. Armed with brass cannons, such ships could sink enemy vessels without ramming or boarding at close range. They could also batter down coastal defenses. Even the much larger Chinese junks were no match for the European ships' maneuverability and firepower.

A strong religious motivation augmented Iberian naval efficiency. Long and bitter wars with the Muslim Moors had left the Portuguese and Spanish with an obsessive drive to convert non-Christians or destroy them in the name of Christ. Sailors with Columbus recited prayers every night, and Portuguese seamen were equally devout. Every maritime mission was regarded as a holy crusade.

For two centuries Iberians had hoped to expand their influence in Muslim lands by launching a new Christian crusade in concert with Ethiopia. The idea

---

astrolabe—An instrument used in navigation for calculating latitude.

lateen sail—A triangular sail that is set at a 45-degree angle to the mast and takes advantage of winds coming from oblique angles.

originated with twelfth-century crusaders in the Holy Land; it gained strength later with Ethiopian migrants at Rhodes, who boasted of their king's prowess against the infidels. Thus arose the myth of "Prester John," a mighty Ethiopian monarch and potential European ally against Mongols, Turks, and Muslims. In response to a delegation from Zar'a Ya'kob, the reigning emperor, a few Europeans visited Ethiopia after 1450. These and other similar contacts greatly stimulated the determination to find a new sea route to the East that might link the Iberians with the legendary Ethiopian king and bring Islam under attack from two sides.

DOCUMENT
"The Land of Prester John"

This dream of war for the cross was sincere, but it also served to rationalize more worldly concerns. Both Spain and Portugal experienced dramatic population growth between 1400 and 1600. The Spanish population increased from 5 to 8.5 million; the Portuguese population more than doubled, from 900,000 to 2 million, despite a manpower loss of 125,000 in the sixteenth century. Hard times in rural areas prompted migration to cities, where dreams of wealth in foreign lands encouraged fortune seeking overseas. Despite the obvious religious zeal of many Iberians, particularly among those in holy orders, a fervent desire for gain was the driving motivation for most migrants.

The structures of the Iberian states provided further support for overseas expansion. In both, the powers of the monarchs had been recently expanded and were oriented toward maritime adventure as a means to raise revenues, divert the Turkish menace, spread Catholic Christianity, and increase national unity. The Avis dynasty in Portugal, after usurping the throne and alienating the great nobles in 1385, made common cause with the gentry and middle classes, who prospered in commercial partnership with the government. In contrast, Spanish nobles, particularly the Castilians, were very much like Turkish aristocrats, who regarded conquest and plunder as their normal functions and sources of income. Thus, the Portuguese and Spanish political systems worked in different ways toward similar imperial ends.

Staking Claims

During the late fifteenth century, both Portugal and Spain staked claims abroad. Portugal gained a long lead over Spain in Africa and Asia. But after conquering Granada, the last Moorish state on the Iberian peninsula, and completely uniting the country, the Spanish monarchs turned their attention overseas. The resulting historic voyage of Columbus established Spanish claims to most of the Western Hemisphere.

The man most responsible for Portugal's ambitious exploits was Prince Henry (1394–1460), known as "the Navigator" because of his famous observatory at

Using ships like these broad-beamed carracks, the Portuguese controlled much of the carrying trade with the East in the fifteenth and sixteenth centuries.

Sagres (SAH-greesh), where skilled mariners planned voyages and recorded their results. As a young man in 1415, Henry directed the Portuguese conquest of Ceuta (see-YOO-tah), a Muslim port on the Moroccan coast, at the western entrance to the Mediterranean. This experience imbued him with a lifelong desire to divert the West African gold trade from Muslim caravans to Portuguese ships. He also shared the common dream of winning Ethiopian Christian allies against the Turks. Such ideas motivated him for 40 years as he sent expeditions down the West African coast, steadily charting and learning from unknown waters.

Before other European states began extensive explorations, the Portuguese had navigated the West African coast to its southern tip. Henry's captains claimed the Madeira Islands in 1418 and the Azores in 1421. A thousand miles to the west of Portugal, these uninhabited islands were settled to produce, among other things, wheat for bread-starved Lisbon.

By 1450 the Portuguese had explored the Senegal River and then traced the Guinea coast during the next decade. After Henry's death in 1460, they pushed

Motivated by a desire to find a sea route to India that bypassed the overland caravan routes controlled by Muslim states, Prince Henry the Navigator was a leading figure in promoting Portuguese explorations down the West African coast. Ironically he seldom left Portugal himself. When he died in 1460, his sailors had reached the Canary Islands, but by the end of that century, Vasco da Gama had sailed from Portugal to India.

south, reaching Benin in the decade after 1470 and Kongo, on the southwest coast, in 1482. Six years later, Bartolomeu Dias rounded southern Africa, but his disgruntled crew forced him to turn back. Nevertheless, King John II of Portugal (1481–1495) was so excited by the prospect of a direct route to India that he named Dias's discovery the "Cape of Good Hope."

Spain soon challenged Portuguese supremacy. The specific controversy was over the Canary Islands, some of which were occupied by Castilians in 1344 and others by Portuguese after the 1440s. The issue, which produced repeated incidents, was ultimately settled in 1479 by the Treaty of Alcacovas (ahl-KAHS-ko-vahsh), which recognized exclusive Spanish rights in the Canaries but banned Spain from the Madeiras, the Azores, the Cape Verdes, and West Africa. Spanish ambitions were thus temporarily frustrated until Columbus provided new hope.

Christopher Columbus (1451–1506), a Genoese sailor with an impossible dream, had been influenced by Marco Polo's journal to believe that Japan could be reached by a short sail directly westward. Although he underestimated the distance by some 7000 miles and was totally ignorant of the intervening continents, Columbus persistently urged his proposals on King John of Portugal and Queen Isabella of Spain, who was captivated by Columbus's dream and became his most steadfast supporter until her death in 1504. Having obtained her sponsorship, Columbus sailed from Palos, Spain, in three small ships on August 3, 1492. He landed on San Salvador in the West Indies on October 12, thinking he had reached his goal. In three more attempts he continued his search for an Asian passage. His voyages touched the major Caribbean islands, Honduras, the Isthmus of Panama, and Venezuela. Although he never knew it, he had claimed a new world for Spain.

VIDEO

Christopher Columbus and the Round World

Columbus's first voyage posed threats to Portuguese interests in the Atlantic and called for compromise if war was to be averted. At Spain's invitation, the pope issued a "bull of demarcation," establishing a north-south line about 300 miles west of the Azores. Beyond this line all lands were opened to Spanish claims. The Portuguese protested, forcing direct negotiations, which produced the Treaty of Tordesillas (tordhai-SEE-lyahs) in 1494. It moved the line some 500 miles farther west. Later explorations showed that the last agreement gave Spain most of the New World but left eastern Brazil to Portugal.

The Developing Portuguese Empire

Through the first half of the sixteenth century, the Portuguese developed a world maritime empire while maintaining commercial supremacy. They established trading posts around both African coasts and a falter-

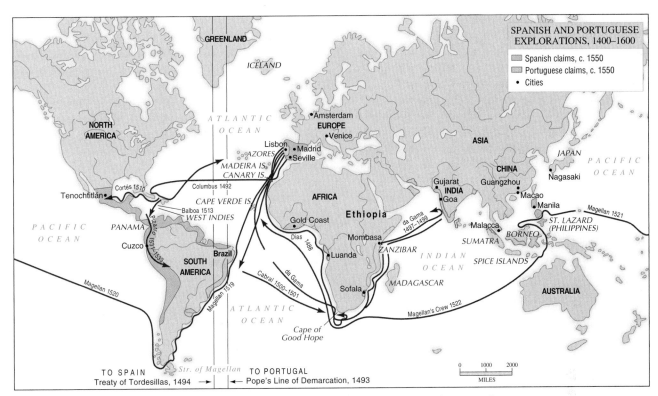

From the mid-fifteenth to the mid-sixteenth centuries, Portugal and Spain took advantage of new naval technology and tactics to become the leading seafaring nations in the world.

ing colony in Brazil, but their most extensive operations were in southern Asia, where they gained control of shipping routes and dominated the Indian Ocean spice trade.

Two voyages at the turn of the sixteenth century laid the foundations for the Portuguese interests in the Americas and the Orient. In 1497 Vasco da Gama (1469–1524) left Lisbon, Portugal, in four ships, rounding the Cape of Good Hope after 93 days on the open sea. While visiting and raiding the East African ports, da Gama picked up an Arab pilot, who brought the fleet across the Indian Ocean to Calicut (KAL-i-kut), on the western coast of India. When he returned to Lisbon in 1499, da Gama had lost two ships and a third of his men, but his cargo of pepper and cinnamon returned the cost of the expedition 60 times over. Shortly afterward, Pedro Cabral (1468–1520), commanding a large fleet on a second voyage to India, bore too far west and sighted the east coast of Brazil. The new western territory was so unpromising that it was left unoccupied until 1532, when a small settlement was established at São Vicente. In the 1540s it had attracted only some 2000 settlers, mostly men, although a few Portuguese women came after the arrival of the lord protector's wife and her retinue in 1535. The colony served mostly as a place to send convicts, and by 1600 it had only 25,000 European residents.

Brazil was neglected in favor of extensive operations in the Indian Ocean and Southeast Asia, where the Portuguese sought to gain control of the spice trade by taking over flourishing port cities, places strategically located on established trade routes. The most striking successes were achieved under Alfonso de Albuquerque, eastern viceroy from 1509 to 1515. He completed subjugation of the Swahili city-states and established fortified trading posts in Mozambique and Zanzibar. After a decisive naval victory over an Arab fleet (1509), Albuquerque's force captured Hormuz (hor-MOOZ) six years later, thus disrupting Arab passage from the Persian Gulf. In 1510 the Portuguese acquired Goa on the west coast of India; it became a base for aiding Hindus against Indian Muslims and conducting trade with Gujerat (goo-ja-RAHT), a major producer of cloth. The next year a Portuguese force took Malacca, a Muslim stronghold in Malaya, which controlled trade with China and the Spice Islands, through the narrow straits opposite Sumatra (soo-MAH-trah). Although a Portuguese goal was to spread the Christian faith at the expense of Islam, the expulsion of Muslim traders had the opposite effect. These traders moved to the Malaysian peninsula and founded new Muslim states.

The Indian Ocean had previously been open to all traders, but the Portuguese network left no room for competitors, and rival traders, especially Muslims, were squeezed out of their previous settlements. Portuguese officials financed their operations from two sources, customs duties and a tax levied on ships trading in the Indian Ocean. All ships were required to stop at Portuguese ports and take a **cartaz.**

The Portuguese presence was largely felt on the ocean; it had very little impact on the land-based empires and trading networks of the Ottomans, the Safavids, the Mughuls, and the Chinese. On the Asian mainland, for instance, the Portuguese were mostly supplicants because they had to interact with well-established and more powerful states. They acquired temporary influence in Laos and Cambodia but were expelled from Vietnam and enslaved in Burma. In China their diplomatic blunders and breaches of etiquette offended Ming officials, who regarded the Portuguese as cannibals. In 1519 a Portuguese representative angered the Chinese by, among other things, starting to erect a fort in Canton harbor without permission and buying Chinese children as slaves. Chinese officials

cartaz—A license issued by the Portuguese that permitted non-Portuguese traders to operate in areas of the Indian Ocean controlled by the Portuguese.

responded by jailing and executing a group of Portuguese emissaries who had been visiting Beijing. After being banished from Chinese ports in 1522 and 1544, the Portuguese cooperated with Chinese smuggling rings off South China before Chinese officials granted them strictly regulated trading rights in Macao (mah-KOU) in 1554. Although the Chinese generally had little interest in European goods, the Portuguese served a useful purpose by supplying the Chinese economy with Indian manufactures such as cloth and Indonesian spices and silver from the Americas reexported through Europe.

The Portuguese developed an extensive relationship with Japan. The connection was established accidentally in 1542 when three Portuguese traders landed off southern Japan after a storm blew their ship off course. At the time Japanese *daimyo* (feudal lords) were contending with each other for power, and Portuguese traders prospered by selling matchlock muskets to rival factions.

The Jesuit priests who followed the merchants in 1549 had great success in winning converts. While the *daimyo* Nobunaga was gaining mastery over his opponents, he

A Japanese View of European Missionaries

In the sixteenth century a Japanese artist depicted the Portuguese as "Southern Barbarians" in a decorative screen.

encouraged the Catholics because they were useful allies against Buddhist sects opposing him. By the 1580s, the Catholics were claiming as many as 150,000 adherents. However, as Japan became unified in the late sixteenth century, Nobunaga's successors began regarding Christians as a divisive threat. They perceived the arrival of Spanish Franciscan friars in 1592 as an additional danger because they had recently scored major successes in winning converts in the Philippines. Japanese officials issued a series of anti-Christian edicts that led to the persecution and killing of thousands of Christians. Following the suppression of a Christian peasant revolt in 1637–1638, the Japanese government expelled all Europeans except for a small contingent of Dutch traders who were confined to a small island in the Nagasaki harbor.

Long before this expulsion, the Portuguese Empire had begun to decline. It did not have the special skills or fluid capital required by a global empire and had become dependent on the bankers and spice brokers of northern Europe for financing. This deficiency was magnified by Albuquerque's failure to recruit women from home who might have produced a Portuguese governing elite in the colonies. To make matters worse, the home population dropped steadily after 1600. Thus the relatively few Portuguese men overseas mated with local women. Most were concubines, prostitutes, or slaves—regarded generally as household pets or work animals. These conditions contributed largely to a decided weakening of morale, economic efficiency, and military power. After the turn of the seventeenth century, the Portuguese lost ground to the Omani Arabs in East Africa, the Spanish in the Philippines, and the Dutch in both hemispheres. Despite a mild later revival, their empire never regained its former glory.

THE PORTUGUESE AND AFRICA

■ *How did Africans respond to the opportunities offered by trade with the Portuguese?*

The Portuguese came to Africa as traders rather than settlers. Their original goal was to find a way around

Africa, Europe, and the World

Muslim middlemen who controlled the trans-Saharan caravan trade and to gain direct access to the fabled goldfields of West Africa. Muslim kingdoms of the Sudan, such as Mali, Kanem-Bornu, and the Hausa states, dominated trade in the West African interior and were reluctant to open up their trade to Europeans. Therefore, the Portuguese concentrated their efforts on establishing commercial bases along the West African coast.

The Portuguese in West Africa

Africa was not of primary importance to the Portuguese, especially after they opened up sea routes to Asia. Thus, they selectively established links with African states where they could trade for goods of value such as gold, which could be traded anywhere in the world, and slaves, which were initially taken to southern Portugal as laborers. The first bases of operation for Portuguese seafarers were at Cape Verde, Arguin (ahr-GWEEN), and Senegambia.

CASE STUDY

Portuguese Travelers in Africa

Although the Portuguese conducted hit-and-run raids for slaves and plunder, they soon learned that if they expected to sustain a profitable trade in gold, they could not afford to alienate African rulers. When the Portuguese arrived on the Gold Coast (present-day Ghana) in 1471, they found Akan states carrying on a vigorous trade to the north through Muslim Dyula traders. Still hoping to develop trade links with the kingdom of Mali, the Portuguese sent several envoys with Dyula traders to Mali in the late fifteenth century. However, Mali's king sent a clear signal about his lack of interest in ties with Portugal by informing the envoy that he recognized only three kings beside himself—the rulers of Yemen, Cairo, and Baghdad.

From that point on, the Portuguese concentrated on establishing a profitable relationship with Akan leaders, exchanging firearms (that could not be obtained through Mali), copper and brass objects, textiles, slaves, and later cowrie shells for gold. From their fort at Elmina ("the mine"), established in 1482, the Portuguese exported close to half a ton of gold annually for the next half century. Because the Akan required slave labor to clear forests for arable agricultural land, the Portuguese brought slaves from the region of Benin and Kongo. It took several more

The Portuguese and Africa

1482	Portuguese establish Fort Elmina on Gold Coast; Portuguese reach kingdom of Kongo
1506–1543	Reign of Nzinga Mbemba, king of Kongo
1506	Portuguese seize Sofala
1571	Portuguese establish colony of Angola
1607	King of Mutapa kingdom signs treaty with Portugal
1698	Portuguese driven from East African coast by Omani Arabs

centuries before Akan states actively participated in selling rather than buying slaves.

The Portuguese also initiated contacts with the kingdom of Benin, located in the forests of southwestern Nigeria. The kings of Benin, called *obas,* had governed their land since the eleventh century. When the Portuguese arrived, Benin possessed a formidable army and was at the peak of its power. Edo, the walled capital, was a bustling metropolis with wide streets, markets, and an efficient municipal government. The huge royal palace awed Europeans who chanced to see it, although the Portuguese—and later the Dutch— were generally prohibited from living in the city. The few European visitors who gained entrance were amazed by Benin's metalwork, such as copper birds on towers, copper snakes coiled around doorways, and beautifully cast bronze statues.

Benin artists cast brass plaques that adorned the oba's palace walls. The plaques depicted important events in Benin's history, including the engagement with the Portuguese. The two Portuguese soldiers in this plaque are notable for their long wavy hair and military uniforms.

The first Portuguese emissary who arrived at oba Ozuola's court in 1486 was sent back to Lisbon with gifts, including a Maltese-type cross. The cross excited the Portuguese who interpreted it as a sign that Benin was near Prester John's kingdom and that its inhabitants would be receptive to conversion to Christianity. However, when Ozuola admitted Catholic missionaries to his kingdom in the early 1500s in the hope of securing Portuguese muskets, the Portuguese made acceptance of Christianity a precondition for receiving arms. Although the missionaries converted several of Ozuola's sons and high-ranking officials, their influence ended at Ozuola's death.

Portugal believed that it could manipulate Benin's rulers to extend Portuguese trade over a much wider area, but the obas did not regard trade with the Portuguese as a vital necessity and did not allow them to establish a sizable presence in the kingdom. The obas controlled all transactions, and Portuguese traders duly paid taxes, observed official regulations, and conducted business only with the obas' representatives.

The Portuguese traded brass and copper items, textiles, and cowrie shells for pepper, cloth, beads, and slaves. Because Benin did not have access to sources of gold, the Portuguese took the slaves from Benin and traded them for gold with the Akan states, which needed laborers for clearing forests for farmland. However, in 1516, Benin decided to curtail the slave trade and offered only female slaves for purchase.

Although effectively limited in Benin, Portuguese traders openly operated among nearby coastal states, where they gained some political influence. They were particularly successful in the small kingdom of Warri, a Niger delta vassal state of Benin. Shortly after 1600, the Warri crown prince was educated in Portugal and brought home a Portuguese queen. Warri supplied large numbers of slaves, as did other nearby states, which were now competing fiercely with one another. Before long, even Benin would accept dependence on the slave trade in order to control its tributaries and hold its own against Europeans.

The Portuguese and the Kongo Kingdom

Farther south, near the mouth of the Congo River, the Portuguese experienced their most intensive involvement in Africa. There, Portuguese seafarers found the recently established Kongo kingdom of several million people, ruled by a king who was heavily influenced by the queen mother and other women on his royal council. Although the Kongo initially perceived the Europeans as water or earth spirits, Kongo's king, Nzinga Nkuwu, soon came to regard them as a potential ally against neighboring African

Loango, Capital of the Kingdom of the Congo

Discovery Through Maps

Savage Pictures: Sebastian Munster's Map of Africa

AFRICA XVIII· NOVA TABVLA

V oyages of exploration in the fifteenth and six-teenth centuries greatly expanded European knowledge of the rest of the world. However, map-makers who knew very little about the geography and peoples of continents such as Africa still tended to rely on outdated information or stereotypical repre-sentations. Thus, when Sebastian Munster (1489–1552 C.E.), a professor of Hebrew and mathematics at Basel, the home of Switzerland's oldest university, de-veloped an interest in maps, he turned to Ptolemy (90–168 C.E.), a celebrated astronomer, geographer, and mathematician of Alexandria, Egypt, whose the-ories about the universe influenced the European and Arab worlds for many centuries. When Ptolemy's *Guide to Geography* was published in Florence around 1400, it was the first atlas of the world.

Ptolemy's view of the world heavily influenced Mun-ster when he began drawing his own world atlas. First published in 1544, Munster's *Cosmographia Universalis* went through 46 editions and was translated into six languages. It was the first collection to feature individ-ual maps of Europe, Asia, the Americas, and Africa.

Munster's map of Africa relied not only on Ptolemy but also on Portuguese and Arab sources. However, it still contained many errors. The map identified the source of the Nile far to the south and, based on the assumption that the Senegal was con-nected to the Niger River in West Africa, showed a river flowing westward to the Atlantic.

The *Cosmographia* was also a descriptive geogra-phy, providing an accompanying narrative and draw-ings of prominent figures, the customs and manners of societies, and the products, animals, and plants of regions. Munster's Africa map depicted a lone human figure that bore no resemblance to Africans and a large elephant at the southern end of the continent. His rendering of Africa conformed to Jonathan Swift's satirical lines:

So Geographers in Africa-Maps
With Savage-Pictures fill their Gaps;
And o'er unhabitable Downs
Place Elephants for want of Towns.

Questions to Consider

1. Why do you think Muster chose to rely on Ptolemy's views rather than on more recent information?

2. Compare the portrayal of Africa in Munster's map with that in Abraham Cresque's Catalan map. Why does Cresque's map contain so much more detail than Munster's?

states. In the 1480s he invited the Portuguese to send teachers, technicians, missionaries, and soldiers. His son, Nzinga Mbemba (1506–1543), who converted to Catholicism in 1491, consolidated the control of the Catholic faction at his court, making Portuguese the official language and Catholicism the state religion. He encouraged his court to adopt European dress and manners while changing his own name to Don Afonso. Many friendly letters subsequently passed between him and King Manuel of Portugal.

This mutual cooperation did not last long. While the Portuguese were prepared to assist Afonso's kingdom, their desire for profits won out over their humanitarian impulses. Portuguese traders, seeking slaves for their sugar plantations at São Tomé (SAH-o TO-mai) and Principe, ranged over Kongo. By 1530 some 4000 to 5000 slaves were being taken from Kongo annually. No longer satisfied with treaty terms that gave them prisoners of war and criminals, the traders ignored the laws and bought everyone they could get, thus creating dissension and weakening the country. Driven to despair, Afonso wrote to his friend and ally Manuel: "There are many traders in all corners of the country. They bring ruin. . . . Every day, people are enslaved and kidnapped, even nobles, even members of the King's own family."[1] Such pleas brought no satisfactory responses. For a while, Afonso tried to curb the slave trade; however, he was shot by disgruntled Portuguese slavers while he was attending Mass in 1430. Afonso's successors were no more successful, and Portuguese slavers operated with impunity throughout Kongo and in neighboring areas.

The Portuguese crown also turned its attention to the Mbundu kingdom to the south of Kongo. In 1520 Manuel established contact with the Mbundu king, Ngola. However, when the Portuguese government agreed to deal with Ngola through Kongo, São Tomé slavers were given a free hand to join with Mbundu's rulers to attack neighboring states. Using African mercenaries known as pombeiros equipped with firearms and sometimes allied with feared Imbangala warriors, the slavers and their allies began a long war of conquest. In 1571 the Portuguese crown issued a royal charter to establish the colony of Angola, situated on the Atlantic coast south of the Kongo kingdom. Although Portugal had ambitious plans to create an agricultural colony for white settlement and to gain control over a silver mine and the salt trade in the interior, Angola was never a successful venture. Few settlers immigrated, and Angola remained a sleepy outpost, consisting of a handful of Portuguese men, even fewer Portuguese women, a growing population of Afro-Portuguese, and a majority of Africans. The colony functioned primarily as a haven for slavers. By the end of the sixteenth century, 10,000 slaves were flowing annually through Luanda (loo-AHN-dah), Angola's capital.

The Portuguese in East Africa

Portuguese exploits in East Africa were similar to those in Kongo and Angola. The Swahili city-states along the coast north of the Zambezi (zam-BEE-zee) River were tempting targets for Portuguese intervention because they were strategically well located for trade with Asia. However, because they rarely engaged in wars with each other or supported sizeable militaries, they could not effectively defend themselves against a ruthless Portuguese naval force that sacked and plundered city-states from Kilwa to Mombasa. At Mombasa Portuguese sailors broke into houses with axes, looted, and killed before setting the town afire. The sultan of Mombasa wrote to the sultan of Malindi: "[They] raged in our town with such might and terror that no one, neither man nor woman, neither the old or the young, nor even the children, however small, was spared to live."[2]

DOCUMENT

"Of the Coasts of East Africa and Malabar"

Although a few city-states such as Malindi (mah-LEEN-dee) escaped the wrath of the Portuguese by becoming allies, the Portuguese usually relied on coercion to keep the city-states in line. They constructed fortified stations from which they attempted to collect tribute and maintain trade with the interior. An early station at Mozambique became the main port of call for vessels on the Asia route. In the 1590s the Portuguese built a fort at Mombasa, hoping to intimidate other cities and support naval operations against Turks and Arabs in the Red Sea. Although the Portuguese dominated trade in gold and ivory along the East African coast, they could not control the whole coastline and Swahili merchants continued to trade with their traditional partners. However, local industries such as ironworking and weaving virtually disappeared under Portuguese rule. When Omani Arabs expelled the Portuguese from the Swahili coast in 1698, the Swahili did not lament their departure. A Swahili proverb captured Swahili sentiment: "Go away, Manuel [the king of Portugal], you have made us hate you; go, and carry your cross with you."[3]

On the southeast coast the Portuguese were drawn to the Zimbabwean plateau by reports of huge gold mines. The Portuguese needed gold to finance their trade for spices in the Indian Ocean, while Shona kingdoms desired beads and cotton cloth from India. The Portuguese seized Sofala in 1506, diminishing the role of Muslim traders and positioning themselves as the middlemen for the gold trade with the coast. After establishing trading settlements along the Zambezi River at Sena and Tete, the Portuguese developed a close relationship with the Karanga kingdom of Mutapa, which received Portuguese traders and Catholic missionaries. This relationship soured when the king of Mutapa ordered the death of a Jesuit missionary in 1560. In the 1570s the Portuguese retaliated

Document   Portuguese Encounters with Africans

The Portuguese had very specific objectives in Africa. They usually established amicable relations with stronger states, while they were more likely to coerce weaker states such as the Swahili city-states in East Africa. When Vasco da Gama dealt with the ruler of Kilwa, an island off the East African coast, he showed little patience for the subtleties of diplomacy and quickly resorted to threats to achieve his aims. This document records an exchange between da Gama and the King of Kilwa.

In the case of the Kingdom of the Kongo, the Portuguese were dealing with a state that clearly defined its interests and did not regard Portugal as a superior nation. Kongo's king, Don Afonso, who converted to Catholicism, wrote a series of letters to the king of Portugal in 1526. These letters demonstrate the complex relationship between the Kongolese leadership and the Portuguese. Afonso complains about Portuguese involvement in the slave trade but also conveys a request for doctors and apothecaries to treat illnesses.

KING IBRAHIM OF KILWA: Good friendship was to friends like brothers are and that he would shelter the Portuguese in his city and harbor . . . to pay tribute each year in money or jewelry was not a way to a good friendship, it was tributary subjugation . . . to pay tribute was dishonor . . . it would be like to be a captive . . . such friendship he did not want with subjugation . . . because even the sons did not want to have that kind of subjugation with their own parents.

VASCO DA GAMA: Take it for certain that if I so decide your city would be grounded by fire in one single hour and if your people wanted to extinguish the fire in town, they would all be burned and when you see all this happen, you will regret all you are telling me now and you will give much more than what I am asking you now, it will be too late for you. If you are still in doubt, it is up to you to see it.

KING IBRAHIM: Sir, if I had known that you wanted to enslave me, I would not have come and I would have fled into the forest, for it is better for me to be a fox but free, than a dog locked up in a golden chain.

From Chapurukha M. Kusimba, *The Rise and Fall of Swahili States* (Walnut Creek: AltaMira Press, 1999), pp. 161–162.

Moreover, Sir, in our Kingdom there is another great inconvenience which is of little service to God, and this is that many of our people [*naturaes*], keenly desirous as they are of the wares and things of your Kingdoms, which are brought here by your people, freed and exempt men; and very often it happens that they kidnap even noblemen and the sons of noblemen, and our relatives, and take them to be sold to the white men who are in our Kingdoms; and for this purpose they have concealed them, and others are brought during the night so that they might not be recognized. And as soon as they are taken by the white men they are immediately ironed and branded with fire, and when they are carried to be embarked, if they are caught by our guards' men the whites allege that they

have brought them but they cannot say from whom, so that it is our duty to do justice and to restore to the freemen their freedom, but it cannot be done if your subjects feel offended, as they claim to be.

And to avoid such a great evil we passed a law so that any white man living in our Kingdoms and wanting to purchase goods in any way should first inform three of our noblemen and officials of our court . . . who should investigate if the mentioned goods are captives or freemen, and if cleared by them there will be no further doubt nor embargo for them to be taken and embarked. But if the white men do not comply with it they will lose the aforementioned goods. . . .

[1526] Sir, Your Highness has been kind enough to write to us saying that we should ask in our letters for anything we need, and that we shall be provided with everything, and as the peace and health of our Kingdom depend on us . . . it happens that we have continuously many and different diseases which put us very often in such a weakness that we reach almost the last extreme; and the same happens to our children, relatives and natives owing to the lack in this country of physicians and surgeons who might know how to cure properly such diseases.

And to avoid such a great error and inconvenience, since it is from God in the first place and then from your Kingdoms and from Your Highness that all the good and drugs and medicines have come to save us, we beg of you to be agreeable and kind enough to send us two physicians and two apothecaries and all the necessary things to stay in our kingdoms. . . .

From Basil Davidson, *African Past* (Boston: Little, Brown and Co., 1964), pp. 192–194.

Questions to Consider

1. Why did the Portuguese treat the kings of Kongo and Kilwa in different ways?
2. What do the letters from the King of the Kongo reveal about the involvement of his people and the Portuguese in the slave trade?

by sending several expeditionary forces up the Zambezi to seize control over the gold-producing areas. The Portuguese believed the gold came from rich mines, when, in reality, African peasants recovered most of the gold from riverbeds during the winter months. In any event, these adventures ended disastrously as drought, disease (especially malaria), and African resisters decimated the Portuguese forces.

A series of internal rebellions and wars with neighboring states, however, forced Mutapa's rulers to turn to the Portuguese for assistance. In 1607 they signed a treaty that ceded control of gold production to the Portuguese. For the rest of the century the Portuguese regularly intervened in Mutapa's affairs until the forces of Mutapa and a rising power, Changamire, combined to expel the Portuguese from the Zimbabwean plateau. Along the Zambezi River the Portuguese crown granted huge land concessions *(prazos)* to Portuguese settlers *(prazeros)* who ruled them as feudal estates. Over time, the *prazeros* loosened their ties with Portugal's officials and became virtually independent. In the absence of Portuguese women, *prazeros* intermarried with Africans and adopted African culture.

The tale of Prester John, the mythical Ethiopian Christian monarch who held the Muslims at bay, had long captivated Portugal's monarchs. Thus, they initially responded positively when the astute Ethiopian empress Eleni made diplomatic overtures. Eleni, the daughter of a Muslim king, had married the Ethiopian emperor Baeda Maryam and converted to Christianity. After his death in 1478, she remained an influential figure as regent during the reigns of two of her sons and two grandsons. Recognizing that the interests of both Ethiopia and Portugal would be served by defeating Muslim states on the Red Sea coast, she wrote Portugal's king in 1509 proposing an alliance against the Ottoman Turks. She reasoned that the combination of Ethiopia's army and Portugal's sea forces would be very potent. However, the Portuguese, disappointed that Ethiopia did not meet their grand expectations of a kingdom ruled by Prester John, were reluctant to sign a pact.

After Eleni's death in 1522, her projected alliance was not completed for several decades. In 1541, the army of Muslim leader Ahmad Gran of the kingdom of Adal had come close to conquering Ethiopia. This time, the Portuguese responded to Ethiopian appeals by dispatching 400 Portuguese musketeers who helped to defeat the Muslims. The following year, however, Muslim forces, augmented by Turkish soldiers, rallied and defeated the Portuguese contingent,

killing its commander, Christopher da Gama, Vasco's son. When the Ethiopians eventually pushed the Muslims out, they enticed some of the Portuguese soldiers to stay on by granting them large estates in the countryside. Subsequent Ethiopian rulers called on descendants of the Portuguese in their conflicts with the Turks.

The Portuguese impact on Africa was not as immediately disastrous as Spanish effects on the New World. The Portuguese did not have the manpower or arms to dictate the terms of trade with most African states. However, they did inflict severe damage in Kongo, Angola, Zimbabwe, and the Swahili city-states. Their most destructive involvement was the slave trade.

By the end of the sixteenth century the Portuguese had moved an estimated 240,000 slaves from West and Central Africa; 80 percent were transported after 1575. These trends foreshadowed much greater disasters for African societies in the seventeenth and eighteenth centuries as the Atlantic slave trade expanded (see Chapter 19).

THE GROWTH OF NEW SPAIN

■ *What factors contributed to the Spanish conquest of Amerindian societies?*

While Portugal concentrated on Asian and African trade, Spain won a vast empire in America. Soon after 1492, Spanish settlements were established in the West Indies, most notably on Hispaniola (ees-pah-nee-O-lah) and Cuba. By 1500, as the American continents were recognized and the passage to Asia remained undiscovered, a host of Spanish adventurers—the ***conquistadora***—set out for the New World with dreams of acquiring riches. From the West Indies they crossed the Caribbean to eastern Mexico, fanning out from there in all directions, toward Central America, the Pacific, and the vast North American hinterlands.

In Mexico the Spaniards profited from internal problems within the Aztec Empire. By the early 1500s, the Aztecs ruled over several million people in a vast kingdom that stretched from the Gulf of Mexico to the Pacific Ocean and from present-day central Mexico to Guatemala. However, unrest ran rampant among many recently conquered peoples, who were forced to pay tribute and taxes and furnish sacrificial victims to their Aztec overlords.

In 1519 Spanish officials in Cuba, excited by reports of a wealthy Amerindian civilization from two

---

prazo—A land grant from the Portuguese crown to a Portuguese settler (*prazero*) in the Zambezi river valley in Mozambique that gave the settler control over tribute and labor service from local residents.

conquistadora—The Spanish soldiers who conquered Mexico and Peru.

expeditions to the Yucatán (yoo-kah-TAHN) peninsula, dispatched Hernando Cortés (1485–1574) with 11 ships, 600 fighting men, 200 servants, 16 horses, 32 crossbows, 13 muskets, and 14 mobile cannons. Before marching against the Aztec capital, he destroyed 10 of his 11 ships to prevent his men from turning back. He had the good luck to secure two interpreters. One was an Amerindian woman, Malitzin, later christened Doña Marina, who became a valuable interpreter and intelligence gatherer as well as bearing Cortés a son. As Cortés's band marched inland, he added thousands of Amerindian warriors to his small force. He easily enlisted Amerindian allies, such as the Cempoala who had suffered under Aztec rule. By contrast, the loyalty of the Tlaxcalan (tlash-KAH-lahn) was secured only after Cortez's force demonstrated the superiority of its firearms, steel swords, and armor and horses (that the Aztecs initially thought were deer).

The Aztec emperor Moctezuma II's initial view of the Spaniards was shaped by an Aztec belief that the Spaniards were representatives of the white-skinned and bearded Teotihuacán (tay-o-tee-wah-KAHN) god, Quetzalcoatl (KAT-SAL-KWA-tel), who had been exiled by the Toltecs in the tenth century C.E. He forbade human sacrifice and had promised to return from across the sea to enforce his law. However, as reports of Spanish victories came to his attention, Moctezuma had second thoughts as Cortés approached the Aztec capital, Tenochtitlán (te-noch-teet-lahn), a city of more than 150,000 people. Thus, Moctezuma warily welcomed Cortés as a guest in his father's palace. Although surrounded by a host of armed Aztecs, Cortés seized the ruler and informed

him that he must cooperate or die. The bold scheme worked temporarily. But when Cortés left the capital to return to the coast, his commander attacked an unarmed crowd at a religious festival, killing many Aztec notables. The massacre touched off a popular uprising. Cortés returned with reinforcements, but when he placed Moctezuma on a wall to pacify the Aztecs, they renounced their former ruler as a traitor and stoned and killed him. Neither the Aztecs nor the Spaniards showed any mercy in the fierce fighting that followed. The Aztecs ultimately drove a battered band of terrified Spaniards from the city in the narrowest of escapes. Later, having regrouped and gained new Amerindian allies, Cortés wore down the Aztecs in a bloody siege during which some Spanish prisoners were sacrificed in full view of their comrades. The outcome of the fighting was in doubt when a smallpox epidemic, accidentally introduced by a Spanish soldier, broke out, killing many thousands of Aztecs who had no immunity to the disease. Finally, in August 1521, some 60,000 exhausted and half-starved defenders surrendered.

As the inheritors of the Aztec empire, the Spaniards found the Aztec's hierarchical system suited to their needs. They replaced an urbanized Aztec elite with their own and gave privileged positions to Amerindian allies such as the Tlaxcalans. The Spanish ruled from Tenochtitlán, rebuilt as Mexico City, which became the capital of an expanding Spanish empire.

Although *conquistadora* steadily penetrated the interior, the fierce Mayas of Yucatán and Guatemala put up a determined resistance until the 1540s. By then, Spanish settlements had been established throughout Central America. The first colony in North America was founded at St. Augustine, on Florida's

An illustration from the Codex Azacatitlán of the Spanish arriving in Mexico. Standing next to Cortés is Malitzin, the Aztec woman who served as his interpreter.

east coast, in 1565. Meanwhile, numerous expeditions, including those of Hernando de Soto (1500–1542) and Francisco de Coronado (1510–1554), explored what is now California, Arizona, New Mexico, Colorado, Texas, Missouri, Louisiana, and Alabama. Spanish friars established a mission at Santa Fe in 1610, providing a base for later missions. All these new territories, known as New Spain, were administered from Mexico City after 1542.

The viceroyalty of Mexico later sponsored colonization of the Philippines, a project justified by the historic voyage of Ferdinand Magellan (1480–1521). Encouraged by the exploits of Vasco de Balboa (1479–1519), who had crossed Panama and discovered the Pacific Ocean in 1513, Magellan sailed from Spain in 1520, steered past the ice-encrusted straits at the tip of South America, and endured a 99-day voyage to the Philippines. He made an unwise choice by intervening in a conflict between two sheikdoms, and he lost his life in a battle with the inhabitants of Mactan Island. Many of Magellan's crew died after terrible suffering from **scurvy.** This illness explains why only one of Magellan's five ships completed this first circumnavigation of the world. However, the feat established a Spanish claim to the Philippines. It also prepared the way for the first tiny settlement of 400 Mexicans at Cebu in 1571. By 1580, when the Philippine capital at Manila had been secured against attacking Portuguese, Chinese, and Moro fleets, the friars were beginning conversions that would reach half a million by 1622. The colony prospered in trade with Asia but remained economically dependent on annual galleons bearing silver from Mexico. Because the Spanish were excluded from China, they relied on a community of Chinese merchants in Manila to trade the silver in the Chinese market for luxury items such as porcelain, silk, and lacquer ware.

The Development of Spanish South America

As in Mexico, the Spanish exploited unique opportunities as well as epidemics in their process of empire building in Peru. Just before they arrived, the recently formed Inca state had been torn apart by a succession crisis. When the emperor Huayna Capac and his heir apparent suddenly died of smallpox in 1526, the claim of his son Huascar (was-KAR) to the throne was contested by Atahualpa, a half-royal son who had been Huayna Capac's favorite. Their conflict, which soon

destroyed nearly every semblance of imperial unity, was a major factor in the surprisingly easy triumph of a handful of Spanish freebooters over a country of more than ten million people, scattered through Peru and Ecuador in hundreds of mountain towns and coastal cities.

Francisco Pizarro (1470–1541), the son of an illiterate peasant, was the conqueror of Peru. After two earlier exploratory visits, he landed on the northern coast in January 1531 with a tiny privately financed army of 207 men and 27 horses. For more than a year he moved south, receiving some reinforcements as he plundered towns and villages. Leaving a garrison of 60 soldiers in a coastal base, he started inland in September 1532 with a Spanish force of fewer than 200. About the same time, word came that Altahualpa's forces had defeated Huascar's in battle and were poised to capture the imperial capital, Cuzco. Pizarro now posed as a potential ally to both sides. At Cajamarca he met and captured Altahualpa, slaughtering some 6000 unarmed retainers of the Inca monarch. He next forced Altahualpa to fill a room with 26,000 pounds of silver and over 13,000 pounds of gold. Then, having collected the ransom, Pizarro executed his royal prisoner and proclaimed Manco, the young son of Altahualpa's dead brother, as emperor.

Thus, upon arriving in Cuzco with their puppet ruler, the Spaniards were welcomed as deliverers and quickly secured tentative control of the country. Manco, after suffering terrible indignities from the Spaniards, organized a rebellion in 1536. Although his army of 60,000 heavily outnumbered Pizarro's 200 Spaniards, they could not score a decisive victory. Manco and his supporters retreated to the northwest to a mountain outpost at Vilacamba where an independent Inca kingdom survived until the Spanish captured and executed the last Inca emperor in 1572.

Although the *conquistadora* had triumphed over the Incas, political anarchy still reigned in Peru as the *conquistadora* split into two factions led by the Pizarro and Almagro families. When Pizarro was assassinated in his palace in 1542, it touched off a bloody civil war that raged for six years.

The period was marked by an obsessive Spanish rape of the country, along with cruel persecution of its Amerindian population, and by ruthless contention, involving every degree of greed and brutality, among the conquerors. Meanwhile, marauding expeditions moved south into Chile and north through Ecuador into Colombia. Expeditions from Chile and Peru settled in Argentina, founding Buenos Aires. Relationships between *conquistadora* and Amerindian women were common, and they

---

scurvy—A disease contracted on voyages of longer than a month because sailors' diets lacked sufficient quantities of vitamins B and C.

produced a new *mestizo* population in Paraguay. Despite this dynamic activity, there was no effective government at Lima, the capital, until the end of the sixteenth century.

Along with brutality, Spaniards in the post-conquest era also demonstrated unprecedented fortitude and courage. Pizarro's Spaniards were always outnumbered in battle. They faced nearly unendurable torments, including scorching heat, disease-carrying insects, air too thin for breathing, and cold that at times could freeze a motionless man into a lifeless statue. Amid the terrible hardships of this male-dominated era, both Amerindian and Spanish women played significant roles. As in Mexico, Amerindian women were camp-following concubines who prepared food and bore children; in addition to traditional feminine tasks, some Spanish women fought beside the men when necessary. Ines Suarez achieved distinction by donning armor and leading the defense of Santiago, Chile, shortly after its founding in 1541. Some women were present on all the pioneering ventures, and others were direct participants in the terrible sacrifices of the civil wars.

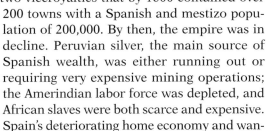

To govern Mexico and Peru the Spanish established two viceroyalties that by 1600 contained over 200 towns with a Spanish and mestizo population of 200,000. By then, the empire was in decline. Peruvian silver, the main source of Spanish wealth, was either running out or requiring very expensive mining operations; the Amerindian labor force was depleted, and African slaves were both scarce and expensive. Spain's deteriorating home economy and waning sea power presented even more serious problems.

European Empires in Latin America, 1660

IBERIAN SYSTEMS IN THE NEW WORLD

■ *What role did Amerindian and African labor play in the Spanish and Portuguese economic systems?*

European expansion overseas after the fifteenth century brought revolutionary change to all the world's peoples, but the Iberian period before 1600 was unique in its violence and ruthless exploitation. Not only were highly organized states destroyed in the New World, but whole populations were wiped out by European diseases,

shock, and inhumane treatment. This tragic catastrophe was accompanied by a decided change in the racial composition of Iberian America as an influx of African slaves, along with continued Spanish and Portuguese immigration, led to a variegated racial mixture, ranging through all shades of color between white and black. Fortunately, the

The arrival of the Spanish and Portuguese in America led to a mixing of three cultures: European, African, and Amerindian. This painted wooden bottle, done in Inca style and dating from about 1650, shows the mix. The three figures are an African drummer, a Spanish trumpeter, and an Amerindian official.

Amerindian population began recovering in the mid-1600s, and their cultures, combining with Iberian and African, formed a new configuration, to be known later as Latin American.

The General Nature of Regimes

Iberian regimes in America faced serious problems. Their vast territories, far greater than the homelands, contained nearly impassable deserts, mountains, and dense rain forests. Supplies had to be moved thousands of miles, often across open seas. Communications were difficult, wars with indigenous peoples were frequent, and disease was often rampant. Such conditions help explain, if not justify, the brutality of Iberian imperialism.

DOCUMENT

New Laws for the Treatment and Preservation of the Indians

With all their unique features, Iberian overseas empires were similar to Roman or Turkish provinces: they were meant to produce revenues. In theory, all Spanish lands were the king's personal property. The Council of the Indies, which directed the viceroys in Mexico City and Lima, advised him on colonial affairs. The highborn Spanish viceroys were aided (and limited) by councils *(audiencias),* made up of aristocratic lawyers from Spain. Local governors, responsible to the viceroys, functioned with their advisory councils **(cabildos)** of officials. Only the rich normally sat in such bodies; poor Spaniards and mestizos had little voice, even in their own taxation. Most taxes, however, were collected by Amerindian chiefs **(caciques),** still acting as rulers of Amerindian peasant villages.

---

mestizo—A person of Spanish and Indian descent.

cabildos—Town councils whose members were usually appointed by the governor.

cacique—An Amerindian chief who assisted the Spanish in collecting taxes from his subjects.

Portuguese Brazil was less directly controlled than the Spanish colonies. It languished for years under almost unrestricted domination of 15 aristocratic "captains" who held hereditary rights of taxing, disposing lands, making laws, and administering justice. In return, they sponsored settlement and paid stipulated sums to the king. This quasi-feudal administration was abandoned in 1548. When Philip II became king of Portugal in 1580, he established municipal councils, although these were still dominated by the hereditary captains.

Iberian Economies in America

Both the philosophies and the structures of the Iberian states limited colonial trade and industry. Most Spanish and Portuguese immigrants were disinclined toward productive labor. With few exceptions, commercial contacts were limited to the homelands; Mexican merchants fought a steadily losing battle to maintain independent trade with Peru and the Philippines. Local trade grew modestly in supplying the rising towns, some crafts developed into large-scale industrial establishments, and a national transport system, based on mule teams, became a major Mexican industry. So did smuggling, as demand for foreign goods rose higher and higher.

Agriculture, herding, and mining silver, however, were the main economic pursuits. The early gold sources soon ran out, but silver strikes in Mexico and Peru poured a stream of wealth back to Spain in the annual treasure fleets, convoyed by warships from Havana to Seville. Without gold to mine, many Spanish aristocrats acquired conquered Amerindian land, raising wheat, rice, indigo, cotton, coffee, and sugarcane. Cattle, horses, and sheep were imported and bred on ranches in the West Indies, Mexico, and Argentina. Brazil developed similar industries, particularly those related to brazilwood (for which the country was given its name), sugar, livestock, and coffee. Although Iberian economic pursuits in America were potentially productive, revealing numerous instances of initiative and originality, they were largely repressed by bureaucratic state systems.

Before 1660, plantations (large estates that used servile labor to grow crops) were not typical for agriculture in Iberian America, although they were developing in certain areas. The Spanish tried plantations in the Canaries, later establishing them in the West Indies, the Mexican lowlands, and Central America and along the northern coasts of South America. Even in such areas, which were environmentally suited for intensive single-crop cultivation, it was not easy to raise the capital, find the skilled technicians, and pay for the labor the system required.

The Spanish initially dealt with the labor problem in Mexico and Peru by forcing Amerindians on the labor market with taxation, but so many died from the devastating impact of European diseases that the Spanish turned to Africans for slave labor. Besides being separated from their families and societies, Africans slaves were mobile and could be shipped anywhere (see p. 563). By the 1550s, some 3000 African slaves were in Peru, working in gold mines and on cattle ranches and participating in a variety of unskilled and skilled occupations in the capital, Lima. At the end of the century, Africans, although replaced in the mines by Amerindians, continued to labor on coastal plantations and serve in elite households. Some 75,000 slaves were in the

Amerindian slaves work a Spanish sugar plantation on the island of Hispaniola. Spanish treatment of the Amerindians was often brutal.

Spanish colonies by 1600; more than 100,000 more arrived in the next four decades.

Portugal established sugar plantations on its Atlantic islands (Madeira, Cape Verde, and São Tomé). São Tomé was uninhabited when the Portuguese settled on it in 1485. Because the island is situated on the equator and receives abundant rainfall, it was an ideal setting to begin sugar production a half century later. São Tomé was also near Angola, a primary source of slaves. This experience created a direct link between the production of sugar and African slave labor. São Tomé also witnessed the resistance of slaves, who, much like the Maroons in Jamaica, fled the sugar plantations for the safety of the mountainous interior.

São Tomé, Cape Verde, and Madeira were the models when the Portuguese introduced the plantation system into northern Brazil around 1550. Like the Spanish, the Portuguese initially recruited Amerindian labor, but after a smallpox epidemic in the 1560s killed off many Amerindians, they began to rely on African slaves as the primary laborers on plantations. By the early 1600s, 30,000 Africans were annually being brought to Brazil. After 1650, as Dutch, British, and French possessions in the Caribbean islands were drawn into the sugar economy, they, as well as Portuguese Brazil, became the largest importers of unfree labor from Africa.

Some slaves were brutally oppressed as laborers in the mines, and others sweated on Spanish or Brazilian plantations. Slaves were also teamsters, overseers, personal servants, and skilled artisans. Particularly in the Spanish colonies, a good many earned their freedom, attaining a social status higher than that of Amerindian peasants. Free blacks, both men and women, operated shops and small businesses. Prostitution was common among black and **mulatto** women, a profession that went hand-in-hand with the sexual exploitation of female slaves as concubines and breeders.

Iberian Effects on Amerindian Life

The Spanish and Portuguese brought terrible disaster to most Amerindians. Having seen their gods mocked and their temples destroyed, many accepted Christianity as the only hope for survival, as well as salvation, while toiling for their Iberian masters. Some died from overwork, some were killed, and others simply languished as their cultures disintegrated. The most dangerous adversity was disease—European or African—to which Amerindians had no immunities.

---

mulatto—A person of European and African descent.

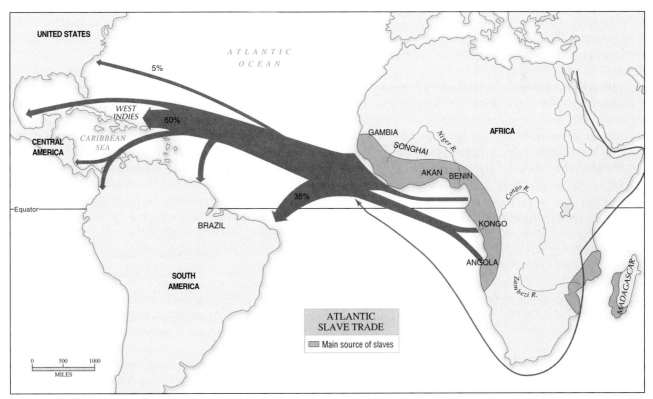

Africans were forcibly captured in raids and kidnappings in the interior of Africa and taken to the coast.
After they were sold to European traders, the slaves were transported across the Atlantic to work on sugar
plantations in the New World.

Epidemics arrived with Columbus and continued throughout the sixteenth century. Smallpox on Hispaniola in 1518 left only 1000 Amerindians alive there. Cortés's men carried the pox to Mexico, where it raged while he fought his way out of Tenochtitlán. From Mexico the epidemic spread through Central America, reaching Peru in 1526. It killed the reigning emperor and helped start the civil war that facilitated Pizarro's conquest. Following these smallpox disasters in the 1540s and 1570s, a wave of measles, along with other successive epidemics, continued depleting the population.

Depopulation of Amerindians was caused in part by their enslavement, despite disapproval by the Catholic Church and the Spanish government. The worst excesses came early. Original settlers on Hispaniola herded the Arawaks to work like animals; they soon became extinct. A whole indigenous population of the Bahamas—some 40,000 people—were carried away as slaves to Hispaniola, Cuba, and Puerto Rico. Cortés captured slaves before he took Tenochtitlán; other Amerindians, enslaved in Panama, were regularly sent to Peru. Before Africans arrived in appreciable numbers, the Portuguese organized "Indian hunts" in the forests to acquire slaves.

Another more common labor system in the Spanish colonies was the ***encomienda.*** This system was instituted in Mexico by Cortés as a way of using Amerindian caciques to collect revenues and provide labor. It was similar to European feudalism and manorialism, involving a royal grant that permitted the holder *(encomendero)* to take income or labor from specified lands and the people living on them. Many

---

encomienda—A system of control over land and Indian labor granted to a Spanish colonist *(encomendero)*.

Document   Disease and the Spanish Conquest

Diseases introduced by Europeans had a devastating impact on indigenous societies in the New World. This account of the impact of a smallpox epidemic among the Aztecs appeared in the Florentine Codex, an invaluable history of the Aztecs published in the mid-sixteenth century. Written in Nahuátl, the Aztec language and translated into Spanish, the books were based on information gathered by Aztec scribes under the supervision of a Franciscan priest Bernadino de Sahagún. This story of the smallpox epidemic drew on eyewitness accounts of individuals who lived through the Spanish conquest.

Before the Spanish appeared to us, first an epidemic broke out, a sickness of pustules. . . . Large bumps spread on people, some were entirely covered. They spread everywhere, on the face, the head, the chest, etc. The disease brought great desolation; a great many died of it. They could no longer walk about, but lay in their dwellings and sleeping places, no longer able to move or stir. They were unable to change position, to stretch out on their sides or face down, or raise their heads. And when they made a motion, they called out loudly. The pustules that covered people caused that covered people caused great desolation. very many people died of them, and many just starved to death; starvation reigned, and no one took care of others any longer.

On some people, the pustules appeared only far apart, and they did not suffer greatly, nor did many of them die of it. But many people's faces were spoiled by it, their faces and noses were made rough. Some lost an eye or were blinded.

This disease of pustules lasted a full sixty days; after sixty days it abated and ended. When people were convalescing and reviving, the pustules disease began to move in the direction of Chalco. And many were disabled or paralyzed by it, but they were not disabled forever. . . . The Mexica warriors were greatly weakened by it.

And when things were in this state, the Spaniards came, moving toward us from Tetzcoco.

Questions to Consider

1. What was more responsible for the Spanish conquest of the Aztecs—Spanish weapons, armor, horses or the diseases that accompanied the Spanish?

2. What was the overall impact of diseases such as smallpox on the indigenous populations of the Americas?

From James Lockhart, *We People Here: Nahuatl Accounts of the Conquest of Mexico* (Berkeley: University of California Press, 1993), pp. 180–182.

encomenderos lashed and starved their Amerindian laborers, working men and women to exhaustion or renting them to other equally insensitive masters. Amerindian women on the *encomiendas* were generally used as wet nurses, cooks, or maids or as sex slaves by the owners and the caciques, who served as overseers.

The *encomienda* system was slowly but steadily abandoned after the 1550s largely because of the efforts of a former *conquistadore* and *encomendero*, Bartolomé de Las Casas (1474–1566). A Dominican friar, he protested the cruel treatment of Amerindians and persuaded Charles V that they should hold the same rights as other subjects. His efforts led to the New Law of 1542, which ended existing *encomiendas* upon the death of their holders, prohibited Amerindian slavery, and gave Amerindians full protection under Spanish law. Most of these provisions, however, were rescinded when the law evoked universal protest and open rebellion in Peru. Although later governors gradually eliminated *encomiendas,* many Amerindians were put on reservations and hired out as contract laborers under the direction of their caciques and local officials *(corrigodores).* This practice eliminated some of the worst excesses of the *encomiendas,* but corrupt officials often exploited their wards, particularly in Peru.

Such physical hardships were matched by others of a psychological nature, which were almost equally damaging to Amerindians. The Spaniards insisted on forcing Christian conversion even while they raped and destroyed, as Pizarro did before executing Atahualpa. Except when they used Amerindian authorities to support their regimes, the Spaniards went out of their way to insult, shame, and degrade their unfortunate subjects. In the new social milieu, Amerindians were constantly reminded of their lowly status, unworthy of human consideration. For example, Cortés, who had multiple Amerindian mistresses, passed off Malitzin to one of his captains; Pizarro forced Manco, while still an ally, to give his young Inca queen to the conqueror. Such indignities, repeated by the hundreds among both Spanish and Portuguese, left many Amerindians demoralized to the point of utter despair.

Their distress was alleviated to some extent by missions, established by the Dominican and Jesuit religious orders. These afforded Amerindians the most effective protection and aid. Las Casas led the way in founding such settlements, where Amerindians were shielded from white exploitation, instructed in Christianity, and educated or trained in special skills. The prevailing philosophy in the missions stressed patient persuasion. Large mission organizations developed in Brazil, Venezuela, Paraguay, and upper California. But even the Amerindians protected by the missions died rapidly in this alien way of life.

Moved by the simplicity and gentle nature of the Amerindians, Bartolomé de Las Casas launched a vigorous campaign to ensure their protection. His Apologetic History of the Indies *(1566) is an indictment of the Spaniards' harsh treatment of the Amerindians.*

Although most Amerindians were demoralized by their misfortunes, some resisted. In Yucatán and Guatemala, where the Mayas did not believe the Spaniards were gods, bloody fighting lasted until the 1540s. About that time, the Spanish put down a revolt on the Mexican Pacific coast with great difficulty. As the silver mines opened in northern Mexico into the 1590s, the Chichimecs, relatives of the Apaches of North America, conducted a border war, using horses and captured muskets. In Peru an Inca rebellion, led first by Manco, was subdued only in 1577. The most stubborn resistance came from the Araucanians of southern Chile, who fought the Spaniards successfully until the close of the sixteenth century.

The full Iberian impact on Amerindian culture is difficult to assess, although there can be no denying that it was disastrous. A conservative estimate of Amerindian population losses puts the proportion at 25 percent during the era to 1650, but some recent figures place losses much higher, up to 95 percent of the pre-1492 total of 100 million. Signs of mental deterioration were also evident in prevalent alcoholism, which began among Amerindians shortly after the conquest.

Spanish Colonial Society and Culture

Spanish colonial society was stratified but somewhat flexible. A small elite of officials and aristocrats contended over politics, policy toward subject peoples, and foreign trade. Merchants and petty officials were on a lower social level but above mestizos, mulattoes, and **zambos.** Amerindians were considered incompetent wards of the home government, and African slaves were legally designated as beneath the law, but there were numerous individual exceptions. Many Amerindians went from their rural homes to the towns, mines, or **haciendas;** some caciques enjoyed wealth and privilege; and a few established Amerindian families retained their nobility as early Spanish allies. Similarly, some African slaves were overseers, privileged personal servants, and involved in urban crafts such as tailoring, shoemaking, carpentry, and blacksmithing; others acquired freedom and became prosperous merchants; still others escaped slavery, organized free communities, and successfully defended their independence.

Women in Spanish American society were a numerical minority. They played ambiguous roles, reflecting the traditional ideal of male superiority. They were excluded from male contacts throughout childhood, not allowed to join in dinner conversations, educated in cloistered schools to become wives and mothers, married in their teens to further family interests, and legally subordinated to their husbands. Most could not serve in public office or qualify as lawyers. Those who did not marry, particularly women of the upper classes, usually entered convents. There was, however, another side to the story. Spanish law guaranteed a wife's dowry rights, a legal protection against the squandering of her wealth, and leverage to limit her husband's activities. The courts recognized separations and at times even granted annulments in cases of wife abuse. Women, particularly widows, operated businesses. Some were wealthy, powerful, and even cruel *encomenderas,* supervising thousands of workers. Whatever their special roles, Iberian matrons defended religion, sponsored charities, dictated manners, and taught their children family values. They civilized the empires conquered by their men.

zambo—A person of African and Indian descent.

hacienda—An estate or plantation belonging to elite families.

Both the unique environment and the mix of peoples shaped Spanish colonial culture toward a new distinctive unity. From southwestern Europe came its aristocratic government, disdain for manual labor, a preference for dramatic over precise expression, and ceremonial Catholic Christianity. From Amerindian traditions came characteristic foods, art forms, architecture, legends, and practical garments like the poncho and serape, as well as substantial vocabulary. From Africa came agricultural knowledge, crafts, and animal husbandry. By 1650 this characteristic colonial culture was being preserved in its own universities, such as those at Lima and Mexico City, both founded more than a century earlier.

BEGINNINGS OF NORTHERN EUROPEAN EXPANSION

■ *What were the experiences of the Dutch, French, and British with their colonies of European settlement?*

European overseas expansion after 1600 entered a second phase, comparable to developments at home. As Spain declined, so did the Spanish Empire and that of Portugal, which was unified with Spain by a Habsburg king after 1580 and plagued with its own developing imperial problems. These conditions afforded opportunities for the northern European states. The Dutch between 1630 and 1650 almost cleared the Atlantic of Spanish warships while taking over most of the Portuguese posts in Brazil, Africa, and Asia. The French and English also became involved on a smaller scale, setting up a global duel for empire in the eighteenth century.

The Shifting Commercial Revolution

Along with this second phase of expansion came a decisive shift in Europe's Commercial Revolution. Expanding foreign trade, new products, an increasing supply of bullion, and rising commercial risks created new problems, calling for energetic initiatives. Because the Spanish and Portuguese during the sixteenth century had depended on quick profits, weak home industries, and poor management, wealth flowed through their hands to northern Europe, where it was invested in productive enterprises. Later it generated a new imperial age.

European markets after the sixteenth century were swamped with a bewildering array of hitherto rare or unknown goods. New foods from America included potatoes, peanuts, maize (Indian corn), tomatoes, and fish from Newfoundland's Grand Banks. In an era without refrigeration, imported spices—such as pepper, cloves, and cinnamon—were valued for making spoiled

Marketplace at Antwerp. In the sixteenth century, Antwerp was the leading city in international commerce. As many as 500 ships a day docked in its bustling harbor, and as many as 1000 wagons arrived each week carrying the overland trade.

foods palatable. Sugar became a common substitute for honey, and the use of cocoa, the Aztec sacred beverage, spread throughout Europe. Coffee and tea from the New World and Asia would also soon change European social habits. Similarly, North American furs, Chinese silks, and cottons from India and Mexico revolutionized clothing fashions. Furnishings of rare woods and ivory and luxurious oriental carpets appeared more frequently in the homes of the wealthy. The use of American tobacco became almost a mania among all classes, further contributing to the booming European market.

Imported gold and, even more significant, silver probably affected the European economy more than all other foreign goods. After the Spaniards had looted Aztec and Inca treasure rooms, the gold flowing from America and Africa subsided to a respectable trickle; but 7 million tons of silver poured into Europe before 1660. Spanish prices quadrupled, and because most new bullion went to pay for imports, prices more than tripled in northern Europe. Rising inflation hurt landlords who depended on fixed rents and creditors who were paid in cheap money, but the bullion bonanza ended a centuries-long gold drain to the East, with its attendant money shortage. It also increased the profits of merchants selling on a rising market, thus greatly stimulating northern European capitalism.

At the opening of the sixteenth century, Italian merchants and moneylenders, mainly Florentines, Venetians, and Genoese, dominated the rising Atlantic economy. The German Fugger banking house at Augsburg also provided substantial financing. European bankers, particularly the Fuggers and the Genoese, suffered heavily from the Spanish economic debacles under Charles V and Philip II. As the century passed, Antwerp, in the southern Netherlands, became the economic hub of Europe. It was the center for the English wool trade as well as a transfer station, drawing southbound goods from the Baltic and Portuguese goods from Asia. It was also a great financial market, dealing in commercial and investment instruments. The Spanish sack of the city in 1576 ended Antwerp's supremacy, which passed to Amsterdam and furthered Dutch imperial ventures.

Meanwhile, northern European capitalism flourished in nearly every category. Portuguese trade in Africa and Asia was matched by that of the Baltic and the North Atlantic. Northern joint-stock companies pooled capital for privateering, exploring, and commercial venturing. The Dutch and English East India companies, founded early in the seventeenth century, were but two of the better-known stock companies. In England common fields were enclosed for capitalistic sheep runs. Throughout western Europe, domestic manufacturing, in homes or workshops, was competing with the guilds. Large industrial enterprises, notably in mining, shipbuilding, and cannon casting, were becoming common. Indeed, the superiority of English and Swedish cannons caused the defeat of the Spanish Armada and Catholic armies in the Thirty Years' War.

The Dutch Empire

By 1650 the Dutch were supreme in both southern Asia and the South Atlantic. Their empire, like that of the Portuguese earlier, was primarily commercial; even their North American settlements specialized in fur trading with the Indians. They acquired territory where necessary to further their commerce but tried to act pragmatically in accordance with Asian cultures rather than by conquest. An exception was their colony in Java, where the Dutch drive for monopolizing the spice trade led them to take direct control of the island. Unlike the Spanish and the Portuguese, the Dutch made little attempt to spread Christianity.

Dutch involvement in the Indian Ocean was the direct result of the Spanish absorption of Portugal in 1580. The Spanish restricted the flow of spices, especially pepper, to Northern Europe, and Dutch seafarers set out to control the sources of the trade. Systematic Dutch naval operations commenced in 1595 when the first Dutch fleet entered the East Indies. Dutch captains soon drove the Portuguese from the Spice Islands. Malacca, the Portuguese bastion, fell after a long siege in 1641. The Dutch also occupied Sri Lanka (SHREE-lahn-KAH) and blockaded Goa, thus limiting Portuguese operations in the Indian Ocean. Although largely neglecting East Africa, they seized all Portuguese posts on the west coast north of Angola. Across the Atlantic,

Dutch Exploration and Expansion

1576	Sack of Antwerp; Amsterdam becomes commercial hub of Europe
1595	First Dutch fleet enters East Indies
1609	Henry Hudson explores Hudson River
1621	Dutch form West India Company
1624	Dutch found New Amsterdam on Manhattan Island
1641	Dutch drive Portuguese out of Malacca

they conquered and held part of Brazil for a few decades, drove Spain from the Caribbean, and captured a Spanish treasure fleet. Decisive battles off the English Channel coast near Kent (1639) and off Brazil (1640) delivered final blows to the Spanish navy. What the English began in 1588, the Dutch completed 50 years later.

Five Dutch trading companies initially conducted trade with Asia, but the Dutch state decided their competition with each other cut into profits and established the Dutch East India Company. Chartered in 1602 and given a monopoly over all operations between the Cape of Good Hope in South Africa and the Strait of Magellan, it conserved resources and cut costs. In addition to its trade and diplomacy, the company sponsored explorations of Australia, Tasmania, New Guinea, and the South Pacific.

The Dutch Empire in the East was established primarily by Jan Pieterszoon Coen, governor-general of the Indies for two periods between 1619 and 1629 and founder of the company capital at Batavia in northwestern Java. At first he cooperated with local rulers in return for a monopoly over the spice trade. When this involved him in costly wars against local sultans as well as their Portuguese and English customers, Coen determined to control the trade at its sources. In the ensuing numerous conflicts and negotiations, which outlasted Coen, the Dutch acquired all of Java, most of Sumatra, the spice-growing Moluccas (mol-U-kuz), and part of Sri Lanka. They began operating their own plantations, overseen by Dutch settlers and worked by thousands of slaves brought in from such diverse areas as East Africa, Bengal, Persia, and Japan. The plantations produced cinnamon, nutmeg, cloves, sugar, tea, tobacco, and coffee, but it was pepper that reaped the highest profits. In the seventeenth century 7 million pounds of pepper were shipped to Europe annually.

Although commercially successful in Asia, the Dutch were not able to found flourishing colonial settlements. Many Dutchmen who went to the East wanted to make their fortunes and return home; those willing to stay were usually mavericks, uninterested in establishing families but instead pursuing temporary sexual liaisons with female slaves or servants. For a while after 1620 the company experimented with a policy of bringing European women to the Indies, but such efforts were abandoned when the venture failed to enlist much interest at home or in the foreign stations. Consequently, the Dutch colonies in Asia, as well as those in Africa, the Caribbean, and Brazil, remained primarily business ventures with less racial mixing than in the Iberian areas.

After resuming war with Spain in 1621, the Dutch formed the West India Company, charged with overtaking the diminishing Spanish and Portuguese holdings in West Africa and America. The company wasted no time. It soon supplanted the Portuguese in West Africa; by 1630 it had taken over the slave trade with America. After driving the Spanish from the Caribbean, the Dutch

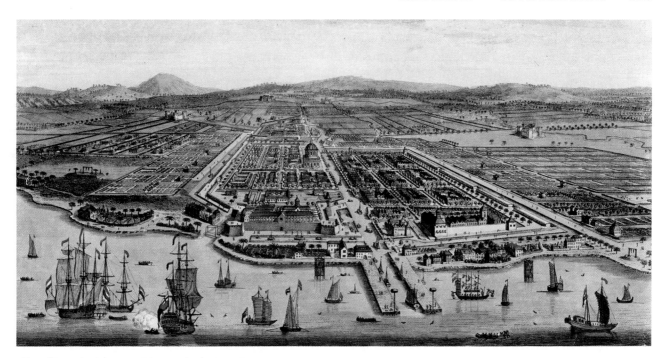

City of Batavia, Java, c.1780, aquatint by Ivan Rynne.

invited other European planters to the West Indies as customers, keeping only a few bases for themselves. The company then launched a successful naval conquest of Brazil, from the mouth of the Amazon south to the San Francisco River. In Brazil the Dutch learned sugar planting, passing on their knowledge to the Caribbean and applying it directly in the East Indies.

Dutch settlements in North America never amounted to much because of the company's commercial orientation. In 1609 Henry Hudson (d. 1611), an Englishman sailing for the Dutch, explored the river (ultimately named for him) and established Dutch claims while looking for a northwest passage. Fifteen years later the company founded New Amsterdam on Manhattan Island; over the next few years it built a number of frontier trading posts in the Hudson valley and on the nearby Connecticut and Delaware Rivers. Some attempts were made to encourage planting by selling large tracts to wealthy proprietors *(patroons)*. Agriculture, however, remained secondary to the fur trade, which the company developed in alliance with the Iroquois tribes. This arrangement hindered settlement; in 1660 only 5000 Europeans were in the colony.

The French Empire

French exploration began early, but no permanent colonies were established abroad until the start of the seventeenth century. The country was so weakened by

patroon—An owner of a landed estate granted by the Dutch West India Company in New York and New Jersey.

religious wars that most of its efforts, beyond fishing, privateering, and a few failed attempts at settlement, had to be directed toward internal stability. While the Dutch were winning their empire, France was involved in the land campaigns of the Thirty Years' War. Serious French empire building thus had to be delayed until after 1650, during the reign of Louis XIV.

Early French colonization in North America was based on claims made by Giovanni da Verrazzano (1485–1528) and Jacques Cartier (1491–1557). The first, a Florentine mariner commissioned by Francis I in 1523, traced the Atlantic coast from North Carolina to Newfoundland. Eleven years later Cartier made one of two voyages exploring the St. Lawrence River. These French expeditions duplicated England's claim to eastern North America.

French colonial efforts during the sixteenth century were dismal failures. They resulted partly from French experiences in exploiting the Newfoundland fishing banks and conducting an undeclared naval war in the Atlantic against Iberian treasure ships and trading vessels after 1520. In 1543 Cartier tried unsuccessfully to establish a colony in the St. Lawrence valley. No more serious efforts were made until 1605, when a French base was established at Port Royal, on Nova Scotia. It was meant to be a fur-trading center and capital for the whole St. Lawrence region. In 1608, Samuel de Champlain (1567–1635), who had been an aide to the governor of the Nova Scotia colony, acted for a French-chartered company in founding Quebec on the St. Lawrence. The company brought in colonists, but the little community was disrupted in 1627 when

British troops took the town and forced Champlain's surrender. Although when Champlain came back as governor the fort was returned to France by a treaty in 1629, growth was slowed by the company's emphasis on fur trading, the bitterly cold winters, and skirmishes with Indians. Only a few settlers had arrived by Champlain's death in 1635, and just 2500 Europeans were in Quebec as late as 1663. Nevertheless, Montreal was established in 1642, after which French trapper-explorers began penetrating the region around the headwaters of the Mississippi.

Elsewhere, the French seized opportunities afforded by the decline of Iberian sea power. They acquired the isle of Bourbon (BOOR-bon), later known as Réunion, in the Indian Ocean (1642) for use as a commercial base. In West Africa they created a sphere of commercial interest at the mouth of the Senegal River, where they became involved in the slave trade with only slight opposition from the Dutch. Even more significant was the appearance of the French in the West Indies. They occupied part of St. Kitts in 1625 and later acquired Martinique, Guadeloupe, and Santo Domingo. Fierce attacks by Carib Indians limited economic development before 1650. However, by the late eighteenth century, Santo Domingo had become the crown jewel of France's Caribbean possessions. Possessing half of the Caribbean's slave population, the island was the largest producer of sugar in America, and—after coffee was introduced in 1723—the world's largest coffee producer until the Haitian revolution of 1791.

British and French Exploration and Colonization

1485–1528	Giovanni da Verrazzano
1491–1557	Jacques Cartier
1497–1498	John Cabot establishes English claims in North America
1567–1635	Samuel de Champlain founds Quebec
1605	French establish base at Port Royal, in Nova Scotia
1607	First English colony in North America founded at Jamestown
1627	British conquer Quebec
1629	Puritans settle near Boston
1632–1635	English Catholics found colony of Maryland
1642	Montreal established

The English Empire

In terms of power and profit, English foreign expansion before 1650 was not impressive. Like French colonialism, it was somewhat restricted by internal political conditions, particularly the poor management and restrictive policies of the early Stuart kings, which led to civil war in the 1640s. A number of circumstances, however, promoted foreign ventures. The population increased from 3 to 4 million between 1530 and 1600, providing a large reservoir of potential indentured labor; religious persecution encouraged migration of nonconformists; and holders of surplus capital were seeking opportunities for investment. Such conditions ultimately produced a unique explosion of English settlement overseas.

During the sixteenth century, English maritime operations were confined primarily to exploring, fishing, smuggling, and plundering. English claims to North America were registered in 1497 and 1498 by two voyages of John Cabot, who explored the coast of North America from Newfoundland to Virginia but found no passage to Asia. For the next century, English expeditions sought such a northern passage, both in the East and in the West. All of them failed, but they resulted in explorations of Hudson Bay and the opening of a northeastern trade route to Russia. From the 1540s, English captains, including the famous John Hawkins of Plymouth, indulged in sporadic slave trading in Africa and the West Indies, despite Spanish restrictions.

After failures in Newfoundland and on the Carolina coast, the first permanent English colony in America was founded in 1607 at Jamestown, Virginia. For a number of years the colonists suffered from lack of food and other privations, but they were saved by their leader, Captain John Smith (1580–1631), whose romantic rescue by the Indian princess Pocahontas (1595–1617) is an American legend. Jamestown set a significant precedent for all English colonies in North America. By the terms of its original charter, the London Company, which founded the settlement, was authorized to supervise government for the colonists, but they were to enjoy all the rights of native Englishmen. Consequently, in 1619 the governor called an assembly to assist in governing. This body would later become the Virginia House of Burgesses, one of the oldest representative legislatures still operating.

Shortly after the founding of Jamestown, large-scale colonization began elsewhere. In 1620 a group of English Protestants, known as Pilgrims, landed at Plymouth. Despite severe hardships, they survived, and their experiences inspired other religious dissenters against the policies of Charles I. In 1629 a number of English Puritans formed the Massachusetts Bay Company and settled near Boston, where their charter gave them the rights to virtual self-government. From this first enclave, emigrants moved out to other areas in present-day Maine, Rhode Island, and Connecticut. By 1642 more than 25,000 people had migrated to New England, laying the foundations for a number of future colonies. Around the same time (1632–1635), a group of English Catholics, fleeing Stuart persecution, founded the Maryland colony. These enterprises firmly planted English culture and political institutions in North America.

Life in the English settlements was hard during those first decades, but a pioneering spirit and native colonial pride was already evident. Food was scarce, disease was ever-present, and conflicts with Amerindians were not uncommon. Yet from the beginning, and more than in other European colonies, settlers looked to their future in the new land because they had left so little behind in Europe. Most were expecting to stay, establish homes, make their fortunes, and raise families. The first Puritans included both men and women; a shipload of "purchase brides" arrived in 1619 at Jamestown to lend stability to that colony. This was but the first of many such contingents, all eagerly welcomed by prospective husbands. In addition, many women came on their own as indentured servants.

Anglo-American colonial women faced discrimination but managed to cope with it pragmatically. They were legally dependent on their husbands, who controlled property and children; a widow acquired these rights, but it was not easy to outlive a husband. Hard work and frequent pregnancies—mothers with a dozen children were not uncommon—reduced female life expectancies. Nevertheless, many women developed a rough endurance, using their social value to gain confidence and practical equality with their husbands, although some did this more obviously than others. This independent spirit was exemplified by Anne Hutchinson (1591–1643), who was banished from Massachusetts for her heretical views and founded a dissenting religious settlement in Rhode Island. Another freethinker was Anne Bradstreet (c. 1612–1672), who, although painfully aware that men considered her presumptuous, wrote thoughtful poetry.

The English government considered the rough coasts and wild forests of North America less important in this period than footholds in the West Indies and Africa, where profits were expected in planting and slave trading. Therefore, a wave of English migrants descended on the West Indies after the Dutch opened the Caribbean. In 1613 English settlers invaded Bermuda, and by the 1620s others had planted colonies on St. Kitts, Barbados, Nevis, Montserrat (mawn-suh-RAHT), Antigua (ahn-TEE-gwah), and the Bahamas. Tobacco planting was at first the major enterprise, bringing some prosperity and the promise of more. The white population expanded dramatically, especially on Barbados, which was not subject to Carib Indian attacks. There, the English population increased from 7,000 to 37,000 in seven years. As yet, there were few African slaves on the English islands, although some were already being imported for the sugar plantations.

This is an anonymous engraving made around 1776 of the Mohawk chief and diplomat Tiyanoga. He was an ally for the British and known to them as "King Hendrick." In this portrait, one can see the influence of European trade goods in Tiyanoga's dress. His shirt is made of linen or calico, and his mantle and breechcloth of English wool duffels.

Meanwhile, English slaving posts in West Africa were beginning to flourish, and English adventurers were starting operations in Asia. Captain John Lancaster took four ships to Sumatra and Java in 1601, returning with a profitable cargo of spices. But expansion outside of the Caribbean was difficult because the Dutch were uncooperative. In the Moluccas, for example, they drove out the English in the 1620s, after repeated clashes. The English fared better in India. By 1622 the British East India Company, which had been chartered in 1600, had put the Portuguese out of business in the Persian Gulf. Subsequently, the English established trading posts on the west coast of India at Agra, Bombay, Masulipatam, Balasore, and Surat. The station at Madras, destined to become the English bastion on the east coast, was founded in 1639. The East India Company prospered from the trade in Indian cotton and silk cloth for the English and European markets.

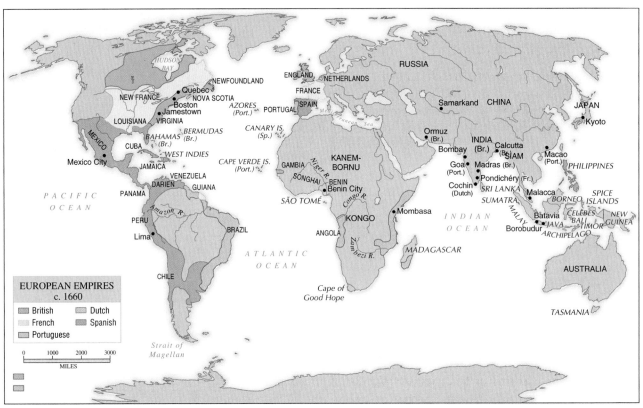

By the late 1600s the Portuguese and Spanish, the pioneers in global exploration, had been displaced in many regions by the English, French, and Dutch.

CONCLUSION

Between 1450 and 1650, the era of the early Commercial Revolution, Europeans faced outwards toward a new world and, following precedents set by earlier Eurasian empires, initiated their own age of oceanic expansion. In the process they stimulated capitalistic development, found a sea route to Asia, became more familiar with Africa, began colonizing America, and proved the world to have a spherical surface. For most of the period Spain and Portugal monopolized the new ocean trade and profited most from exploiting American gold and silver. Only after 1600, when leadership shifted toward the Dutch, French, and English, did European colonialism show signs of developing in new directions.

Overseas expansion exerted a tremendous effect on European culture and institutions. Spain's political predominance in the sixteenth century was largely bought with Amerindian treasure, and Spain's eventual decline was mainly caused by the squandering of wealth on war rather than on investment and the influx of American bullion, which inflated Spanish money and discouraged Spanish economic development. Northern European capitalism, developing in financial organization, shipbuilding, metalworking, manufacturing, and agriculture, brought a new vitality to northern economies in response to Spanish and Portuguese purchasing power. Economic advantages also contributed to Protestant victories in the Thirty Years' War.

By the late seventeenth century, the Europeans had experienced mixed results in their encounters with societies around the world. In the Indian Ocean, where they engaged well-established states, such as in China, Japan, and India, they usually had to respect their laws and authority and even do their bidding and had little impact on land-based trading networks. The Portuguese were run out of China twice before they came to respect Chinese law, and other Europeans fared worse. All were ultimately excluded from Japan. Southern India was not entirely open, as the Portuguese found by the end of the period. In the main, Turks, Arabs, Chinese, Japanese, Thais, and Vietnamese felt superior to Europeans and were usually able to defend their interests with effective action.

Where they dealt with smaller states and city-states, such as in Indonesia and East Africa, Europeans were more likely to directly intervene or dominate their affairs. Sri Lanka and the Spice Islands of the Malay archipelago, which were vulnerable to sea attack, came under domination, direct or indirect, and were exploited by the Portuguese and the Dutch.

In the New World the European impact was both dramatic and tragic. Portuguese captains and Spanish *conquistadora,* as well as diseases such as smallpox, nearly destroyed indigenous peoples and subjected most of the survivors to terrible hardships, indignities, cultural deprivations, and psychological injuries. However, the Portuguese and Spanish in America generated a new cultural synthesis, blending European, Amerindian, and African elements to produce a richness and variety not present in any of the parent cultures. This integration was largely accomplished by racial mixing, which created a new Latin American stock in the Western Hemisphere.

The European impact on Africa was less apparent at the time but perhaps more damaging in the long run than what happened to the Amerindians of Latin America. When the Portuguese began exploring the African coastline, they were more concerned with scoring quick profits through gold exports than with establishing stable, long-term relationships with African states. Moreover, with the exception of Angola or landed estates along the Zambezi River, the Portuguese did not have the manpower or resources to conquer or influence the political affairs of African states. However, as the Atlantic slave trade increased, the Portuguese and African states, especially along the Atlantic and Indian Ocean coasts, became bound up in a destructive process that would run its tragic course over the next few centuries.

Suggestions for Web Browsing

You can obtain more information about topics included in this chapter at the websites listed below. See also the companion website that accompanies this text, **http://www.ablongman.com/ brummett**, which contains an online study guide and additional resources.

Age of Discovery
http://www.win.tue.nl/cs/fm/engels/discovery/#age

An excellent collection of resources that includes text, images, and maps relating to the early years of European expansion.

Internet Medieval History Sourcebook: Exploration and Expansion
http://www.fordham.edu/halsall/sbook1z.html

Extensive online source for links about Western exploration and expansion, including primary documents by or about da Gama, Columbus, Drake, and Magellan.

Columbus Navigation Home Page
http://www1.minn.net/~keithp/

Extensive information regarding the life and voyages of Christopher Columbus.

Internet African History Sourcebook
http://www.fordham.edu/halsall/africa/africasbook.html

Extensive online source for links about African history, including primary documents about the slave trade and by people who opposed it, supported it, and were its victims.

Literature and Film

Two major documentary series marked the quincentennial of Columbus's 1492 voyage in different ways. *Columbus and the Age of Discovery* (1991) is a seven-part series that primarily treats European exploration and expansion in the New World, while *500 Nations* (1995) is an eight-part series that examines Native American history before and after the arrival of Europeans. *Conquistadores* (2001) is Michael Wood's presentation of European explorers/conquerors such as Cortés and Pizarro.

Mexican writer Carlos Fuentes has written a major epic, *Terra Nostra*, trans. Margaret Peden (Farrar, Straus, and Giroux, 1976) and a collection of short stories and novellas, *The Orange Tree*, trans. Alfred MacAdam (Farrar, Straus, and Giroux, 1994), with Spanish exploration and conquest of the New World as their backdrop. James Lackhart's *We People Here: Nahuatl Accounts of the Conquest of Mexico* (University of California Press, 1993) presents indigenous Indian narratives of the Spanish conquest compiled by a Franciscan priest in the sixteenth century.

Suggestions for Reading

Several excellent works, which cover the subject of European exploration and colonization, are Geoffrey V. Scammell, *The First Imperial Age: European Overseas Expansion, 1400–1700* (Unwin Hyman, 1989); Anthony Pagden, eds., *European Encounters with the New World* (Yale University Press, 1993); and Nicholas Canny and Anthony Pagden, *Colonial Identity in the Atlantic World* (Princeton University Press, 1989). European encounters with other peoples are treated in Urs Bitterli, *Cultures in Conflict: Encounters Between European and Non-European Cultures, 1492–1800* (Stanford University Press, 1989), and Stuart Schwartz, ed., *Implicit Understandings: Observing, Reporting, and Reflecting on the Encounters between Europeans and Other Peoples in the Early Modern Era* (Cambridge University Press, 1994).

Books on the Iberian New World are Tzvetan Todorov, *The Conquest of America* (Harper&Row, 1984) and Mark A. Burkholder, *Colonial Latin America* (Oxford University Press, 1989). Works on Columbus include Felipe Fernandez-Armesto, *Columbus* (Oxford University Press, 1992), and John Yewell, Chris Dodge, and Jan De Surey, *Confronting Columbus: An Anthology* (McFarland, 1992).

For a penetrating study of Latin American social conditions, see Louisa Hoberman and Susan M. Socolow, eds., *Cities and Society in Colonial Latin America* (University of New Mexico Press, 1986).

Luis Martin, *Daughters of the Conquistadores* (Southern Methodist University Press, 1989) documents the significant role of women in the grueling process of colonization. Good coverage of the Spanish campaigns in Peru is provided in Susan Ramirez, *The World Upside Down: Cross-Cultural Contact and Conflict in Sixteenth-Century Peru* (Stanford University Press, 1996).

On political, economic, and social conditions, see Leslie B. Simpson, *The Encomienda in New Spain*, 3rd ed. (University of California Press, 1982). Edward Murguca, *Assimilation, Colonialism, and the Mexican American People* (University Press of America, 1989), depicts the racial and cultural synthesis in colonial Mexico.

A respected work on Portuguese exploration and colonization is A. J. R. Russell-Wood, *A World on the Move: The Portuguese in Africa, Asia and America, 1415–1808* (St. Martin's Press, 1992). On the Portuguese in Asia, see Michael Pearson, *The Indian Ocean* (Routledge, 2003).

A sound treatment of Dutch imperial development is Charles R. Boxer, *The Dutch Seaborne Empire* (Penguin, 1989). French colonialism in America is covered in William J. Eccles, *France in America* (Michigan State University Press, 1990), and the British Empire in William R Lewis, Nicholas Canny, P. J. Marshall, and Alaine Low, eds., *The Origins of Empire: British Overseas Enterprise to the Close of the Seventeenth Century* (Oxford University Press, 1998).

Testing Your Understanding—Unit IV

Civilization Past & Present,
Chapter 16: Global Encounters

 Pages 133–140
CHECKING YOUR COMPREHENSION

Identify the following statements as true or false.

1. Catholic missionaries were admitted to Ozuola's kingdom in hopes of securing Portuguese fire arms.

2. Land-based armies were key to Europe's becoming a significant force in various parts of the world.

3. The Chinese gave the Portuguese permission to erect a fort in Canton harbor and to buy Chinese children as slaves.

4. The Portuguese went to West Africa as traders.

Choose the best answer for each of the following questions.

5. According to the text, Prince Henry was known as the "the Navigator" because of
   a. his expeditions down the West African coast.
   b. claiming the Madeira Islands and Azores.
   c. diverting West African gold trade from Muslim caravans to Portuguese ships.
   d. his famous observatory at Sagres.

6. It can be inferred from the text that the Portuguese were important to Japan because
   a. they sold matchlock muskets.
   b. Jesuit priests brought Christianity.
   c. they brought European goods to trade.
   d. they brought fluid capital.

7. Historians have referred to the European economic transformation as the
   a. medieval era.
   b. reformation.
   c. commercial revolution.
   d. modern era.

Answer each of the following questions.

8. Explain what is meant by "bull of demarcation."

9. According to the text, why were Portugal and Spain not able to maintain initial competitive advantages over one another?

10. Discuss why the Portuguese empire began to decline at the end of the sixteenth century.

Define each term as it is used in the chapter.

11. astrolabe

12. lateen sail

13. cartaz

Discussion and Critical Thinking Questions

1. What strategies did the Portuguese use to develop their empire?

2. Discuss the religious motivations of the Iberian navigators.

3. Describe important differences between the Portuguese and Spanish political systems.

Pages 141–149
CHECKING YOUR COMPREHENSION

Identify the following statements as true or false.

1. Francisco Pizarro's assassination set off a civil war that lasted six years.

2. Munster's map of Africa relied solely on Ptolemy's view of the world.

3. The smallpox epidemic was a contributing factor in the Aztecs surrendering their empire to the Spanish.

Choose the best answer for each of the following questions.

4. According to the text, what was the most destructive involvement the Portuguese brought to the African states?
   a. war
   b. slave trade
   c. weapons
   d. disease

5. In his correspondence to the Portuguese, Don Afonso addresses the following items except
   a. request for doctors and medicine.
   b. involvement in the slave trade.
   c. threat of overtaking the city by fire.
   d. enactment of a law requiring white men to inform the Africans of the purchase of goods.

6. According to the text, the main economic pursuits of the Iberian states were
   a. mining gold.
   b. sugarcane.
   c. arts and crafts.
   d. agriculture, herding, and silver mining.

Answer each of the following questions.

7. Why did the tale of Prester John, the mythical Ethiopian Christian monarch, captivate Portugal's monarchs?

8. What territories became known as New Spain?

9. Who was Ines Suarez, and what distinction did she have?

Define each term as it is used in the chapter.

10. conquistadora

11. prazos

12. mestizo

13. cabildos

14. cacique

15. scurvy

Discussion and Critical Thinking Questions

1. Describe how Portuguese exploits were similar to those in Kongo and Angola.

2. It is inferred in the text that the brutality of Iberian imperialism might have been justified by the difficult conditions faced by the Iberian regimes. Explain why.

3. Using information from the text, discuss the use of African slaves in the European labor market.

Pages 150–159
CHECKING YOUR COMPREHENSION

Identify the following statements as true or false.

1. Prior to the arrival of African slaves, the Portuguese hunted Indians in the forests to acquire as slaves.

2. The Dutch empire attempted to spread Christianity much like the Spanish and Portuguese had.

3. The first English colony in America was founded at Plymouth, Massachusetts.

Choose the best answer for each of the following questions.

4. According to the text, what led to Spain's political decline?
   a. their monopoly on ocean trade
   b. American colonization
   c. exploitation of American gold and silver
   d. squandering their wealth on war

5. It can be inferred from the text that which city was the economic hub of Europe in the sixteenth century?
    a. Antwerp
    b. Augsburg
    c. Amsterdam
    d. Venice

6. According to the text, the French exploration did not lead them to establish colonies until the seventeenth century because
    a. they conducted an undeclared naval war in the Atlantic.
    b. they lacked sea power.
    c. the country was weakened internally by religious wars.
    d. British troops overtook their attempts to establish colonies.

Answer each of the following questions.

7. Discuss the challenges Anglo-American colonial women faced.

8. What was the purpose of the document "Disease and the Spanish Conquest" in the text?

9. Describe the hardships the Amerindians faced.

Define each term as it is used in the chapter.

10. encomienda

11. zambos

12. hacienda

13. patroons

Discussion and Critical Thinking Questions

1. The text infers that Spanish colonial society was influenced by several different cultures. Discuss the impact these influences had on Spanish colonial society.

2. Discuss the common thread between the explorations of the Portuguese and Spanish and the later explorations by the English, French, and Dutch.

3. Compare and contrast the differences between the women in Spanish American society and the Puritan women.

Chapter Review
END OF CHAPTER ANALYSIS

Choose the best answer for each of the following questions.

1. The chapter employs all of the following techniques to make it easier to understand except
   a. highlighting.
   b. graphics.
   c. marginal notations.
   d. chapter contents.

2. The authors use which of the following to support the information in the chapter?
   a. historical documents
   b. personal accounts
   c. opinions
   d. analogies

3. The chapter addresses all of the following areas except
   a. the Portuguese's exploration in Africa.
   b. Spain's acquiring an empire in America.
   c. the Amerindian's role in the labor market in the new world.
   d. the rapid growth of U.S. territories.

Group Projects

1. Create a timeline that includes all of the dates and details of the major explorations completed by the Europeans in the fifteenth, sixteenth, and seventeenth centuries.

2. You have been assigned the task of clarifying the information in the chapter. Indicate what the editors of the chapter could add to make it easier to understand the chapter (tables, pictures, additional documents).

Journal Ideas

1. There were many references in the chapter to African slaves who were used for labor. Discuss the treatment of the slaves and how the slave trade practices as you have learned were brought into the United States.

2. List the critical issues during the time of the global exploration. What were the opportunities for women and for families to prosper? Would you have liked to live during that time? Why or why not?

Unit V

From

Yvonne Collioud Sisko

American 24-Karat Gold: 24 Classic American Short Stories
Second Edition

"Salvation" by Langston Hughes
"The Masque of the Red Death" by Edgar Allan Poe

An Introduction to Literature

Literature is defined as the body of written work of a language, period, or culture. It is often noted as creative writing that is recognized for its artistic value. There are many types (or genres) of literature such as poetry, prose fiction, drama, and essays.

Literature courses are required for most college students. Introductory courses often give students an overall view of literature, while upper-level literature courses usually focus on a particular author or time period. A degree in literature will prepare students to enter careers in such diverse fields as education, law, mass media, publishing, communications, and the arts.

Strategies for Reading Literature

When reading literature, it is necessary to pay particular attention to the message (or theme) the author is trying to convey about life, society, or human nature. There are often many literary devices that you need to recognize, identify, interpret, and analyze. The author's careful use of language may include such literary devices as metaphors, similes, rhyme, alliteration, and tone. Other important aspects of literature include the setting, conflict, and point of view. One key aspect of reading literature is to understand that behind every action is a reason, and it is often necessary to delve deep into the literature to reveal the author's intended meaning. Using a double-entry journal while you read may help you organize your thoughts about the story's action and characters. It will also allow you to make comments and ask questions while you read.

Salvation

Langston Hughes

> **Langston Hughes** was born in Joplin, Missouri in 1902. After his parents' separation, he spent his early childhood with his grandmother in Lawrence, Kansas. His grandmother gave him a positive outlook on his African American heritage and on life through her stories filled with characters who triumphed over life's problems with zeal and determination. At twelve, he moved back with his mother and lived in Lincoln, Illinois. Later, he served as a crewman on freighters and traveled to Africa, Holland, and Paris. He returned to Washington, D. C. and then moved to New York City. Sharing the same patron with Zora Neale Hurston, he attended Columbia University and eventually became a central figure in the Harlem Renaissance. He died in 1967.
>
> Hughes enjoyed a fruitful writing career. His writings reflect the rhythms of Harlem and the positive attitudes of his grandmother. His poems and short stories are available in many collections.

I was saved from sin when I was going on thirteen. But not really saved. It happened like this. There was a big revival at my Auntie Reed's church. Every night for weeks there had been much preaching, singing, praying, and shouting, some very hardened sinners had been brought to Christ, and the membership of the church had grown by leaps and bounds. Then just before the revival ended, they held a special meeting for children, "to bring the young lambs to the fold." My aunt spoke of it for days ahead. That night I was escorted to the front row and placed on the mourners' bench with all the other young sinners, who had not yet been brought to Jesus.

2   My aunt told me that when you were saved you saw a light, and something happened to you inside! And Jesus came into your life! And God was with you from then on! She said you could see and hear and feel Jesus in your soul. I believed her. I had heard a great many old people say the same thing and it seemed to me they ought to know. So I sat there calmly in the hot, crowded church, waiting for Jesus to come to me.

3   The preacher preached a wonderful rhythmical sermon, all moans and shouts and lonely cries and dire pictures of hell, and then he sang a song about the ninety and nine safe in the fold, but one little lamb was left out in the cold. Then he said: "Won't you come? Won't you come to Jesus? Young lambs, won't you come?" And he held out his arms to all us young sinners there on the mourners' bench. And the little girls cried. And some of them jumped up and went to Jesus right away. But most of us just sat there.

4   A great many old people came and knelt around us and prayed, old women with jet-black faces and braided hair, old men with work-gnarled hands. And the church sang a song about the lower lights are burning, some poor sinners to be saved. And the whole building rocked with prayer and song.

5   Still I kept waiting to *see* Jesus.

6   Finally all the young people had gone to the altar and were saved, but one boy and me. He was a rounder's son named Westley. Westley and I were surrounded by sisters and deacons praying. It was very hot in the church, and getting late now. Finally Westley said to me in a whisper: "God damn! I'm tired o' sitting here. Let's get up and be saved." So he got up and was saved.

7   Then I was left all alone on the mourners' bench. My aunt came and knelt at my knees and cried, while prayers and songs swirled all around me in the little church. The whole congregation prayed for me alone, in a mighty wail of moans and voices. And I kept waiting serenely for Jesus, waiting, waiting—but he didn't come. I wanted to see him, but nothing happened to me. Nothing! I wanted something to happen to me, but nothing happened.

8   I heard the songs and the minister saying: "Why don't you come? My dear child, why don't you come to Jesus? Jesus is waiting for you. He wants you. Why don't you come? Sister Reed, what is this child's name?"

9   "Langston," my aunt sobbed.

10   "Langston, why don't you come? Why don't you come and be saved? Oh, Lamb of God! Why don't you come?"

11   Now it was really getting late. I began to be ashamed of myself, holding everything up so long. I began to wonder what God thought about Westley, who certainly hadn't seen Jesus either, but who was now sitting proudly on the platform, swinging his knickerbockered legs and grinning down at me, surrounded by deacons and old women on their knees praying. God had not struck Westley dead for taking his name in vain or for lying in the temple. So I decided that maybe to save further trouble, I'd better lie, too, and say that Jesus had come, and get up and be saved.

12   So I got up.

13   Suddenly the whole room broke into a sea of shouting, as they saw me rise. Waves of rejoicing swept the place. Women leaped in the air. My aunt threw her arms around me. The minister took me by the hand and led me to the platform.

14   When things quieted down, in a hushed silence, punctuated by a few ecstatic "Amens," all the new young lambs were blessed in the name of God. Then joyous singing filled the room.

15   That night, for the last time in my life but one—for I was a big boy twelve years old—I cried. I cried, in bed alone, and couldn't stop. I buried my head under the quilts, but my aunt heard me. She woke up and told my uncle I was crying because the Holy Ghost had come into my life, and because I had seen Jesus. But I was really crying because I couldn't bear to tell her that I had lied, that I had deceived everybody in church, that I hadn't seen Jesus, and that now I didn't believe there was a Jesus any more, since he didn't come to help me.

Follow-up Questions

10 Short Questions

*Select the **best** answer for each.*

____ 1. The narrator and the author are probably
    a. different people.
    b. relatives.
    c. the same person.

____ 2. This occasion is probably
    a. a religious ceremony.
    b. a school graduation.
    c. a birthday party.

____ 3. The narrator probably lives with
    a. his parents.
    b. Westley.
    c. his aunt.

____ 4. In this story, sinners need
    a. to stay the same.
    b. to change.
    c. to sing.

____ 5. The narrator feels he needs
    a. to hear God.
    b. to see God.
    c. to feel God.

____ 6. Compared to the girls, the boys
    a. take longer.
    b. take less time.
    c. take the same amount of time.

____ 7. "Lambs" refers to
    a. the children to be saved.
    b. the older people.
    c. the minister.

____ 8. The ceremony is generally
    a. very quiet.
    b. very active.
    c. very reserved.

____ 9. In the end, Westley
    a. does see God.
    b. does feel God.
    c. lies about seeing God.

____ 10. In the end, the narrator
    a. does see God.
    b. does feel God.
    c. lies about seeing God.

5 Significant Quotations

Explain the importance of each of these quotations.

1. "That night I was escorted to the front row and placed on the mourners' bench with all the other young sinners, who had not yet been brought to Jesus."

2. "She said you could see and hear and feel Jesus in your soul. I believed her."

3. "Westley and I were surrounded by sisters and deacons praying."

4. "Suddenly the whole room broke into a sea of shouting, as they saw me rise."

5. "That night, for the last time in my life but one—for I was a big boy twelve years old—I cried."

2 Comprehension Essay Questions

Use specific details and information from the story to answer these questions as completely as possible.

1. How would you describe the narrator's experience? Use specific details and information from the story to support your answer.

2. What significant roles do the setting and the supporting characters play? Use specific details and information from the story to support your answer.

Discussion Questions

Be prepared to discuss these questions in class.

1. When have you told a lie to get yourself out of a difficult position? How is your experience similar to or different from the narrator's experience?

2. What are the ironies in this story? Use specific details from the story to support your thinking.

Writing

Use each of these ideas for writing an essay.

1. Discuss a time when you have been expected to do more—or less—than you could do, and discuss the results of that unmet expectation.

2. Discuss a spiritual experience you have had or someone you know has had, and discuss the results of that experience.

Further Writing

1. Research evangelistic religions and the impact of congregations and rituals on their members' conduct and beliefs.

2. Research religious passage rites among either mainstream and/or tribal religions.

The Masque of the Red Death

EDGAR ALLAN POE

Edgar Allan Poe was born in 1809 and orphaned at a young age. He was adopted by John Allan, a rather militaristic businessman from Richmond, Virginia. Adoption by a person of means was not uncommon and would have been fortunate for the young Poe, except that his free spirit and his father's precision clashed. John Allan provided Poe with study at the University of Virginia—but Poe withdrew, due to drinking problems—and then at West Point—but Poe was dismissed, due to a disciplinary problem. Poe later married his very young cousin, Virginia Clemm, but the probable nonconsummation of this marriage and the early death of young Virginia contributed to Poe's idealization of both real and imagined women. His life, in fact, was one of continual disappointments. After Virginia's death, Poe sank into intermittent depressions, suffered bouts of insanity, and experienced hallucinations. Writing for many others, he wanted to publish his own magazine, but this dissolved in financial failure. He eventually died in Baltimore in 1849.

However, it is from these very problems that Poe's genius soars. He envelops the reader with his perceived worlds of the sane and insane, the rational and macabre, with equal ease. Credited with developing the modern mystery form, Poe's every word and every action draw the reader in, mixing reality with irreality, sane with insane. His other works include "The Pit and the Pendulum" and "The Fall of the House of Usher."

The "Red Death" had long devastated the country. No pestilence had ever been so fatal, or so hideous. Blood was its Avatar and its seal—the redness and the horror of blood. There were sharp pains, and sudden dizziness, and then profuse bleeding at the pores, with dissolution. The scarlet stains upon the body and especially upon the face of the victim, were the pest ban which shut him out from the aid and from the sympathy of his fellow-men. And the whole seizure, progress, and termination of the disease, were the incidents of half an hour.

2   But the Prince Prospero was happy and dauntless and sagacious. When his dominions were half depopulated, he summoned to his presence a thousand hale and light-hearted friends from among the knights and dames of his court, and with these retired to the deep seclusion of one of his castellated abbeys. This was an extensive and magnificent structure, the creation of the prince's own eccentric yet august taste. A strong and lofty wall girdled it in. This wall had gates of iron. The courtiers, having entered, brought furnaces and massy hammers and welded the bolts. They resolved to leave means neither of ingress nor egress to the sudden impulses of despair or of frenzy from within. The abbey was amply provisioned. With such precautions the courtiers might bid defiance to contagion. The external world could take care of itself. In the meantime it was folly to grieve, or to think. The prince had provided all the appliances of pleasure. There were buffoons, there were improvisatori, there were ballet-dancers, there were musicians, there was Beauty, there was wine. All these and security were within. Without was the "Red Death."

3   It was toward the close of the fifth or sixth month of his seclusion, and while the pestilence raged most furiously abroad, that the Prince Prospero entertained his thousand friends at a masked ball of the most unusual magnificence.

4   It was a voluptuous scene, that masquerade. But first let me tell of the rooms in which it was held. There were seven—an imperial suite. In many palaces, however, such suites form a long and straight vista, while the folding doors slide back nearly to the walls on either hand, so that the view of the whole extent is scarcely impeded. Here the case was very different; as might have been expected from the duke's love of the *bizarre.* The apartments were so irregularly disposed that the vision embraced but little more than one at a time. There was a sharp turn at every twenty or thirty yards, and at each turn a novel effect. To the right and left, in the middle of each wall, a tall and narrow Gothic window looked out upon a closed corridor which pursued the windings of the suite. These windows were of stained glass whose color varied in accordance with the prevailing hue of the decorations of the chamber into which it opened. That at the eastern extremity was hung, for example, in blue—and vividly blue were its windows. The second chamber was purple in its ornaments and tapestries, and here the panes were purple. The third was green throughout, and so were the casements. The fourth was furnished and lighted with orange—the fifth with white—the sixth with violet. The seventh apartment was closely shrouded in black velvet tapestries that hung all over the ceiling and down the walls, falling in heavy folds upon a carpet of the same material and hue. But in this chamber only, the color of the windows failed to correspond with the decorations. The panes here were scarlet—a deep blood color. Now in no one of the seven apartments was there any lamp or candelabrum, amid the profusion of golden ornaments that lay scattered to and fro or depended from the roof. There was no light of any kind emanating from lamp or candle within the suite of chambers. But in the corridors that followed the suite, there stood, opposite to each window, a heavy tripod, bearing a brazier of fire, that projected its rays through the tinted glass and so glaringly illumined the room. And thus were produced a multitude of gaudy and fantastic appearances. But in the western or black chamber the effect of the fire-light that streamed upon the dark hangings through the blood-tinted panes was ghastly in the extreme, and produced so wild a look upon the countenances of those who entered, that there were few of the company bold enough to set foot within its precincts at all.

5   It was in this apartment, also, that there stood against the western wall, a gigantic clock of ebony. Its pendulum swung to and fro with a dull, heavy, monotonous clang; and when the minute-hand made the circuit of the face, and the hour was to be stricken, there came from the brazen lungs of the clock a sound which was clear and loud and deep and exceedingly musical, but of so peculiar a note and emphasis that, at each lapse of an hour, the musicians of the orchestra were constrained to pause, momentarily, in their performance, to hearken to the sound; and thus the waltzers perforce ceased their evolutions; and there was a brief disconcert of the whole gay company; and, while the chimes of the clock yet rang, it was observed that the giddiest grew pale, and the more aged and sedate passed their hands over their brows as if in confused revery or meditation. But when the echoes had fully ceased, a light laughter at once pervaded the assembly; the musicians looked at each other and smiled as if at their own nervousness and folly, and made whispering vows, each to the other, that the next chiming of the clock should produce in them no similar emotion; and then, after the lapse of sixty minutes (which embrace three thousand and six hundred seconds of the Time that flies), there came yet another chiming of the clock, and then were the same disconcert and tremulousness and meditation as before.

6   But, in spite of these things, it was a gay and magnificent revel. The tastes of the duke were peculiar. He had a fine eye for colors and effects. He disregarded the *decora* of mere fashion. His plans were bold and fiery, and his conceptions glowed with barbaric lustre. There are some who would have thought him mad. His followers felt that he was not. It was necessary to hear and see and touch him to be *sure* that he was not.

7   He had directed, in great part, the movable embellishments of the seven chambers, upon occasion of this great *fête;* and it was his own guiding taste which had given character to the masqueraders. Be sure they were grotesque. There were much glare and glitter and piquancy and phantasm—much of what has been since seen in "Hernani." There were arabesque figures with unsuited limbs and appointments. There were delirious fancies such as the madman fashions. There were much of the beautiful, much of the wanton, much of the *bizarre,* something of the terrible, and not a little of that which might have excited disgust. To and fro in the seven chambers there stalked, in fact, a multitude of dreams. And these—the dreams—writhed in and about, taking hue from the rooms, and causing the wild music of the orchestra to seem as the echo of their steps. And, anon, there strikes the ebony clock which stands in the hall of the velvet. And then, for a moment, all is still, and all is silent save the voice of the clock. The dreams are stiff-frozen as they stand. But the echoes of the chime die away—they have endured but an instant—and a light, half-subdued laughter floats after them as they depart. And now again the music swells, and the dreams live, and writhe to and fro more merrily than ever, taking hue from the many-tinted windows through which stream the rays from the tripods. But to the chamber which lies most westwardly of the seven there are now none of the maskers who venture; for the night is waning away; and there flows a ruddier light through the blood-colored panes; and the blackness of the sable drapery appals; and to him whose foot falls upon the sable carpet, there comes from the near clock of ebony a muffled peal more solemnly emphatic than any which reaches *their* ears who indulge in the more remote gaieties of the other apartments.

8   But these other apartments were densely crowded, and in them beat feverishly the heart of life. And the revel went whirlingly on, until at length there commenced the sounding of midnight upon the clock. And then the music ceased, as I have told; and the evolutions of the waltzers were quieted, and there was an uneasy cessation of all things as before. But now there were twelve strokes to be sounded by the bell of the clock; and thus it happened, perhaps, that more of thought crept, with more of time, into the meditations of the thoughtful among those who revelled. And thus too, it happened, perhaps, that before the last echoes of the last chime had utterly sunk into silence, there were many individuals in the crowd who had found leisure to become aware of the presence of a masked figure which had arrested the attention of no single individual before. And the rumor of this new presence having spread itself whisperingly around, there arose at length from the whole company a buzz, or murmur, expressive of disapprobation and surprise—then, finally, of terror, of horror, and of disgust.

9   In an assembly of phantasms such as I have painted, it may well be supposed that no ordinary appearance could have excited such sensation. In truth the masquerade license of the night was nearly unlimited; but the figure in question had out-Heroded Herod, and gone beyond the bounds of even the prince's indefinite decorum. There are chords in the hearts of the most reckless which cannot be touched without emotion. Even with the utterly lost, to whom life and death are equally jests, there are matters of which no jest can be made. The whole company, indeed, seemed now deeply to feel that in the costume and bearing of the stranger neither wit nor propriety existed. The figure was tall and gaunt, and shrouded from head to foot in the habiliments of the grave. The mask which concealed the visage was made so nearly to resemble the countenance of a stiffened corpse that the closest scrutiny must have had difficulty in detecting the cheat. And yet all this might have been endured, if not approved, by the mad revellers around. But the mummer had gone so far as to assume the type of the Red Death. His vesture was dabbled in *blood*—and his broad brow, with all the features of the face, was besprinkled with the scarlet horror.

10   When the eyes of Prince Prospero fell upon this spectral image (which, with a slow and solemn movement, as if more fully to sustain its *rôle,* stalked to and fro among the waltzers) he was seen to be convulsed, in the first moment with a strong shudder either of terror or distaste; but, in the next, his brow reddened with rage.

11   "Who dares"—he demanded hoarsely of the courtiers who stood near him—"who dares insult us with this blasphemous mockery? Seize him and unmask him—that we may know whom we have to hang, at sunrise, from the battlements!"

12   It was in the eastern or blue chamber in which stood the Prince Prospero as he uttered these words. They rang throughout the seven rooms loudly and clearly, for the prince was a bold and robust man, and the music had become hushed at the waving of his hand.

13   It was in the blue room where stood the prince, with a group of pale courtiers by his side. At first, as he spoke, there was a slight rushing movement of this group in the direction of the intruder, who, at the moment was also near at hand, and now, with deliberate and stately step, made closer approach to the speaker. But from a certain nameless awe with which the mad assumptions of the mummer had inspired the whole party, there were found none who put forth hand to seize him; so that, unimpeded, he passed within a yard of the prince's person; and, while the vast assembly, as if with one impulse, shrank from the centres of the rooms to the walls, he made his way uninterruptedly, but with the same solemn and measured step which had distinguished him from the first, through the blue chamber to the purple—through the purple to the green—through the green to the orange—through this again to the white—and even thence to the violet, ere a decided movement had been made to arrest him. It was then, however, that the Prince Prospero, maddening with rage and the shame of his own momentary cowardice, rushed hurriedly through the six chambers, while none followed him on account of a deadly terror that had seized upon all. He bore aloft a drawn dagger, and had approached, in rapid impetuosity, to within three or four feet of the retreating figure, when the latter, having attained the extremity of the velvet apartment, turned suddenly and confronted his pursuer. There was a sharp cry—and the dagger dropped gleaming upon the sable carpet, upon which, instantly afterward, fell prostrate in death the Prince Prospero. Then, summoning the wild courage of despair, a throng of the revellers at once threw themselves into the black apartment, and, seizing the mummer, whose tall figure stood erect and motionless within the shadow of the ebony clock, gasped in unutterable horror at finding the grave cerements and corpse-like mask, which they handled with so violent a rudeness, untenanted by any tangible form.

14   And now was acknowledged the presence of the Red Death. He had come like a thief in the night. And one by one dropped the revellers in the blood-bedewed halls of their revel, and died each in the despairing posture of his fall. And the life of the ebony clock went out with that of the last of the gay. And the flames of the tripods expired. And Darkness and Decay and the Red Death held illimitable dominion over all.

FOLLOW-UP QUESTIONS

10 SHORT QUESTIONS

*Select the **best** answer for each.*

_____ 1. As a victim of the Red Death bleeds, one
    a. has the help and support
      of friends.
    b. does not have the help
      and support of friends.
    c. gets better rapidly.

_____ 2. Prince Prospero
    a. cares about the general population.
    b. is kind to the general population.
    c. shows little concern for
      the general population.

_____ 3. Prince Prospero
    a. thinks he can escape
      the Red Death.
    b. thinks he cannot escape the Red Death.
    c. does not know about
      the Red Death.

_____ 4. He and his court
    a. think they will be infected with the disease.
    b. think they will not be infected with the
      disease.
    c. do not know about the disease.

_____ 5. The castle rooms are
    a. all the same.
    b. one big room.
    c. separated and different.

_____ 6. The black room's only other color is
    a. white.
    b. blue.
    c. blood red.

_____ 7. The clock has
    a. an unsettling chime.
    b. a pleasant chime.
    c. a sweet, musical chime.

_____ 8. The mummer enters
    a. an afternoon party.
    b. a formal ball.
    c. a masked ball.

_____ 9. The mummer
    a. is wearing a mask.
    b. is not wearing a mask.
    c. is wearing heavy makeup.

_____ 10. The prince and his guests
    a. escape the Red Death.
    b. never see the Red Death.
    c. die from the Red Death.

5 SIGNIFICANT QUOTATIONS

Explain the importance of each of these quotations.

1. "No pestilence had ever been so fatal, or so hideous."

2. "When his dominions were half depopulated, he summoned to his presence a thousand hale and light-hearted friends [. . .] and with these retired to the deep seclusion of one of his castellated abbeys."

3. "It was toward the close of [. . .] his seclusion, and while the pestilence raged most furiously abroad, that the Prince Prospero entertained his thousand friends at a masked ball of the most unusual magnificence."

4. "It was in this apartment, also, that there stood against the western wall, a gigantic clock of ebony."

5. "Then, summoning the wild courage of despair, a throng of revellers at once threw themselves into the black apartment, and, seizing the mummer [. . .] gasped in unutterable horror at finding the grave cerements and corpse-like mask [. . .] untenanted by any tangible form."

2 Comprehension Essay Questions

*Use specific details and information from the story to answer these questions
as completely as possible.*

1. How does the black chamber prepare you for the figure's appearance? Use specific details and information from the story to support your explanation.

2. What happens to Prince Prospero? Use specific details and information from the story to support your explanation.

Discussion Questions

Be prepared to discuss these questions in class.

1. To what current concerns might you compare the masked character? Use specific details from the story to support your ideas.

2. How does the illustration demonstrate this story? Use specific details from the story to support your thinking.

Writing

Use each of these ideas for writing an essay.

1. We have all been to strange places. Describe a place you have been to that seemed to reek of disease or evil.

2. We have all met scary or gloomy people. Describe your encounter with a scary person and how you handled the situation.

Further Writing

1. Read literary analyses of "The Masque of the Red Death" (available in a library). Then discuss whom or what beyond biological disease the figure of Red Death might represent in this story.

2. Research the AIDS/HIV virus, and use this story in your introduction to your research.

Testing Your Understanding—Unit V

American 24-Karat Gold,
"Salvation" by Langston Hughes

 Paragraphs 1–5
CHECKING YOUR COMPREHENSION

Choose the best answer for each of the following questions.

1. It can be inferred that the old people who knelt and prayed around the children
   a. had already been saved.
   b. were getting tired of waiting for the children to go to the platform.
   c. knew that Jesus wasn't really visiting each child in the church.
   d. all had children who were sitting on the mourner's bench that day.

2. It can be concluded that the child in the story
   a. was a sinner and didn't want to be saved.
   b. thought it was all make believe and didn't want to play their game.
   c. was excited about spending time with his aunt in church.
   d. believed his aunt and thought he'd see Jesus that day.

Identify the following statements as true or false.

3. The boy in the story did not like being referred to as a lamb.

4. The church was a quiet place reserved for prayer and reflection.

5. Langston continued to sit on the mourner's bench because Jesus didn't appear.

Answer the following questions.

6. Explain the metaphor used by Hughes in paragraph 1.

7. Why isn't it possible to know why the young girls cried in paragraph 3?

Discussion and Critical Thinking Question

1. Why do you think the young girls "jumped up and went to Jesus right away" while most of the boys "just sat" on the mourner's bench?

 Paragraphs 6–10
CHECKING YOUR COMPREHENSION

Choose the best answer for each of the following questions.

1. Why did Westley finally get up from the mourner's bench?
   a. He saw Jesus and was finally saved.
   b. He didn't want to be the last one left on the bench.
   c. He was tired of sitting there so he joined the others.
   d. He was upset with Langston.

2. It can be inferred that Langston's aunt was crying because
   a. she wanted her nephew to be saved.
   b. she didn't want Langston to embarrass her in church.
   c. she felt he wasn't being true to himself.
   d. she was sick and scared of dying.

Identify the following statements as true or false.

3. The minister asked Langston's name so he could reprimand him.

4. Langston was confused when Jesus didn't appear in front of him.

5. The congregation was scared that Langston would never be saved.

Answer the following questions.

6. Why didn't the minister ask the other children's names?

7. How can you tell that Langston wasn't trying to cause trouble?

Discussion and Critical Thinking Question

1. How do you think Langston felt when he saw all of the other children around him get up and be saved?

 Paragraphs 11–15
CHECKING YOUR COMPREHENSION

Choose the best answer for each of the following questions.

1. Langston did not want to pretend to see Jesus because he was concerned
   a. Jesus would never appear to him during his lifetime.
   b. that God would be upset with him.
   c. that his aunt would be very upset with him.
   d. that Westley would tell everyone he lied.

2. In paragraph 13, what two words are used as metaphors?
   a. room and platform
   b. broke and rise
   c. sea and waves
   d. suddenly and leaped

Identify the following statements as true or false.

3. Everyone in the church believed that Langston saw Jesus.

4. Westley suffered no repercussions for lying about seeing Jesus.

Answer the following questions.

5. Why was it so ironic that Langston cried in his bed that night?

6. Why did Langston decide that there was no Jesus?

Discussion and Critical Thinking Questions

1. How do you think Langston felt the next time he went to church?

2. If you were Langston, what would you have done differently?

"The Masque of the Red Death" by Edgar Allan Poe

Paragraphs 1–4
CHECKING YOUR COMPREHENSION

Choose the best answer for each of the following questions.

1. Why did Prince Prospero hide in his castle with strong lofty walls and iron gates?
   a. He was afraid the peasants wanted to steal all of his money.
   b. He was trying to hide from the Red Death.
   c. He was sick and needed time to recuperate.
   d. He was concerned that the people in the next town were going to attack.

2. The seven rooms that held the masquerade ball are symbolic of
   a. the belief that everyone's life has seven stages.
   b. the seven months that the prince lived in seclusion.
   c. the number of people who survived the Red Death.
   d. the seven soldiers Prince Prospero lost to the Red Death.

Identify the following statements as true or false.

3. Prince Prospero sent out for provisions each month to ensure they had enough food.

4. The seven rooms of the masquerade were laid out from east to west.

5. Those who suffered from the Red Death expelled blood from small holes in their skin.

Answer the following questions.

6. How did Prince Prospero feel about the people over whom he had authority?

7. How did the courtiers ensure that no one could leave the castle?

Discussion and Critical Thinking Question

1. What is so ironic about Prince Prospero having a masquerade ball while in seclusion?

Paragraphs 5–8
CHECKING YOUR COMPREHENSION

Choose the best answer for each of the following questions.

1. When describing the clock in paragraph 5, Poe utilizes which literary device?
   a. alliteration
   b. personification
   c. simile
   d. metaphor

2. The overall feeling that is portrayed when the clock strikes midnight is
   a. gloom and despair.
   b. frustration and disappointment.
   c. enjoyment and pleasure.
   d. murk and bliss.

Identify the following statements as true or false.

3. The clock was not the same color as the velvet walls in the room.

4. When the clock chimed, people became unsettled.

5. The masked figure brought attention to himself by his actions.

Answer the following questions.

6. What was different regarding the fire in the black velvet chamber?

7. Why didn't the masquerade guests venture into the black velvet chamber?

Discussion and Critical Thinking Question

1. What do you think are the "dreams" that Poe continually mentions in the story?

Paragraphs 9–14
CHECKING YOUR COMPREHENSION

Choose the best answer for each of the following questions.

1. What is the theme of this short story?
   a. The rich don't care about the poor.
   b. It's important to stay healthy.
   c. No one escapes death.
   d. There are consequences for every action.

2. What message is the author trying to send his readers?
   a. Money can't buy everything.
   b. It's good to be a prince.
   c. There are many plagues that kill people.
   d. Power can overcome all problems.

Identify the following statements as true or false.

3. Everyone in the castle died from the Red Death.

4. Prince Prospero and the masked figure are the only two people who talk in the story.

Answer the following questions.

5. What is so ironic regarding Prince Prospero's name?

6. What was found when the masked figure was finally detained?

Discussion and Critical Thinking Question

1. What advice would you have given Prince Prospero if he asked you to join him and his friends in the castle to hide from the Red Death?

Chapter Review
END OF CHAPTER ANALYSIS

1. Compare the mood/tone at the end of Hughes' "Salvation" to Poe's "The Masque of the Red Death."

2. Explain the importance of the concept of "waiting" in both Hughes' "Salvation" and Poe's "The Masque of the Red Death."

Group Project

1. Both short stories involve the idea of not believing what you cannot see. Choose a concept in our society that falls into this category and explain what problems people have when they encounter this belief and what can be done to alleviate this dilemma.

Journal Ideas

1. The author of "Salvation" needs some help writing a sequel. Develop an outline that would explain what happens after Langston wakes up the next morning.

2. Make a list of alternative actions that may have proven beneficial for Prince Prospero instead of hiding in his castle.

Unit VI

From

Samuel E. Wood
Ellen Green Wood
Denise Boyd

Mastering the World of Psychology

Second Edition

Chapter 10:
Health and Stress

An Introduction to Psychology

Psychology is defined as the scientific study of human and animal behavior and mental processes. This occurs through the orderly investigation into a problem that involves collecting and analyzing data, drawing conclusions, and communicating findings. Psychology is concerned with explaining how a number of separate facts are related.

Introduction to psychology courses are often required at most liberal arts colleges and universities. A degree in psychology will prepare students to enter careers in such fields as business, public relations, staff training, mental health therapy, research, and education.

Strategies for Reading Psychology

When reading a psychology textbook, it is necessary to define all new terms and understand their relationship to one another. It is also helpful to note the similarities and differences between related ideas. This can be done by utilizing Venn diagrams and concept maps. Applying the concepts introduced to your life and to the world around you will help you understand them better. Be sure that you are able to give examples of the concepts, ideas, and theories that are introduced in your textbook.

Health and

Stress

chapter 10

Sources of Stress

- ◆ *What was the Social Readjustment Rating Scale designed to reveal?*
- ◆ *What roles do hassles and uplifts play in the stress of life, according to Lazarus?*
- ◆ *How do approach-approach, avoidance-avoidance, and approach- avoidance conflicts differ?*
- ◆ *How do the unpredictability and lack of control over a stressor affect its impact?*
- ◆ *For people to function effectively and find satisfaction on the job, what nine variables should fall within their comfort zone?*
- ◆ *How do people typically react to catastrophic events?*
- ◆ *How might historical racism affect the health of African Americans?*

Responding to Stress

- ◆ *What is the general adaptation syndrome?*
- ◆ *What are the roles of primary and secondary appraisals when a person is confronted with a potentially stressful event?*
- ◆ *What is the difference between problem-focused and emotion-focused coping?*

Health and Illness

- ◆ *How do the biomedical and biopsychosocial models differ in their approaches to health and illness?*
- ◆ *What are the Type A and Type B behavior patterns?*
- ◆ *How do psychological factors influence cancer patients' quality of life?*
- ◆ *What are the effects of stress on the immune system?*

- ◆ *What four personal factors are associated with health and resistance to stress?*
- ◆ *What are the relationships among gender, ethnicity, and health?*

Lifestyle and Health

- ◆ *What is the most dangerous health-threatening behavior?*
- ◆ *What are some health risks of alcohol abuse?*
- ◆ *What is the difference between bacterial and viral STDs?*
- ◆ *What are some benefits of regular aerobic exercise?*
- ◆ *What are the benefits and risks associated with alternative medicine?*

Lance Armstrong was, in his own words, "born to race bikes." As a teenager, and the child of a divorced working mother in Plano, Texas, he trained and competed hard. On weekends, he rode his bicycle so far that he sometimes had to phone his mother to pick him up. Armstrong's dedication to his training was so single-minded that he neglected his schoolwork and nearly failed his senior year of high school, but managed to squeak by. After high school, his life was a whirlwind of amateur competitions, the 1992 Olympics, and then the professional cycling circuit.

In his first professional race, Armstrong came  in dead last, but he won ten titles the following year. By 1996, he was a household name in Europe and was gaining fame in the United States as well— heady stuff for any 25-year-old. It seemed that everything was going his way. But one fall day, Armstrong experienced an excruciating pain. Shockingly, tests revealed that he had advanced testicular cancer that had spread to his lungs and his brain. Doctors recommended surgeries to remove his malignant testicle and the cancer in his brain. Following those procedures, he would undergo an aggressive course of chemotherapy. The physicians told Armstrong that, even with the best treatment, he had less than a 50-50 chance to recover. This young, powerful man who had been on top of the world just days before now faced his own mortality.

The chemotherapy weakened Armstrong severely, and he lost 20 pounds. However, his years of training gave him great reserves of physical strength and, at least as importantly, his will was strong. Armstrong has said cancer caused him to take a hard look at himself. He realized that he had relied on his tremendous natural physical abilities and had not learned the discipline, strategy, and teamwork that would be necessary to become a truly great cyclist. He had never given himself the full opportunity to train. He would start, then stop, then start again just a month before a big race. His natural ability was so great that he still won many races, but not the long-distance ones for which more skill is required. Now that Armstrong could take nothing for granted, he realized how important it was to develop into the best cycler he could be. He had a strong network of family and friends he could count on for emotional support. And, even in the midst of his own treatment, he wanted to do something for others. To this end, he established the Lance Armstrong Foundation to help other cancer victims and raise awareness about the importance of early detection. "Having cancer," he says, "was the best thing that ever happened to me."

Armstrong believes that his dedication to rebuilding his health and turning a tragedy into opportunity helped him to recover rapidly. His oncologist described the cyclist as "the most willful person I have ever met...he wasn't *willing* to die." Just 5 months after the diagnosis, he began to train again and vowed to return better than ever. But his sponsors, doubtful that he would ever be able to achieve this goal, dropped him. Armstrong signed a much less lucrative contract with another sponsor and continued to train, but his initial efforts left him exhausted and depressed. Afraid of failing, afraid that his strength would never rebound, afraid of a humiliating loss, afraid that his cancer would return, again and again Armstrong had to fight the desire to quit when things were too tough. One day, riding high in the mountains of North Carolina, he felt his unquenchable spirit return. A few days earlier, his coach had had to coax him to try just one more race. Now he was on top of the world again, spoiling for a competition.

Armstrong won his first post-cancer race in 1998, but his real comeback arrived in 1999, when he won Tour de France, a grueling 21 days of riding totaling 2,110 miles. He became an inspiration and a role model to young people and cancer survivors around the world. In 2001, 5 years after his diagnosis, Armstrong was pronounced cancer free. He undergoes regular testing to ensure that the disease has not recurred. He also continues to work with his foundation. In 2004, Armstrong won his sixth Tour de France race, setting a world record.

Why would someone say, as Armstrong did, that cancer was the best thing that ever happened to him? Such statements represent a deliberate choice to view what anyone would agree is a "stressor" as an opportunity for growth. As you will learn in this chapter, the way that an individual views his or her challenges in life greatly influences whether we succeed in overcoming them. We will begin by considering the various sources of stress in our lives.

Sources of Stress

What do you mean when you say you are "stressed out"? Most psychologists define **stress** as the physiological and psychological response to a condition that threatens or challenges an individual and requires some form of adaptation or adjustment. Stress is associated with the **fight-or-flight response,** in which the body's sympathetic nervous system and the endocrine glands prepare the body to fight or escape from a threat (see Chapter 2). Most of us frequently experience other kinds of **stressors,** stimuli or events that are capable of producing physical or emotional stress.

Holmes and Rahe's Social Readjustment Rating Scale

Researchers Holmes and Rahe (1967) developed the **Social Readjustment Rating Scale (SRRS)** to measure stress by ranking different life events from most to least stressful and assigning a point value to each event. Life events that produce the greatest life changes and require the greatest adaptation are considered the most stressful, regardless of whether the events are positive or negative. The 43 life events on the scale range from death of a spouse (assigned 100 stress points) to minor law violations such as getting a traffic ticket (11 points). Find your life stress score by completing *Try It 10.1* (on page 310).

Holmes and Rahe claim that there is a connection between the degree of life stress and major health problems. People who score 300 or more on the SRRS, the researchers say, run about an 80% risk of suffering a major health problem within the next 2 years. Those who score between 150 and 300 have a 50% chance of becoming ill within a 2-year period (Rahe et al., 1964). More recent research has shown that the weights given to life events by Holmes and Rahe continue to be appropriate for adults in North America and that SRRS scores are correlated with a variety of health indicators (Faisal-Cury et al., 2004; Hobson & Delunas, 2001; Scully et al., 2000).

Some researchers have questioned whether a high score on the SRRS is a reliable predictor of future health problems (Krantz et al., 1985; McCrae, 1984). One of the main shortcomings of the SRRS is that it assigns a point value to each life change without taking into account how an individual copes with that stressor. One study found that SRRS scores did reliably predict disease progression in multiple sclerosis patients (Mohr et al., 2002). But the patients who used more effective coping strategies displayed less disease progression than did those who experienced similar stressors but coped poorly with them.

◆ **stress**

The physiological and psychological response to a condition that threatens or challenges a person and requires some form of adaptation or adjustment.

◆ **fight-or-flight response**

A response to stress in which the sympathetic nervous system and the endocrine glands prepare the body to fight or flee.

◆ **stressor**

Any stimulus or event capable of producing physical or emotional stress.

◆ *What was the Social Readjustment Rating Scale designed to reveal?*

◆ **Social Readjustment Rating Scale (SRRS)**

Holmes and Rahe's measure of stress, which ranks 43 life events from most to least stressful and assigns a point value to each.

Even positive life events, such as getting married, can cause stress.

Try It 10.1

Finding a Life Stress Score

To assess your level of life changes, check all of the events that have happened to you in the past year. Add up the points to derive your life stress score. (Based on Holmes & Masuda, 1974.)

Rank	Life Event	Life Change Unit Value	Your Points
1	Death of spouse	100	____
2	Divorce	73	
3	Marital separation	65	____
4	Jail term	63	
5	Death of close family member	63	____
6	Personal injury or illness	53	
7	Marriage	50	____
8	Getting fired at work	47	
9	Marital reconciliation	45	____
10	Retirement	45	
11	Change in health of family member	44	____
12	Pregnancy	40	
13	Sex difficulties	39	____
14	Gain of new family member	39	
15	Business readjustment	39	____
16	Change in financial state	38	
17	Death of close friend	37	____
18	Change to different line of work	36	
19	Change in number of arguments with spouse	35	____
20	Taking out loan for major purchase (e.g., home)	31	
21	Foreclosure of mortgage or loan	30	____
22	Change in responsibilities at work	29	
23	Son or daughter leaving home	29	____
24	Trouble with in-laws	29	
25	Outstanding personal achievement	28	____
26	Spouse beginning or stopping work	26	
27	Beginning or ending school	26	____
28	Change in living conditions	25	
29	Revision of personal habits	24	____
30	Trouble with boss	23	
31	Change in work hours or conditions	20	____
32	Change in residence	20	
33	Change in schools	20	____
34	Change in recreation	19	
35	Change in church activities	19	____
36	Change in social activities	18	
37	Taking out loan for lesser purchase (e.g., car or TV)	17	____
38	Change in sleeping habits	16	
39	Change in number of family get-togethers	15	____
40	Change in eating habits	15	
41	Vacation	13	____
42	Christmas	12	
43	Minor violation of the law	11	____

Life stress score: _____

Daily Hassles and Uplifts

Which is more stressful—major life events or those little problems and frustrations that seem to crop up every day? Richard Lazarus believes that the little stressors, which he calls **hassles,** cause more stress than major life events do. Daily hassles are the "irritating, frustrating, distressing demands and troubled relationships that plague us day in and day out" (Lazarus & DeLongis, 1983, p. 247). Kanner and others (1981) developed the Hassles Scale to assess various categories of hassles. Unlike the Holmes and Rahe scale, the Hassles Scale takes into account the facts that items may or may not represent stressors to individuals and that the amount of stress produced by an item varies from person to person. People completing the scale indicate the items that have been a hassle for them and rate those items for severity on a 3-point scale. Table 10.1 shows the ten hassles most frequently reported by college students.

DeLongis and others (1988) studied 75 American couples over a 6-month period and found that daily stress (as measured on the Hassles Scale) related significantly to present and future "health problems such as flu, sore throat, headaches, and backaches" (p. 486). Research also indicates that minor hassles that accompany stressful major life events, such as those measured by the SRRS, are better predictors of a person's level of psychological distress than the major events themselves (Pillow et al., 1996).

According to Lazarus, **uplifts,** or positive experiences in life, may neutralize the effects of many hassles. Lazarus and his colleagues also constructed an Uplifts Scale. As with the Hassles Scale, people completing this scale make a cognitive appraisal of what they consider to be an uplift. Research has demonstrated links among hassles, uplifts, and a personal sense of well-being. It appears that a hectic daily schedule increases hassles, decreases uplifts, and diminishes their subjective sense of how well they feel (Erlandsson & Eklund, 2003). However, items viewed as uplifts by some people may actually be stressors for others. For middle-aged people, uplifts are often health- or family-related, whereas for college students uplifts often take the form of having a good time (Kanner et al., 1981).

◆ *What roles do hassles and uplifts play in the stress of life, according to Lazarus?*

◆ **hassles**
Little stressors, including the irritating demands that can occur daily, that may cause more stress than major life changes do.

◆ **uplifts**
The positive experiences in life, which may neutralize the effects of many hassles.

TABLE 10.1 The Ten Most Common Hassles for College Students	
HASSLE	**PERCENTAGE OF TIMES CHECKED**
1. Troubling thoughts about future	76.6
2. Not getting enough sleep	72.5
3. Wasting time	71.1
4. Inconsiderate smokers	70.7
5. Physical appearance	69.9
6. Too many things to do	69.2
7. Misplacing or losing things	67.0
8. Not enough time to do the things you need to do	66.3
9. Concerns about meeting high standards	64.0
10. Being lonely	60.8

Source: Kanner et al. (1981).

Making Choices

◆ *How do approach-approach, avoidance-avoidance, and approach-avoidance conflicts differ?*

What happens when you have to decide which movie to see or which new restaurant to try? Simply making a choice, even among equally desirable alternatives (an **approach-approach conflict**), can be stressful. Some approach-approach conflicts are minor, such as deciding which movie to see. Others can have major consequences, such as the conflict between building a promising career or interrupting that career to raise a child. In an **avoidance-avoidance conflict**, a person must choose between two undesirable alternatives. For example, you may want to avoid studying for an exam, but at the same time you want to avoid failing the test. An **approach-avoidance conflict** involves a single choice that has both desirable and undesirable features. The person facing this type of conflict is simultaneously drawn to and repelled by a choice—for example, wanting to take a wonderful vacation but having to empty a savings account to do so.

Unpredictability and Lack of Control

◆ *How do the unpredictability and lack of control over a stressor affect its impact?*

"Good morning, class. Today, we are going to have a pop quiz," your professor says. Do these words cause a fight-or-flight response in your body? Such reactions are common, because unpredictable stressors are more difficult to cope with than predictable stressors. Laboratory tests have shown that rats receiving electric shocks without warning develop more ulcers than rats given shocks just as often but only after receiving a warning (Weiss, 1972). Likewise, humans who are warned of a stressor before it occurs and have a chance to prepare themselves for it experience less stress than those who must cope with an unexpected stressor.

Our physical and psychological well-being is profoundly influenced by the degree to which we feel a sense of control over our lives (Rodin & Salovey, 1989). Langer and Rodin (1976) studied the effects of control on nursing-home residents. Residents in one group were given some measure of control over their lives, such as choices in arranging their rooms and in the times they could see movies. They showed improved health and well-being and had a lower death rate than another group who were not given such control. Within 18 months, 30% of the residents given no choices had died, compared with only 15% of those who had been given some control over their lives. Control is important for cancer patients, too. Some researchers suggest that a sense of control over their daily physical symptoms and emotional reactions may be even more important for cancer patients than control over the course of the disease itself (Thompson et al., 1993).

Several studies suggest that we are less subject to stress when we have the power to do something about it, whether we exercise that power or not (John, 2004). Glass and Singer (1972) subjected two groups of participants to the same loud noise. Participants in one group were told that they could, if necessary, terminate the noise by pressing a switch. These participants suffered less stress, even though they never did exercise the control they were given. Friedland and others (1992) suggest that when people experience a loss of control because of a stressor, they are motivated to try to reestablish control in the stressful situation. Failing this, they often attempt to increase their sense of control in other areas of their lives.

◆ **approach-approach conflict**

A conflict arising from having to choose between equally desirable alternatives.

◆ **avoidance-avoidance conflict**

A conflict arising from having to choose between undesirable alternatives.

◆ **approach-avoidance conflict**

A conflict arising when the same choice has both desirable and undesirable features.

Stress in the Workplace

◆ *For people to function effectively and find satisfaction on the job, what nine variables should fall within their comfort zone?*

Perhaps there is no more troublesome source of stress than the workplace. Everyone who works is subject to some job-related stress, but the amount and sources of the stress differ, depending on the type of job and the kind of organization. Albrecht (1979) suggests that if people are to function effectively and find satisfaction on the job, the following nine variables must fall within their comfort zone (see also Figure 10.1):

FIGURE 10.1 **Variables in Work Stress**

For a person to function effectively and find satisfaction on the job, these nine variables should fall within the person's comfort zone. *Source:* Albrecht (1979).

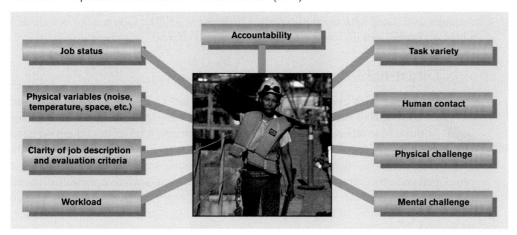

- *Workload.* Too much or too little to do can cause people to feel anxious, frustrated, and unrewarded.
- *Clarity of job description and evaluation criteria.* Anxiety arises from confusion about job responsibilities and performance criteria or from a job description that is too rigidly defined to leave room for individual initiative.
- *Physical variables.* Temperature, noise, humidity, pollution, amount of workspace, and the physical positions (standing or sitting) required to carry out job duties should fall within a person's comfort zone.
- *Job status.* People with very low-paying, low-status jobs may feel psychological discomfort; those with celebrity status often cannot handle the stress that fame brings.
- *Accountability.* Accountability overload occurs when people have responsibility for the physical or psychological well-being of others but only a limited degree of control (air-traffic controllers, emergency room nurses and doctors); accountability underload occurs when workers perceive their jobs as meaningless.
- *Task variety.* To function well, people need a comfortable amount of variety and stimulation.
- *Human contact.* Some workers have virtually no human contact on the job (forest-fire lookouts); others have almost continuous contact with others (welfare and employment office workers). People vary greatly in how much interaction they enjoy or even tolerate.
- *Physical challenge.* Jobs range from being physically demanding (construction work, professional sports) to requiring little to no physical activity. Some jobs (firefighting, police work) involve physical risk.
- *Mental challenge.* Jobs that tax people beyond their mental capability, as well as those that require too little mental challenge, can be frustrating.

Workplace stress can be especially problematic for women because of sex-specific stressors, including sex discrimination and sexual harassment in the workplace and difficulties in combining work and family roles. These added stressors have been shown to increase the negative effects of occupational stress on the health and well-being of working women (Swanson, 2000).

Air-traffic controllers have an extremely high-stress job. The on-the-job stress they experience increases the risk of coronary disease and stroke.

Job stress can have a variety of consequences. Perhaps the most frequently cited is reduced effectiveness on the job. But job stress can also lead to absenteeism, tardiness, accidents, substance abuse, and lower morale (Wilhelm et al., 2004). However, as you might predict, unemployment is far more stressful for most people than any of the variables associated with on-the-job stress (Price et al., 2002). Given a choice between a high-stress job and no job at all, most of us would choose the former.

Catastrophic Events

◆ *How do people typically react to catastrophic events?*

Catastrophic events such as the terrorist attacks of September 11, 2001, and the crash of the space shuttle Columbia in early 2003 are stressful both for those who experience them directly and for people who learn of them via news media. Most people are able to manage the stress associated with such catastrophes. However, for some, these events lead to **posttraumatic stress disorder (PTSD),** a prolonged and severe stress reaction to a catastrophic event (such as a plane crash or an earthquake) or to severe, chronic stress (such as that experienced by soldiers engaged in combat or residents of neighborhoods in which violent crime is a daily occurrence) (Kilpatrick et al., 2003).

The potential impact of catastrophic events on the incidence of PTSD is illustrated by surveys conducted before and after September 11, 2001. Prior to the terrorist attacks, most surveys found that between 1% and 2% of Americans met the diagnostic criteria for PTSD (Foa & Meadows, 1997). Two months after the attacks, about 17% of Americans surveyed by researchers at the University of California–Irvine reported symptoms of PTSD. When the researchers conducted follow-up interviews with survey participants 6 months after the attacks, 6% of them were still experiencing distress. Other researchers have found additional lingering effects associated with September 11 (see Figure 10.2). As you might predict, however, individuals with a personal connection to the events of September 11 were more likely to experience long-term symptoms of PTSD. For example, a survey of flight attendants conducted in summer 2002 found that 17% of them continued to suffer from PTSD symptoms (Lating et al., 2004).

People with PTSD often have flashbacks, nightmares, or intrusive memories that make them feel as though they are actually reexperiencing the traumatic event. They suffer increased anxiety and startle easily, particularly in response to anything that reminds them of the trauma (Green et al., 1985). Many survivors of war or catastrophic events experience *survivor guilt* because they lived while others died; some feel that

◆ **posttraumatic stress disorder (PTSD)**

A prolonged and severe stress reaction to a catastrophic event or to severe, chronic stress.

FIGURE 10.2 Americans' Stress Levels after September 11, 2001

Researchers have found that Americans continued to experience increased levels of stress and anxiety several months after the terrorist attacks of September 11, 2001. *Sources:* Clay (2002), Clay et al. (2002), Schlenger et al. (2002), Silver et al. (2002).

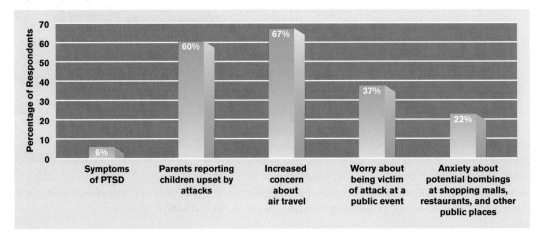

perhaps they could have done more to save others. Extreme combat-related guilt in Vietnam veterans is a risk factor for suicide or preoccupation with suicide (Hendin & Haas, 1991). One study of women with PTSD revealed that they were twice as likely as women without PTSD to experience first-onset depression and three times as likely to develop alcohol problems (Breslau et al., 1997). PTSD sufferers also experience cognitive difficulties, such as poor concentration (Vasterling et al., 2002).

Racism and Stress

A significant source of chronic stress is being a member of a minority group in a majority culture. A study of White and African American participants' responses to a questionnaire about ways of managing stress revealed that a person may experience racial stress from simply being one of the few or only members of a particular race in any of a variety of settings, such as a classroom, the workplace, or a social situation (Plummer & Slane, 1996). The feelings of stress experienced in such situations can be intense, even in the absence of racist attitudes, discrimination, or any other overt evidence of racism.

◆ *How might historical racism affect the health of African Americans?*

Some theorists have proposed that a phenomenon called *historical racism*—experienced by members of groups that have a history of repression—can also be a source of stress (Troxel et al., 2003). Researchers interested in the effects of historical racism have focused primarily on African Americans. Many of these researchers claim that the higher incidence of high blood pressure among African Americans is attributable to stress associated with historical racism. Surveys have shown that African Americans experience more race-related stress than members of other minority groups do (Utsey et al., 2002). Those African Americans who express the highest levels of concern about racism display higher levels of cardiovascular reactivity to experimentally induced stressors, such as sudden loud noises, than do peers who express less concern (Bowen-Reid & Harrell, 2002). At least one study has demonstrated a correlation between African Americans' perceptions of racism and hypertension (Din-Dzietham et al., 2004). Researchers found that African Americans who reported the highest levels of race-related stressors in their workplaces were more likely to have high blood pressure than workers who reported fewer such stressors.

African Americans are also more likely than members of other minority groups to have a strong sense of ethnic identity, a factor that helps moderate the effects of racial stress (Utsey et al., 2002). But some studies show that personal characteristics, such as hostility, may increase the effects of racial stress (Fang & Myers, 2001; Raeikkoenen et al., 2003). So, the relationship between historical racism and cardiovascular health is probably fairly complex and varies considerably across individuals. Moreover, some researchers believe that the association must be studied more thoroughly in other historically oppressed groups, such as Native Americans, before firm conclusions can be drawn (Belcourt-Dittloff & Stewart, 2000).

A strong sense of ethnic identity helps African Americans cope with the stress that may arise from living with racism.

Responding to Stress

◆ general adaptation syndrome (GAS)

The predictable sequence of reactions (alarm, resistance, and exhaustion stages) that organisms show in response to stressors.

How do you respond to stress? Psychologists have different views of the ways in which people respond to stressful experiences. Each approach can help us gain insight into our own experiences and, perhaps, deal more effectively with stress.

Selye and the General Adaptation Syndrome

◆ What is the general adaptation syndrome?

Hans Selye (1907–1982), the researcher most prominently associated with the effects of stress on health, established the field of stress research. At the heart of Selye's concept of stress is the **general adaptation syndrome (GAS),** the predictable sequence of reactions that organisms show in response to stressors. It consists of three stages: the alarm stage, the resistance stage, and the exhaustion stage (Selye, 1956). (See Figure 10.3.)

◆ alarm stage

The first stage of the general adaptation syndrome, in which the person experiences a burst of energy that aids in dealing with the stressful situation.

The first stage of the body's response to a stressor is the **alarm stage,** in which the adrenal cortex releases hormones called *glucocorticoids* that increase heart rate, blood pressure, and blood-sugar levels, supplying a burst of energy that helps the person deal with the stressful situation (Pennisi, 1997). Next, the organism enters the **resistance stage,** during which the adrenal cortex continues to release glucocorticoids to help the body resist stressors. The length of the resistance stage depends both on the intensity of the stressor and on the body's power to adapt. If the organism finally fails in its efforts to resist, it reaches the **exhaustion stage,** at which point all the stores of deep energy are depleted, and disintegration and death follow.

◆ resistance stage

The second stage of the general adaptation syndrome, when there are intense physiological efforts to either resist or adapt to the stressor.

◆ exhaustion stage

The third stage of the general adaptation syndrome, which occurs if the organism fails in its efforts to resist the stressor.

Selye found that the most harmful effects of stress are due to the prolonged secretion of glucocorticoids, which can lead to permanent increases in blood pressure, suppression of the immune system, weakening of muscles, and even damage to the hippocampus (Stein-Behrens et al., 1994). Thanks to Selye, the connection between extreme, prolonged stress and certain diseases is now widely accepted by medical experts.

Lazarus's Cognitive Theory of Stress

◆ What are the roles of primary and secondary appraisals when a person is confronted with a potentially stressful event?

Is it the stressor itself that upsets us, or the way we think about it? Richard Lazarus (1966; Lazarus & Folkman, 1984) contends that it is not the stressor that causes stress, but rather a person's perception of it. According to Lazarus, when people are confronted with a potentially stressful event, they engage in a cognitive process that involves a primary and a secondary appraisal. A **primary appraisal** is an evaluation of the meaning and significance of the situation—whether its effect on one's well-being is positive, irrelevant, or negative. An

◆ primary appraisal

A cognitive evaluation of a potentially stressful event to determine whether its effect is positive, irrelevant, or negative.

FIGURE 10.3

The General Adaptation Syndrome

The three stages in Selye's general adaptation syndrome are (1) the alarm stage, during which there is emotional arousal and the defensive forces of the body are mobilized for fight or flight; (2) the resistance stage, in which intense physiological efforts are exerted to resist or adapt to the stressor; and (3) the exhaustion stage, when the organism fails in its efforts to resist the stressor. *Source:* Selye (1956).

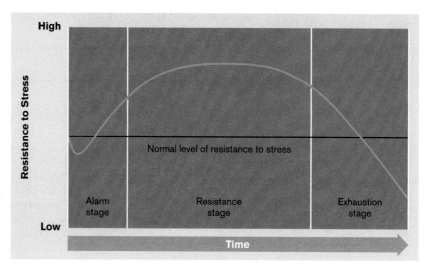

event appraised as stressful could involve (1) harm or loss—that is, damage that has already occurred; (2) threat, or the potential for harm or loss; or (3) challenge—that is, the opportunity to grow or to gain. An appraisal of threat, harm, or loss can occur in relation to anything important to you—a friendship, a part of your body, your property, your finances, your self-esteem. When people appraise a situation as involving threat, harm, or loss, they experience negative emotions such as anxiety, fear, anger, and resentment (Folkman, 1984). An appraisal that sees a challenge, on the other hand, is usually accompanied by positive emotions such as excitement, hopefulness, and eagerness.

During **secondary appraisal,** if people judge the situation to be within their control, they make an evaluation of available resources—physical (health, energy, stamina), social (support network), psychological (skills, morale, self-esteem), material (money, tools, equipment), and time. Then, they consider the options and decide how to deal with the stressor. The level of stress they feel is largely a function of whether their resources are adequate to cope with the threat, and how severely those resources will be taxed in the process. Figure 10.4 summarizes the Lazarus and Folkman psychological model of stress. Research supports their claim that the physiological, emotional, and behavioral reactions to stressors depend partly on whether the stressors are appraised as challenging or threatening.

◆ **secondary appraisal**
A cognitive evaluation of available resources and options prior to deciding how to deal with a stressor.

Coping Strategies

If you're like most people, the stresses you have experienced have helped you develop some coping strategies. **Coping** refers to a person's efforts through action and thought to deal with demands perceived as taxing or overwhelming. **Problem-focused coping** is direct; it consists of reducing, modifying, or eliminating the source of stress itself. If you are getting a poor grade in history and appraise this as a threat, you may study harder, talk over your problem with your professor, form a study group with other class members, get a tutor, or drop the course.

Emotion-focused coping involves reappraising a stressor an effort to reduce its emotional impact. Research has shown that emotion-focused coping can be a very effective way of managing stress (Austenfeld & Stanton, 2004). If you lose your job, you may decide that it isn't a major tragedy and instead view it as a challenge, an opportunity to

◆ *What is the difference between problem-focused and emotion-focused coping?*

◆ **coping**
Efforts through action and thought to deal with demands that are perceived as taxing or overwhelming.

◆ **problem-focused coping**
A direct response aimed at reducing, modifying, or eliminating a source of stress.

◆ **emotion-focused coping**
A response involving reappraisal of a stressor to reduce its emotional impact.

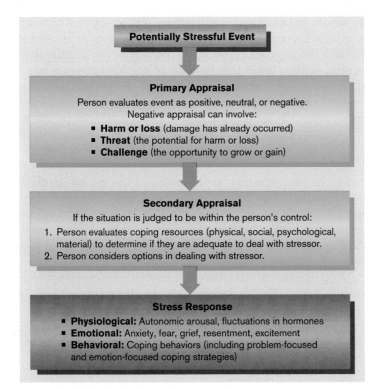

Potentially Stressful Event

Primary Appraisal
Person evaluates event as positive, neutral, or negative. Negative appraisal can involve:
- **Harm or loss** (damage has already occurred)
- **Threat** (the potential for harm or loss)
- **Challenge** (the opportunity to grow or gain)

Secondary Appraisal
If the situation is judged to be within the person's control:
1. Person evaluates coping resources (physical, social, psychological, material) to determine if they are adequate to deal with stressor.
2. Person considers options in dealing with stressor.

Stress Response
- **Physiological:** Autonomic arousal, fluctuations in hormones
- **Emotional:** Anxiety, fear, grief, resentment, excitement
- **Behavioral:** Coping behaviors (including problem-focused and emotion-focused coping strategies)

FIGURE 10.4

Lazarus and Folkman's Psychological Model of Stress

Lazarus and Folkman emphasize the importance of a person's perceptions and appraisal of stressors. The stress response depends on the outcome of the primary and secondary appraisals, whether the person's coping resources are adequate to cope with the threat, and how severely the resources are taxed in the process. *Source:* Folkman (1984).

Theories of Stress Responses

THEORY	DESCRIPTION
Selye's general adaptation syndrome (GAS)	Three stages: alarm, resistance, and exhaustion
Lazarus's cognitive theory	Primary appraisal (evaluation of stressor), followed by secondary appraisal (evaluation of resources and options)
Coping strategies	Problem-focused coping, directed toward stressor; emotion-focused coping, directed toward the emotional response to the stressor

find a better job with a higher salary. Despite what you may have heard, ignoring a stressor—one form of emotion-focused coping—can be an effective way of managing stress. Researchers studied 116 people who had experienced heart attacks (Ginzburg et al., 2002). All of the participants reported being worried about suffering another attack. However, those who tried to ignore their worries were less likely to exhibit anxiety-related symptoms such as nightmares and flashbacks. Other emotion-focused strategies, though, such as keeping a journal in which you write about your worries and track how they change over time, may be even more effective (Pennebaker & Seagal, 1999; Solano et al., 2003).

A combination of problem-focused and emotion-focused coping is probably the best stress-management strategy (Folkman & Lazarus, 1980). For example, a heart patient may ignore her anxiety (emotion-focused coping) while conscientiously adopting recommended lifestyle changes such as increasing exercise (problem-focused coping).

Review and Reflect 10.1 summarizes the key aspects of the various theories concerning humans' response to stress.

Health and Illness

Have you heard the term *wellness* and wondered exactly what was meant by it? This word is associated with a new approach to thinking about health, used by both professionals and laypersons. This approach encompasses a growing emphasis on lifestyle, preventive care, and the need to maintain wellness rather than thinking of health matters only when the body is sick. Health psychologists are discovering how stress, through its influence on the immune system, may affect people's health. They are also examining how personal and demographic factors are related to both illness and wellness.

Two Approaches to Health and Illness

For many decades, the predominant view in medicine was the **biomedical model,** which explains illness in terms of biological factors. Today, physicians and psychologists alike recognize that the **biopsychosocial model** provides a fuller explanation of both health and illness (see Figure 10.5) (Engel, 1977, 1980; Schwartz, 1982). This model considers health and illness to be determined by a combination of biological, psychological, and social factors.

Growing acceptance of the biopsychosocial approach has given rise to a new subfield, **health psychology,** which is "the field within psychology devoted to understanding psychological influences on how people stay healthy, why they become ill, and how they respond when they do get ill" (Taylor, 1991, p. 6). Health psychology is particularly important today because several prevalent diseases, including heart disease and cancer, are related to unhealthy lifestyles and stress (Taylor & Repetti, 1997).

◆ **biomedical model**
A perspective that explains illness solely in terms of biological factors.

◆ **biopsychosocial model**
A perspective that focuses on health as well as illness and holds that both are determined by a combination of biological, psychological, and social factors.

◆ *How do the biomedical and biopsychosocial models differ in their approaches to health and illness?*

◆ **health psychology**
The subfield within psychology that is concerned with the psychological factors that contribute to health, illness, and recovery.

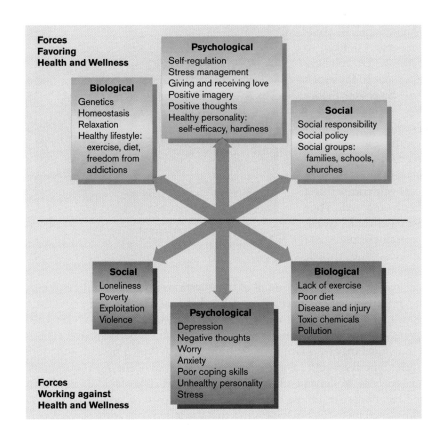

FIGURE 10.5

The Biopsychosocial Model of Health and Illness

The biopsychosocial model focuses on health as well as on illness and holds that both are determined by a combination of biological, psychological, and social factors. Most health psychologists endorse the biopsychosocial model. *Source:* Green & Shellenberger (1990).

Coronary Heart Disease

To survive, the heart muscle requires a steady, sufficient supply of oxygen and nutrients carried by the blood. Coronary heart disease is caused by the narrowing or the blockage of the coronary arteries, the arteries that supply blood to the heart muscle. Although coronary heart disease remains the leading cause of death in the United States, responsible for 28% of all deaths, deaths due to this cause have declined 50% during the past 30 years (National Center for Health Statistics, 2004).

A health problem of modern times, coronary heart disease is largely attributable to lifestyle and is therefore an important field of study for health psychologists. A *sedentary lifestyle*—one that includes a job at which one spends most of the time sitting and less than 20 minutes of exercise three times per week—is the primary modifiable risk factor contributing to death from coronary heart disease (Gallo et al., 2003). Other modifiable risk factors are high serum cholesterol level, cigarette smoking, and obesity.

Though not modifiable, another important risk factor is family history. The association between family history and coronary heart disease is both genetic and behavioral. For instance, individuals whose parents have high blood pressure, but who have not yet developed the disorder themselves, exhibit the same kinds of emotional reactivity and poor coping strategies as their parents (Frazer et al., 2002).

High levels of stress and job strain have also been associated with increased risk for coronary heart disease and stroke (Rosengren et al., 1991; Siegrist et al., 1990). Apparently, the effects of stress enter the bloodstream almost as if they were injected intravenously. Malkoff and others (1993) report that after an experimental group of participants had experienced laboratory-induced stress, their blood platelets (special clotting cells) released large amounts of a substance that promotes the buildup of plaque in blood vessels and may lead to heart attack and stroke. No changes were found in the blood platelets of unstressed control-group participants.

Personality type is also associated with an individual's risk of heart disease. After extensive research, cardiologists Meyer Friedman and Ray Rosenman (1974) concluded that there are two types of personality: Type A, associated with a high rate of coronary

◆ *What are the Type A and Type B behavior patterns?*

◆ Type A behavior pattern

A behavior pattern marked by a sense of time urgency, impatience, excessive competitiveness, hostility, and anger; considered a risk factor in coronary heart disease.

◆ Type B behavior pattern

A behavior pattern marked by a relaxed, easygoing approach to life, without the time urgency, impatience, and hostility of the Type A pattern.

heart disease, and Type B, commonly found in persons unlikely to develop heart disease. Do you have characteristics similar to those of a Type A or a Type B person? Before reading further, complete *Try It 10.2* and find out.

People with the **Type A behavior pattern** have a strong sense of time urgency and are impatient, excessively competitive, hostile, and easily angered. They are "involved in a chronic, incessant struggle to achieve more and more in less and less time" (Friedman & Rosenman, 1974, p. 84).

Hostility is a key component of the Type A behavior pattern.

Type A's would answer "true" to most or all of the questions in the *Try It*. In contrast, people with the **Type B behavior pattern** are relaxed and easygoing and are not driven by a sense of time urgency. They are not impatient or hostile and are able to relax without guilt. They play for fun and relaxation rather than to exhibit superiority over others. Yet, a Type B individual may be as bright and ambitious as a Type A person, and more successful as well. Type B's would answer "false" to most or all of the *Try It* questions.

Using meta-analysis, Miller and others (1991) found that 70% of middle-aged men with coronary heart disease exhibited the Type A behavior pattern, compared to 46% of healthy middle-aged men. Research indicates that the lethal core of the Type A personality is not time urgency but anger and hostility, which fuel an aggressive, reactive

Try It 10.2

Type A or Type B?

Answer true (T) or false (F) for each of the statements below. (Adapted from Friedman & Rosenman, 1974.)

_____ 1. I forcefully emphasize key words in my everyday speech.

_____ 2. I usually walk and eat quickly.

_____ 3. I get irritated and restless around slow workers.

_____ 4. When talking to others, I get impatient and try to hurry them along.

_____ 5. I get very irritated, even hostile, when the car in front of me drives too slowly.

_____ 6. When others are talking, I often think about my own concerns.

_____ 7. I usually think of or do at least two things at the same time.

_____ 8. I get very impatient when I have to wait.

_____ 9. I usually take command and move the conversation to topics that interest me.

_____ 10. I usually feel guilty when I relax and do nothing.

_____ 11. I am usually too absorbed in my work to notice my surroundings.

_____ 12. I keep trying to do more and more in less time.

_____ 13. I sometimes punctuate my conversation with forceful gestures such as clenching my fists or pounding the table.

_____ 14. My accomplishments are due largely to my ability to work faster than others.

_____ 15. I don't play games just for fun. I play to win.

_____ 16. I am more concerned with acquiring things than with becoming a better person.

_____ 17. I usually use numbers to evaluate my own activities and the activities of others.

temperament (Miller et al., 1996; Räikkönen, et al., 2004; Smith & Ruiz, 2002; Williams, 1993). Hostility is not only highly predictive of coronary heart disease but is also associated with ill health in general (Miller et al., 1996).

Cancer

Cancer is the second leading cause of death in the United States, accounting for 22% of all deaths (National Center for Health Statistics, 2004). Cancer strikes frequently in the adult population, and about 30% of Americans—more than 75 million people—will develop cancer at some time in their lives. The young are not spared the scourge of cancer, for it takes the lives of more children aged 3 to 14 than any other disease.

◆ How do psychological factors influence cancer patients' quality of life?

Cancer, a collection of diseases rather than a single illness, can invade cells in any part of a living organism—humans, other animals, and even plants. Normal cells in all parts of the body divide, but fortunately they have built-in instructions about when to stop dividing. Unlike normal cells, cancer cells do not stop dividing. And, unless caught in time and destroyed, they continue to grow and spread, eventually killing the organism. Health psychologists point out that an unhealthy diet, smoking, excessive alcohol consumption, promiscuous sexual behavior, or becoming sexually active in the early teens (especially for females) are all behaviors that increase the risk of cancer.

The more than 1 million people in the United States who are diagnosed with cancer each year have the difficult task of adjusting to a potentially life-threatening disease and the chronic stressors associated with it. Thus, researchers claim that cancer patients need more than medical treatment. Their therapy should include help with psychological and behavioral factors that can influence their quality of life. Carver and others (1993) found that 3 months and 6 months after surgery, breast cancer patients who maintained an optimistic outlook, accepted the reality of their situation, and maintained a sense of humor experienced less distress. Patients who engaged in denial—refusal to accept the reality of their situation—and had thoughts of giving up experienced much higher levels of distress. Dunkel-Schetter and others (1992) found that the most effective elements of a strategy for coping with cancer were social support (such as through self-help groups), a focus on the positive, and distraction. Avoidant coping strategies such as fantasizing, denial, and social withdrawal were associated with more emotional distress.

This group of cancer patients is involved in art therapy, which is believed to lower the stress level associated with having a serious illness.

The Immune System and Stress

◆ *What are the effects of stress on the immune system?*

Composed of an army of highly specialized cells and organs, the immune system works to identify and search out and destroy bacteria, viruses, fungi, parasites, and any other foreign matter that may enter the body. The key components of the immune system are white blood cells known as **lymphocytes,** which include B cells and T cells. *B cells* are so named because they are produced in the bone marrow. *T cells* derive their name from the thymus gland where they are produced. All cells foreign to the body, such as bacteria, viruses, and so on, are known as *antigens*. B cells produce proteins called *antibodies*, which are highly effective in destroying antigens that live in the bloodstream and in the fluid surrounding body tissues (Paul, 1993). For defeating harmful foreign invaders that have taken up residence inside the body's cells, however, T cells are critically important.

Psychoneuroimmunology is a field of study in which psychologists, biologists, and medical researchers combine their expertise to learn the effects of psychological factors—emotions, thinking, and behavior—on the immune system (Fleshner & Laudenslager, 2004). Researchers now know that the immune system is not just a means for fighting off foreign invaders. Rather, it is an incredibly complex, interconnected defense system working with the brain to keep the body healthy (Ader, 2000).

Psychological factors, emotions, and stress are all related to immune system functioning (Kiecolt-Glaser et al., 2002). The immune system exchanges information with the brain, and what goes on in the brain can apparently enhance or suppress the immune system. In one study, researchers gave volunteers nasal drops containing a cold virus. Within the next few days, symptoms of the viral infection rose sharply in some of the 151 women and 125 men who participated in the study, but less so or not at all in others. Participants with a rich social life in the form of frequent interactions with others—spouses, children, parents, co-workers, friends, and volunteer and religious groups—seemed to enjoy a powerful shield of protection against the virus infection. This pattern of protection held across age and racial groups, for both sexes, at all educational levels, and at every season of the year (Ader, 2000; Cohen et al., 1997).

Close social ties—to family, friends, and others—apparently have good effects on the immune system. Ill effects often come from stress. Periods of high stress are correlated with increased symptoms of many infectious diseases, including oral and genital herpes, mononucleosis, colds, and flu. Stress may also decrease the effectiveness of certain kinds of vaccines (Miller et al., 2004; Moynihan et al., 2004) and decrease levels of the immune system's B and T cells. Kiecolt-Glaser and others (1996) found that elderly men and women experiencing chronic stress as a result of years of caring for a spouse with Alzheimer's disease showed an impaired immune response to flu shots. Physicians have long observed that stress and anxiety can worsen autoimmune diseases. And "if fear can produce relapses [in autoimmune diseases], then even the fear of a relapse may become a self-fulfilling prophecy" (Steinman, 1993, p. 112). Stress is also associated with an increase in illness behaviors—reporting physical symptoms and seeking medical care (Cohen & Herbert, 1996; Cohen & Williamson, 1991).

Stress has the power to suppress the immune system long after the stressful experience is over. An experimental group of medical students who were enduring the stress of major exams was compared with a control group of medical students who were on vacation from classes and exams. When tested for the presence of disease-fighting antibodies, participants in the exam group, but not those in the control group, had a significant reduction in their antibody count because of the stress. The lowered antibody count was still present 14 days after the exams were over. At that point, the students were not even aware that they were still stressed and reported feeling no stress (Deinzer et al., 2000).

In addition to academic pressures, poor marital relationships and sleep deprivation have been linked to lowered immune response (Kiecolt-Glaser et al., 1987; Maier & Laudenslager, 1985). Several researchers have reported that severe, incapacitating depression is also related to lowered immune system activity (Herbert & Cohen, 1993). For several months after the death of a spouse, the widow or widower suffers weakened immune system function and is at a higher risk of mortality. Severe bereavement weakens

lymphocytes
◆ **lymphocytes**

The white blood cells—including B cells and T cells—that are the key components of the immune system.

◆ **psychoneuroimmunology**

(sye-ko-NEW-ro-IM-you-NOLL-oh-gee) A field in which psychologists, biologists, and medical researchers combine their expertise to study the effects of psychological factors on the immune system.

the immune system, increasing a person's chance of suffering from a long list of physical and mental ailments for as long as 2 years following a partner's death (Prigerson et al., 1997).

Personal Factors Reducing the Impact of Stress and Illness

There are several personal factors that seem to offer protection against the effects of stress and illness. People who are generally optimistic tend to cope more effectively with stress, which, in turn may reduce their risk of illness (Seligman, 1990). An important characteristic shared by optimists is that they generally expect good outcomes. Such positive expectations help make them more stress-resistant than pessimists, who tend to expect bad outcomes. Similarly, individuals who are optimistic seem to be able to find positives even in the darkest of circumstances (Rini et al., 2004). An especially lethal form of pessimism is hopelessness. A longitudinal study of a large number of Finnish men revealed that participants who reported feeling moderate to high hopelessness died from all causes at two to three times the rates of those reporting low or no hopelessness (Everson et al., 1996).

In addition, studying male executives with high levels of stress, psychologist Suzanne Kobasa (1979; Kobasa et al., 1982) found three psychological characteristics that distinguished those who remained healthy from those who had a high incidence of illness. The three qualities, which she referred to collectively as **hardiness,** are *commitment, control,* and *challenge.* Hardy individuals feel a strong sense of commitment to both their work and their personal life. They see themselves not as victims of whatever life brings, but as people who have control over consequences and outcomes. They act to solve their own problems, and they welcome challenges in life, viewing them not as threats but as opportunities for growth and improvement. Other researchers have found that the dimensions of hardiness are related to the subjective sense of well-being among the elderly (Smith et al., 2004).

Another personal factor that contributes to resistance to stress and illness is religious faith (Dedert et al., 2004; Miller & Thoresen, 2003). A meta-analysis of 42 separate studies combined data on some 126,000 individuals and revealed that religious involvement is positively associated with measures of physical health and lower rates of cancer, heart disease, and stroke (McCullough et al., 2000). Why is religious involvement linked to health? Researchers are currently examining a number of hypotheses (Powell et al., 2003). One proposal is that individuals who frequent religious services experience proportionately more positive emotions than those who do not attend.

Religious involvement may also provide people with a stronger form of social support than is available to those who are not religious (Seeman et al., 2003). **Social support** is support provided, usually in time of need, by a spouse, other family members, friends, neighbors, colleagues, support groups, or others. It can involve tangible aid, information, and advice, as well as emotional support. It can also be viewed as the feeling of being loved, valued, and cared for by those toward whom we feel a similar obligation.

Social support appears to have positive effects on the body's immune system as well as on the cardiovascular and endocrine systems (Moynihan et al., 2004; Holt-Lunstad et al., 2003; Miller et al., 2002; Uchino et al., 1996). Social support may help encourage health-promoting behaviors and reduce the impact of stress so that people are less likely to resort to unhealthy methods of coping, such as smoking or drinking. Further, social support has been shown to reduce depression and enhance self-esteem in individuals who suffer from chronic illnesses such as kidney disease (Symister & Friend, 2003). A large study of soldiers who had enlisted in the U.S. Army showed that a high level of social support from peers

◆ *What four personal factors are associated with health and resistance to stress?*

◆ **hardiness**
A combination of three psychological qualities—commitment, control, and challenge—shared by people who can handle high levels of stress and remain healthy.

◆ **social support**
Tangible and/or emotional support provided in time of need by family members, friends, and others; the feeling of being loved, valued, and cared for by those toward whom we feel a similar obligation.

A strong social support network can help a person recover faster from an illness.

was an essential ingredient in reducing stress (Bliese & Castro, 2000). People with social support recover more quickly from illnesses and lower their risk of death from specific diseases. Social support may even increase the probability of surviving a heart attack because it buffers the impact of stress on cardiovascular function (Steptoe, 2000).

Gender, Ethnicity, and Health

◆ *What are the relationships among gender, ethnicity, and health?*

The degree of wellness and the leading health risk factors are not the same for all Americans (CDC, 2003a). For example, researchers have found that women are more likely than men to seek medical care (Addis & Mahalik, 2003). Nevertheless, most medical research in the past, much of it funded by the U.S. government, rejected women as participants in favor of men (Matthews et al., 1997). One area where the failure to study women's health care needs has been particularly evident is in research examining mortality risk following open-heart surgery. Women are more likely to die after such surgery than are men. To date, studies have shown that the gender gap in surgical survival narrows with age, but researchers are still investigating why women's postsurgical mortality rate is higher than men's (Vaccarino et al., 2002). Women are also slighted in general health care and treatment (Rodin & Ickovics, 1990). Physicians are more likely to see women's health complaints as "emotional" in nature rather than due to physical causes (Council on Ethical and Judicial Affairs, American Medical Association [AMA], 1991).

There are health disparities across ethnic groups as well. For example, African American infants are at twice the risk of death within their first year of life as White American infants (CDC, 2005). Compared to White Americans, African Americans have higher rates of diabetes, arthritis, and, as you learned earlier in this chapter, high blood pressure (National Center for Health Statistics, 2004). African Americans are 40% more likely than White Americans to die of heart disease and 30% more likely to die of cancer. Even when African and White Americans of the same age suffer from similar illnesses, the mortality rate of African Americans is higher (CDC, 2003a). And the rate of AIDS is more than three times higher among African Americans than among White Americans.

Hispanic Americans account for more than 20% of new tuberculosis cases in the United States (CDC, 2003a). Hypertension and diabetes are also more prevalent among Hispanic Americans than among non-Hispanic White Americans, but heart problems are less prevalent (CDC, 2005). Rates of diabetes are also dramatically higher among Native Americans than for other groups (CDC, 2005). In addition, the infant mortality rate among Native Americans is two times higher than among Whites (CDC, 2005).

Asian Americans, who make up 3.6% of the U.S. population, are comparatively very healthy. However, there are wide disparities among subgroups. For example, Vietnamese women are five times more likely to suffer from cervical cancer than White women are (CDC, 2005). Similarly, the overall age-adjusted death rate for Asian American males is 40% lower than that for White American males, but their death rate from stroke is 8% higher. Of all U.S. ethnic groups, infant mortality is lowest for Chinese Americans, at 3 deaths per 1,000 births, compared with 7 per 1,000 for the overall population (National Center for Health Statistics, 2000).

Some of the variations in health across ethnic groups can be explained by socioeconomic status (Franks, et al., 2003). African Americans, Hispanic Americans, and Native Americans are more likely to be poor than their White counterparts. Health psychologist Edith Chen points out that poverty predisposes individuals—and particularly children—to poor health for a number of reasons (Chen, 2004). One important reason is lack of access to health care. Another is stress—individuals who live in poverty are exposed to more physical and psychological stress than others. Nevertheless, changes in health-related behaviors such as dietary choices and exercise benefit individuals who are poor just as much as they do more affluent people, so taking steps to ensure that individuals across all racial groups are aware of these behaviors are likely to bring about improvements in health for all concerned (Beets & Pitetti, 2004; CDC, 2005).

Edith Chen

Where would you expect to find a gifted 14-year-old with a keen interest in science? You might be surprised to learn that adolescents with these characteristics, such health psychology researcher Edith Chen, are often accepted as volunteeer research assistants in university labs.

That route is precisely how Chen got her start in research. While still in high school, she worked at the University of Miami doing research on the effects of neurotransmitters on muscle fiber contraction. The professor she assisted even let Chen present a paper at a scientific conference, as she puts it, "before [I] was old enough to appreciate (and be intimidated by) the reputation of established leaders in the field" ("Edith Chen," 2004, p. 707).

Ever the ambitious student, Chen began her undergraduate work at Harvard University intending to pursue a double major in chemistry and philosophy. However, when she found out that she would have to do a senior thesis integrating the two fields, she looked elsewhere for a major. She inadvertently discovered the interdisciplinary major known as history of science and was intrigued by the opportunity it offered to take a combination of science and liberal arts courses. When she took an abnormal psychology course in her junior year, the professor invited her to work on a research project examining memory bias and anxiety. The project sparked her interest in applying to graduate programs in clinical psy-

chology. Because Chen had taken only one psychology course, she thought she wouldn't be able to get in. Her professor encouraged her to take introductory psychology and a statistics class prior to applying to graduate school. With his help, she was admitted to the program at the University of California–Los Angeles.

At UCLA, Chen initially continued the work on memory bias and anxiety that had first interested her at Harvard. Eventually, UCLA's health psychology program caught her attention. She worked with faculty in the program to apply her interests in anxiety to issues related to pain management. Her dissertation dealt with helping children with cancer learn to reflect on their memories of treatment in ways that helped to minimize their anxiety responses to future treatments.

After receiving her Ph.D., Chen worked as a postdoctoral fellow at the University of Pittsburgh. While there, she began the research program examining correlations between immune system functioning and socioeconomic status that she continues to pursue today. Currently, Chen is investigating these correlations in children who suffer from asthma.

Chen's story is similar to that of many young researchers in that her career path has been strongly shaped by mentors. If her first psychology professor hadn't been willing to help her get into graduate school, Chen might have dismissed her interest in graduate work in psychology as beyond her reach as a nonpsychology major. If you have an interest in a particular field, seek out an experienced person who can advise you about the best strategy for pursuing a career in that area.

Lifestyle and Health

Think about your own health for a moment. What do you think is the greatest threat to your personal well-being and longevity? For most Americans, health enemy number one is their own habits—lack of exercise, too little sleep, alcohol or drug abuse, an unhealthy diet, and overeating. What can make someone change an unhealthy lifestyle? Perhaps vanity is the key. Researchers have found that people are more likely to adopt healthy behaviors if they believe behavioral change will make them look better or appear more youthful than if they simply receive information about the health benefits of the suggested change (Mahler et al., 2003). Still, there are some health-threatening behaviors that carry such grave risks that everyone ought to take them seriously. The most dangerous unhealthy behavior of all is smoking.

Smoking and Health

Smoking remains the foremost cause of preventable diseases and deaths in the United States (U.S. Department of Health and Human Services, 2000). That message appears to be taking root because the prevalence of smoking among American adults has been decreasing and is currently less than 25% (National

◆ *What is the most dangerous health-threatening behavior?*

Center for Health Statistics, 2004). Moreover, smoking is more likely to be viewed as a socially unacceptable behavior now than in the past (Chassin et al., 2003). But there are wide variations in smoking habits according to gender and ethnic group. The highest rates of smoking are found among Native American men (41%) and women (29%), while the lowest rates are reported for Asian American men (18%) and women (11%) (U.S. Department of Health and Human Services, 2000).

Even though the prevalence of smoking is decreasing, every year more than 1 million young Americans become regular smokers, and more than 400,000 American adults die from diseases related to tobacco use (U.S. Department of Health and Human Services, 2000). Smoking increases the risk for heart disease, lung cancer, other smoking-related cancers, and emphysema. It is now known that smoking suppresses the action of T cells in the lungs, increasing susceptibility to respiratory tract infections and tumors (McCue et al., 2000).

Other negative consequences from smoking include the widespread incidence of chronic bronchitis and other respiratory problems; the deaths and injuries from fires caused by smoking; and the low birth weight and retarded fetal development in babies born to smoking mothers. Furthermore, mothers who smoke during pregnancy tend to have babies who are at greater risk for anxiety and depression and are five times more likely to become smokers themselves (Cornelius et al., 2000). And millions of non-smokers engage in *passive smoking* by breathing smoke-filled air—with proven ill effects. Research indicates that nonsmokers who are regularly exposed to *second-hand smoke* have twice the risk of heart attack of those who are not exposed (Kawachi et al., 1997)

Because smoking is so addictive, smokers have great difficulty breaking the habit. Even so, 90% of ex-smokers quit smoking on their own (Novello, 1990). The average smoker makes five or six attempts to quit before finally succeeding (Sherman, 1994). Some aids, such as nicotine gum and the nicotine patch, help many people kick the habit. A meta-analysis involving 17 studies and more than 5,000 participants revealed that 22% of people who used the nicotine patch stopped smoking compared with only 9% of those who received a placebo. And 27% of those receiving the nicotine patch plus antismoking counseling or support remained smoke-free (Fiore, cited in Sherman, 1994). But even with the patch, quitting is difficult, because the patch only lessens withdrawal symptoms, which typically last 2 to 4 weeks (Hughes, 1992). Half of all relapses occur within the first 2 weeks after people quit, and relapses are most likely when people are experiencing stressful negative emotions or are using alcohol. It takes just one cigarette, sometimes only one puff, to cause a relapse.

Alcohol Abuse

◆ *What are some health risks of alcohol abuse?*

Do you use alcohol regularly? Many Americans do. Recall from Chapter 4 that *substance abuse* is defined as continued use of a substance that interferes with a person's major life roles at home, in school, at work, or elsewhere and contributes to legal difficulties or any psychological problems (American Psychiatric Association, 1994). Alcohol is perhaps the most frequently abused substance of all, and the health costs of alcohol abuse are staggering—in fatalities, medical bills, lost work, and family problems.

Approximately 10 million Americans are alcoholics (Neimark et al., 1994). Alcohol abuse is three times more prevalent in males than in females (American Psychiatric Association, 2000). And people who begin drinking before age 15 are four times more likely than those who begin later to become alcoholics (Grant & Dawson, 1998). For many, alcohol provides a method of coping with life stresses they feel otherwise powerless to control (Seeman & Seeman, 1992). As many as 80% of men and women who are alcoholics complain of episodes of depression. The presence of depression or other psychiatric problems decreases the likelihood that an alcoholic who enters treatment will recover (Green et al., 2004). A large study of almost 3,000 alcoholics concluded that some depressive episodes are independent of alcohol, whereas others are substance-induced (Schuckit et al., 1997).

Alcohol can damage virtually every organ in the body, but it is especially harmful to the liver and is the major cause of cirrhosis, which kills 26,000 people each year (Neimark et al., 1994). Other causes of death are more common in alcoholics than in nonalcoholics as well. One Norwegian longitudinal study involving more than 40,000 male participants found that the rate of death prior to age 60 was significantly higher among alcoholics than nonalcoholics (Rossow & Amundsen, 1997). Alcoholics are about three times as likely to die in automobile accidents or of heart disease as nonalcoholics, and they have twice the rate of deaths from cancer.

Shrinkage in the cerebral cortex of alcoholics has been found by researchers using MRI scans (Jernigan et al., 1991). CT scans also show brain shrinkage in a high percentage of alcoholics, even in those who are young and in those who show normal cognitive functioning (Lishman, 1990). Moreover, heavy drinking can cause cognitive impairment that continues for several months after the drinking stops (Sullivan et al., 2002). The only good news in recent studies is that some of the effects of alcohol on the brain seem to be partially reversible with prolonged abstinence.

Since the late 1950s, the American Medical Association has maintained that alcoholism is a disease, and once an alcoholic, always an alcoholic. According to this view, even a small amount of alcohol can cause an irresistible craving for more, leading alcoholics to lose control of their drinking (Jellinek, 1960). Thus, total abstinence is seen as the only acceptable and effective method of treatment. Alcoholics Anonymous (AA) also endorses both the disease concept and the total abstinence approach to treatment. And there is a drug that may make abstinence somewhat easier. German researchers report that the drug acamprosate helps prevent relapse in recovering alcoholics (Sass et al., 1996).

Some studies suggest a genetic influence on alcoholism and lend support to the disease model. For example, neuroscientist Henri Begleiter and his colleagues have accumulated a large body of evidence suggesting that the brains of alcoholics respond differently to visual and auditory stimuli than those of nonalcoholics (Hada et al., 2000, 2001; Prabhu et al., 2001). Further, many relatives of alcoholics, even children and adults who have never consumed any alcohol in their lives, display the same types of response patterns (Zhang et al., 2001). The relatives of alcoholics who do display these patterns are more likely to become alcoholics themselves or to suffer from other types of addictions (Anokhin et al., 2000; Beirut et al., 1998). Consequently, Begleiter has suggested that the brain-imaging techniques he uses in his research may someday be used to determine which relatives of alcoholics are genetically predisposed to addiction (Porjesz et al., 1998).

Sexually Transmitted Diseases

What is the most common infectious disease in the United States? You might be surprised to learn that it is *chlamydia*, a sexually transmitted disease (CDC, 2003b). **Sexually transmitted diseases (STDs)** are infections spread primarily through sexual contact. Each year, approximately 15 million Americans contract an STD. The incidence of many STDs has increased dramatically over the past 30 years or so. This trend can be partly explained by more permissive attitudes toward sex and increased sexual activity among young people, some of whom have had several sexual partners by the time they graduate from high school (look back at Figure 8.4 on page 259). Another factor is the greater use of nonbarrier methods of contraception, such as the birth control pill, which do not prevent the spread of STDs. Barrier methods, such as condoms and vaginal spermicide, provide some protection against STDs.

Chlamydia is one of many **bacterial STDs,** diseases that can be cured by antibiotics. It can be transmitted through many kinds of physical contact involving the genitals as well as actual intercourse (CDC, 2003b). Women are about three times as likely as men to suffer from chlamydia. The prevalence of another bacterial STD, *gonorrhea*, has declined considerably in recent years, but the strains that exist today are far more resistant to antibiotics than those that existed decades ago (CDC, 2003b). One of the long-term effects of both chlamydia and gonorrhea is *pelvic inflammatory disease*, an infection of the female reproductive tract that can cause infertility.

◆ What is the difference between bacterial and viral STD's?

◆ **sexually transmitted diseases**

Infections that are spread primarily through intimate sexual contact.

◆ **bacterial STDs**

Sexually transmitted diseases that are caused by bacteria and can be treated with antibiotics.

◆ **viral STDs**

Sexually transmitted diseases that are caused by viruses and are considered to be incurable.

◆ **acquired immune deficiency syndrome (AIDS)**

A devastating and incurable illness that is caused by infection with the human immunodeficiency virus (HIV) and progressively weakens the body's immune system, leaving the person vulnerable to opportunistic infections that usually cause death.

◆ **human immunodeficiency virus (HIV)**

The virus that causes AIDS.

Another bacterial STD is *syphilis*, which can lead to serious mental disorders and death if it is not treated in the early stages of infection. At one time, syphilis had been almost completely eradicated. However, in 2002, about 7,000 cases were reported to the Centers for Disease Control and Prevention (CDC, 2003b). Most of these cases involved homosexual males who live in urban areas (CDC, 2003b). Educating such men about the dangers of syphilis and measures that may be taken to prevent its transmission has become a major focus of public health officials in recent years.

Unlike STDs caused by bacteria, **viral STDs** cannot be treated with antibiotics and are considered to be incurable. One such disease is *genital herpes*, a disease that can be acquired through either intercourse or oral sex. The Centers for Disease Control and Prevention reports that 20% of the adult population in the United States is infected with herpes (CDC, 2001a). Outbreaks of the disease, which include the development of painful blisters on the genitals, occur periodically in most people who carry the virus.

A more serious viral STD is *genital warts* caused by infection with *human papillomavirus (HPV)*. The primary symptom of the disease, the presence of growths on the genitals, is not its most serious effect, however. HPV is strongly associated with cervical cancer (CDC, 2003b). Studies indicate that, in the United States, 25% of women in their twenties, and 10% of women older than the age 30 are infected with HPV (Stone et al., 2002).

The most feared STD is **acquired immune deficiency syndrome (AIDS),** caused by infection with the **human immunodeficiency virus (HIV).** The virus attacks the T cells, gradually but relentlessly weakening the immune system until it is essentially nonfunctional. Although the first case was diagnosed in this country in 1981, there is still no cure for AIDS. However, efforts to develop a way to immunize people against HIV have yielded several potential vaccines, at least one of which is currently being tested on humans (Beyrer, 2003). By the end of 2001, 816,249 cases of AIDS and 467,910 deaths from AIDS had been reported to the Centers for Disease Control and Prevention (2002). Worldwide, in 2001, 3 million people died from AIDS and 40 million people were living with HIV infection (CDC, 2002). Concerns about the HIV-AIDS crisis has been heightened by the recent discovery of a strain of the virus that leads to full-blown AIDS in as short a period as a few months (Lombardi, 2005). Test your knowledge about AIDS in *Try It 10.3*.

Try It 10.3

AIDS Quiz

Answer true or false for each statement.

1. AIDS is a single disease. (true/false)

2. AIDS symptoms vary widely from country to country, and even from risk group to risk group. (true/false)

3. Those at greatest risk for getting AIDS are people who have sex without using condoms, drug users who share needles, and infants born to AIDS-infected mothers. (true/false)

4. AIDS is one of the most highly contagious diseases. (true/false)

5. One way to avoid contracting AIDS is to use an oil-based lubricant with a condom. (true/false)

Answers:

1. False: AIDS is not a single disease. Rather, a severely impaired immune system leaves a person with AIDS highly susceptible to a whole host of infections and diseases.

2. True: In the United States and Europe, AIDS sufferers may develop Kaposi's sarcoma (a rare form of skin cancer), pneumonia, and tuberculosis. In Africa, people with AIDS usually waste away with fever, diarrhea, and symptoms caused by tuberculosis.

3. True: Those groups are at greatest risk. Screening of blood donors and testing of donated blood have greatly reduced the risk of contracting AIDS through blood transfusions today,

women make up the fastest-growing group of infected people worldwide, as AIDS spreads among heterosexuals, especially in Africa.

4. False: AIDS is not among the most highly infectious diseases. You cannot get AIDS from kissing, shaking hands, or using objects handled by people who have AIDS.

5. False: Do not use oil-based lubricants, which can eat through condoms. Latex condoms with an effective spermicide are safer. Learn the sexual history of any potential partner, including HIV test results. Don't have sex with prostitutes.

HIV attacks the immune system, leaving it severely impaired and virtually unable to function. The diagnosis of AIDS is made when the immune system is so damaged that victims develop rare forms of cancer or pneumonia or other so-called opportunistic infections. The average time from infection with HIV to advanced AIDS is about 10 years, but the time may range from 2 years to as long as 15 years or more (Nowak & McMichael, 1995). The disease progresses faster in smokers, in the very young, in people older than 50, and, apparently, in women. AIDS also progresses faster in those who are repeatedly exposed to the virus and in those who were infected by someone in an advanced stage of the disease.

Researchers believe that HIV is transmitted primarily through the exchange of blood, semen, or vaginal secretions during sexual contact or when IV (intravenous) drug users share contaminated needles or syringes. Figure 10.6 illustrates the proportion of AIDS cases attributable to each means of transmitting the disease. The rate of AIDS among gay men is higher than in other groups because gay men are likely to have anal intercourse. Anal intercourse is more dangerous than coitus because rectal tissue often tears during penetration, allowing HIV ready entry into the bloodstream.

It is a mistake to view AIDS as a disease confined to gay men, however. About 25% of the AIDS cases reported in the United States in 2001 were females, 40% of whom contracted it through heterosexual contact and 20% through IV drug abuse (CDC, 2002). In Africa, where AIDS is currently epidemic and is believed to have originated, it strikes men and women about equally, and heterosexual activity is believed to be the primary means of transmission (Quinn, 2002). AIDS is transmitted 12 times more easily from infected men to women than vice versa (Padian et al., 1991). AIDS may also be transmitted from mother to child during pregnancy or breast-feeding (Prince, 1998).

What are the psychological effects on people who struggle to cope with this fearsome disease? The reaction to the news that one is HIV-positive is frequently shock, bewilderment, confusion, or disbelief. Stress reactions to the news are typically so common and so acute that experts strongly recommend pretest counseling so that those who do test positive may know in advance what to expect (Maj, 1990). Another common reaction is anger—at past or present sexual partners, family members, health care professionals, or society in general. Often, a person's response includes guilt, a sense that one is being punished for homosexuality or drug abuse. Other people exhibit denial, ignoring medical advice and continuing to act as if nothing has changed in their lives. Then, of course, there is fear—of death; of mental and physical deterioration; of rejection by friends, family, and co-workers; of sexual rejection; of abandonment. Experiencing emotional swings ranging from shock to anger to guilt to fear can lead to serious clinical depression and apathy (Tate et al., 2003). Once apathy sets in, HIV-positive patients may become less likely to comply with treatment (Dorz et al., 2003).

There are only two foolproof ways to protect oneself from becoming infected with an STD through intimate sexual contact. The first is obvious: Abstain from sexual contact. The second is to have a mutually faithful (monogamous) relationship with a partner who is free of infection. Any other course of action will place a person at risk. Much has been written in recent decades about the joy of sex. It is true that the pleasures sex brings to life are many, but fear of STDs may interfere with those pleasures. Thus, safe sex practices are essential—not only for health, but also for the enjoyment of sex.

The producers of *Sesame Street* introduced an HIV-positive Muppet to the show's cast to help educate young viewers about the plight of children living with the infection.

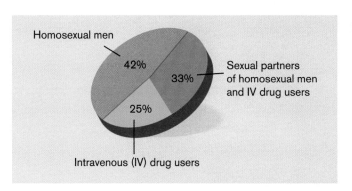

FIGURE 10.6

How HIV Has Been Transmitted in AIDS Cases in the United States
Source: CDC (2001b).

Homosexual men 42%

Sexual partners of homosexual men and IV drug users 33%

Intravenous (IV) drug users 25%

Discharges, blisters, sores, rashes, warts, odors, or any other unusual symptoms are warning signs of STDs. Yet, many people who have no visible symptoms carry STDs. What you don't know can hurt you. People who choose to practice risky sex cannot be safe but can reduce the risks by using a latex condom along with a spermicide such as an intravaginal contraceptive foam, jelly, or cream.

The potential for risky sexual behavior is increased when people are under the influence of alcohol and other drugs (Leigh & Stall, 1993). People put themselves at risk for AIDS when they have multiple sex partners or have sex with prostitutes, IV drug users, or anyone carrying HIV (Bellis et al., 2002). Anyone who fears that he or she might have been exposed to an STD should go to a doctor or clinic to be tested. Many STDs are easily treated, and serious complications can be avoided if the treatment is prompt. Initiating a discussion of sexual history with a potential partner can be stressful but will enable you to make informed decisions about your behavior. And, anyone who has an STD should discuss it with his or her partner so that the partner can be checked and treated.

Exercise

◆ *What are some benefits of regular aerobic exercise?*

How much exercise do you get? Many studies show that regular exercise pays rich dividends in the form of physical and mental fitness. However, many people still express reluctance to exercise. More than 30% of Americans get no exercise at all (National Center for Health Statistics, 2004). Some simply prefer not to be physically active; others blame such factors as the cost of joining a health club or even the unpredictability of the weather for their lack of physical activity (Salmon et al., 2003). Such individuals are missing out on one of the simplest and most effective ways of enhancing one's health.

Aerobic exercise (such as running, swimming, brisk walking, bicycling, rowing, and jumping rope) is exercise that uses the large muscle groups in continuous, repetitive action and increases oxygen intake and breathing and heart rates. To improve cardiovascular fitness and endurance and to lessen the risk of heart attack, an individual should perform aerobic exercise regularly—three or four times a week for 20–30 minutes, with additional 5–10-minute warm-up and cool-down periods (Alpert et al., 1990; Shepard, 1986). Less than 20 minutes of aerobic exercise three times a week has "no measurable effect on the heart," and more than 3 hours per week "is not known to reduce cardiovascular risk any further" (Simon, 1988, p. 3). However, individuals who engage in more than 3 hours of aerobic activity each week are more successful at losing excess weight and keeping it off than are those who exercise less (Votruba et al., 2000).

In case you are not yet convinced, consider the following benefits of exercise (Fiatarone et al., 1988):

■ Increases the efficiency of the heart, enabling it to pump more blood with each beat, and reduces the resting pulse rate and improves circulation

◆ **aerobic exercise**
(ah-RO-bik) Exercise that uses the large muscle groups in continuous, repetitive action and increases oxygen intake and breathing and heart rates.

Regular aerobic exercise improves cardiovascular fitness in people of all ages.

- Raises levels of HDL (the good blood cholesterol), which (1) helps rid the body of LDL (the bad blood cholesterol) and (2) removes plaque buildup on artery walls
- Burns up extra calories, enabling you to lose weight or maintain your weight
- Makes bones denser and stronger, helping to prevent osteoporosis in women
- Moderates the effects of stress
- Gives you more energy and increases your resistance to fatigue
- Benefits the immune system by increasing natural killer cell activity

Alternative Medicine

Do you take vitamins or herbal supplements in hopes of positively influencing your health? According to surveys, Americans spend billions of dollars each year on unconventional treatments—herbs, massage, self-help groups, megavitamins, folk remedies, and homeopathy—for a variety of illnesses and conditions. In one such survey, the National Science Foundation (NSF, 2002) found that 88% of Americans believe that there are valid ways of preventing and curing illnesses that are not recognized by the medical profession. Moreover, a growing number of people are turning to alternative health care providers for treatment of their mental health problems (Simon et al., 2004). And college-educated Americans are more likely to use unconventional treatments than those who have less education.

The National Science Foundation (2002) defines **alternative medicine** as any treatment or therapy that has not been scientifically demonstrated to be effective. Even a simple practice such as taking vitamins sometimes falls into this category. For instance, *scurvy* (a condition whose symptoms include bleeding gums and easy bruising) has been scientifically determined to be caused by Vitamin C deficiency. So, taking Vitamin C to prevent or cure scurvy is not considered an alternative therapy. However, if you take Vitamin C to protect yourself against the common cold, you are using alternative medicine because Vitamin C has not been scientifically proven to prevent colds.

If alternative treatments lack scientific support, why do so many people believe in them? One possibility is that it is easier to take a vitamin than to make a lifestyle change. But it is also true that people who do their own research about alternative therapies may happen upon effective treatments of which their physicians are unaware. However, most patients who use alternative treatments do not inform their physicians about them. Health professionals cite this tendency toward secrecy as a major risk factor in the use of alternative medicine (Yale–New Haven Hospital, 2003). They point out that many therapies, especially those that involve food supplements, have pharmacological effects that can interfere with treatments prescribed by physicians. Consequently, individuals who use alternative treatments should tell their physicians about them. While doctors may be skeptical about the utility of the alternative treatments, they need to have this information about their patients to practice conventional medicine effectively. Moreover, faith in an alternative treatment may cause an individual to delay seeking necessary conventional medical treatment.

Although it is true that some alternative therapies may be helpful in both preventing and treating illness, most health professionals agree that lifestyle changes bring greater health benefits than do any methods of alternative medicine. Unfortunately, many people resist making lifestyle changes because they see them as taking too long to be effective or being too difficult to carry out. A smoker may think, "I've been smoking so long, quitting now won't make a difference." An obese person may be so overwhelmed by the amount of weight loss necessary to attain an ideal weight that she or he gives up. However, Table 10.2 (on page 332) shows that the benefits of various lifestyle changes, some of which are fairly easy to achieve, can be well worth the effort. And remember, to be healthier, you don't have to make *all* of the changes. You might consider starting with just one. Even if you never make another change, you are likely to live longer and be healthier than you would have otherwise.

◆ *What are the benefits and risks associated with alternative medicine?*

◆ **alternative medicine**
Any treatment or therapy that has not been scientifically demonstrated to be effective.

TABLE 10.2 ◆ Benefits of Lifestyle Changes

LIFESTYLE CHANGE	BENEFITS
If overweight, lose just 10 pounds.	34% reduction in triglyceride levels; 16% decrease in total cholesterol; 18% increase in HDL ("good" cholesterol); significant reduction in blood pressure; decreased risk of diabetes, sleep apnea, and osteoarthritis (Still, 2001).
Add 20 to 30 grams of fiber to your diet each day.	Improved bowel function; reduced risk of colon cancer and other digestive system diseases; decrease in total cholesterol; reduced blood pressure; improved insulin function in both diabetics and nondiabetics (HCF, 2003).
Engage in moderate physical activity every day (e.g., walk up and down stairs for 15 minutes; spend 30 minutes washing a car).	Reduced feelings of anxiety and sadness; increased bone density; reduced risk of diabetes, heart disease, high blood pressure, and many other life-shortening diseases (CDC, 1999).
Stop smoking at any age, after any number of years of smoking.	*Immediate:* improved circulation; reduced blood level of carbon monoxide; stabilization of pulse rate and blood pressure; improved sense of smell and taste; improved lung function and endurance; reduced risk of lung infections such as pneumonia and bronchitis.
	Long-term: reduced risk of lung cancer (declines substantially with each year of abstinence); decreased risk of other smoking-related illnesses such as emphysema and heart disease; decreased risk of cancer recurrence in those who have been treated for some form of cancer (National Cancer Institute, 2000).

Looking Back   At the beginning of the chapter, you read about the remarkable recovery of Lance Armstrong. What were the keys to his success? To put it succinctly, Armstrong took control of those things that he realistically could control, such as what he ate and how much exercise he got, and sought the best medical treatment available. At the same time, he approached the challenges he faced with an optimistic outlook. In doing so, he provided others in his circumstances with a superb role model.

Apply It 10.1   Interpreting Health Information on the Internet

An increasing number of people are turning to the Internet for information about their health. One study of 188 women with breast cancer found that about half of them used the Internet to find out more about the disease (Fogel et al., 2002). Surveys of older adults and HIV-positive individuals have shown that using the Internet helps them gain a sense of control over their health care decisions (Benotsch et al., 2004; Kalichman et al., 2003; McMellon &

Schiffman, 2002). Chat rooms devoted to specific diseases may represent an important source of social support for patients, especially those suffering from rare disorders (Kummervold et al., 2002). And using e-mail to coach and encourage patients in the management of chronic diseases such as diabetes has proven to be effective both for patients' health and for health care professionals' time management (McKay et al., 2002).

But how reliable is the information available on the Internet? In a large-scale study of health-related websites sponsored by the American Medical Association, researchers found that the quality of information varied widely from one site to another (Eysenbach et al., 2002). A study of Internet-based advice for managing children's fever sponsored by the British Medical Association found that most websites contained erroneous information. Moreover, in a follow-up

Apply It 10.1

study done 4 years later, the researchers found that about half of the sites were no longer available; those that remained showed little improvement in the quality of information.

Despite these difficulties, physicians' organizations acknowledge the potential value of the Internet in helping patients learn about and manage their own health. And because so many older adults are using the Internet to learn about health issues, the American Association of Retired Persons (2002) has published a list of points to keep in mind when surfing the Web for health information and advice:

- *Remember that there are no rules governing what is published on the Internet.* Unlike scientific journal articles, which are usually written and reviewed by experts in the field, Internet articles can be posted by anyone, without review of any kind. Without expert knowledge, it is extremely difficult to tell whether the information and advice these articles contain are valid.

- *Consider the source.* Generally, websites sponsored by medical schools, government agencies, and public health organizations are reliable. Others, especially those promoting a health-related product, should be considered suspect.

- *Get a second opinion.* Ask your health care provider about Internet-based information, or read what's available from several different sources on the topic.

- *Examine references.* Sites that refer to credible sources (e.g., books, other websites) that you can find on the Internet or in a library or bookstore are probably more reliable than sites that offer no references to support their advice.

- *How current is the information?* Health-related information changes frequently. Be certain that you are reading the most current findings and recommendations.

- *Is it too good to be true?* As in all areas of life, if something sounds too good to be true (e.g., a vitamin that cures cancer), it probably is. Try to find experimental, placebo-controlled studies that support any claims.

Using these guidelines, you can become a better consumer of Internet-based health information.

Chapter 10 Summary

Sources of Stress p. 189

◆ **What was the Social Readjustment Rating Scale designed to reveal?** p. 189

The SRRS assesses stress in terms of life events, positive or negative, that necessitate change and adaptation. Holmes and Rahe found a relationship between degree of life stress (as measured on the scale) and major health problems.

◆ **What roles do hassles and uplifts play in the stress of life, according to Lazarus?** p. 191

According to Lazarus, daily hassles typically cause more stress than major life changes. Positive experiences in life—or uplifts—can neutralize the effects of many of the hassles, however.

◆ **How do approach-approach, avoidance-avoidance, and approach-avoidance conflicts differ?** p. 192

In an approach-approach conflict, a person must decide between equally desirable alternatives. In an avoidance-avoidance conflict, the choice is between two undesirable alternatives. In an approach-avoidance conflict, a person is both drawn to and repelled by a single choice.

◆ **How do the unpredictability and lack of control over a stressor affect its impact?** p. 192

Stressors that are unpredictable and uncontrollable have greater impact than those that are predictable and controllable.

◆ **For people to function effectively and find satisfaction on the job, what nine variables should fall within their comfort zone?** p. 192

The nine variables that should fall within a worker's comfort zone are workload, clarity of job description and evaluation criteria, physical variables, job status, accountability, task variety, human contact, physical challenge, and mental challenge.

◆ **How do people typically react to catastrophic events?** p. 194

Most people cope quite well with catastrophic events. However, some people develop posttraumatic stress disorder (PTSD), a prolonged, severe stress reaction, often characterized by flashbacks, nightmares, or intrusive memories of the traumatic event.

◆ **How might historical racism affect the health of African Americans?** p. 195

Some researchers believe that African Americans have higher levels of high blood pressure than members of other groups because of stress due to historical racism. African Americans who express high levels of concern about racism display larger cardiovascular responses to experimentally induced stressors than do their peers who express lower levels of concern.

◆ Responding to Stress p. 196

◆ What is the general adaptation syndrome? p. 196

The general adaptation syndrome (GAS) proposed by Selye is the predictable sequence of reactions that organisms show in response to stressors. It consists of the alarm stage, the resistance stage, and the exhaustion stage.

◆ What are the roles of primary and secondary appraisals when a person is confronted with a potentially stressful event? p. 196

Lazarus maintains that, when confronted with a potentially stressful event, a person engages in a cognitive appraisal process consisting of (1) a primary appraisal, to evaluate the relevance of the situation to one's well-being (whether it will be positive, irrelevant, or negative), and (2) a secondary appraisal, to evaluate one's resources and determine how to cope with the stressor.

◆ What is the difference between problem-focused and emotion-focused coping? p. 197

Problem-focused coping is a direct response, aimed at reducing, modifying, or eliminating the source of stress; emotion-focused coping involves reappraising a stressor in an effort to reduce its emotional impact.

◆ Health and Illness p. 198

◆ How do the biomedical and biopsychosocial models differ in their approaches to health and illness? p. 198

The biomedical model focuses on illness rather than on health and explains illness in terms of biological factors. The biopsychosocial model focuses on health as well as on illness and holds that both are determined by a combination of biological, psychological, and social factors.

◆ What are the Type A and Type B behavior patterns? p. 199

The Type A behavior pattern, often cited as a risk factor for coronary heart disease, is characterized by a sense of time urgency, impatience, excessive competitive drive, hostility, and easily aroused anger. The Type B behavior pattern is characterized by a relaxed, easy-going approach to life, without the time urgency, impatience, and hostility of the Type A pattern.

◆ How do psychological factors influence cancer patients' quality of life? p. 201

Cancer patients can improve their quality of life by maintaining an optimistic outlook, accepting the reality of their situation, and maintaining a sense of humor. Social support and psychotherapy can help them do so.

◆ What are the effects of stress on the immune system? p. 202

Stress has been associated with lowered immune response and with increased symptoms of many infectious diseases.

◆ What four personal factors are associated with health and resistance to stress? p. 203

Personal factors related to health and resistance to stress are optimism, hardiness, religious involvement, and social support.

◆ What are the relationships among gender, ethnicity, and health? p. 204

Women are more likely than men to seek medical care, but women's needs have often been ignored by medical researchers and health care providers. African Americans, Hispanic Americans, and Native Americans have higher rates of many diseases than do White Americans. Asian Americans are comparatively very healthy.

◆ Lifestyle and Health p. 205

◆ What is the most dangerous health-threatening behavior? p. 205

Smoking is considered the most dangerous health-related behavior because it is directly related to more than 400,000 deaths each year, including deaths from heart disease, lung cancer, respiratory diseases, and stroke.

◆ What are some health risks of alcohol abuse? p. 206

Alcohol abuse damages virtually every organ in the body, including the liver, stomach, skeletal muscles, heart, and brain. Alcoholics are three times as likely to die in motor vehicle accidents as nonalcoholics.

◆ What is the difference between bacterial and viral STDs? p. 207

Bacterial STDs can be treated and, in most cases, cured with antibiotics. Viral STDs are considered to be incurable.

◆ What are some benefits of regular aerobic exercise? p. 210

Regular aerobic exercise reduces the risk of cardiovascular disease, increases muscular strength, moderates the effects of stress, makes bones denser and stronger, and helps one maintain a desirable weight.

◆ What are the benefits and risks associated with alternative medicine? p. 211

Alternative medicine, or the use of any treatment that has not been proven scientifically to be effective, can benefit individuals who find alternative treatments that are effective. However, many patients increase their risk of poor outcomes by not telling their physicians about their use of alternative treatments. And some people delay seeking necessary conventional medical treatment because they believe that alternative approaches will work.

acquired immune deficiency
  syndrome (AIDS), p. 208
aerobic exercise, p. 210
alarm stage, p. 196
alternative medicine, p. 211
approach-approach conflict, p. 192
approach-avoidance conflict, p. 192
avoidance-avoidance conflict, p. 192
bacterial STDs, p. 207
biomedical model, p. 198
biopsychosocial model, p. 198
coping, p. 197
emotion-focused coping, p. 197
exhaustion stage, p. 196

fight-or-flight response, p. 189
general adaptation syndrome (GAS),
  p. 196
hardiness, p. 203
hassles, p. 191
health psychology, p. 198
human immunodeficiency virus
  (HIV), p. 208
lymphocytes, p. 202
posttraumatic stress disorder (PTSD)
  p. 194
primary appraisal, p. 196
problem-focused coping, p. 197
psychoneuroimmunology, p. 202

resistance stage, p. 196
secondary appraisal, p. 197
sexually transmitted diseases
  (STDs), p. 207
Social Readjustment Rating Scale
  (SRRS), p. 189
social support, p. 203
stress, p. 189
stressor, p. 189
Type A behavior pattern, p. 200
Type B behavior pattern, p. 200
uplifts, p. 191
viral STDs, p. 208

Study Guide 10

Answers to all the Study Guide questions are provided at the end of the book.

◆ SECTION ONE: Chapter Review

Sources of Stress (pp. 189–195)

1. On the Social Readjustment Rating Scale, only negative life changes are considered stressful. (true/false)

2. The Social Readjustment Rating Scale takes account of the individual's perceptions of the stressfulness of the life change in assigning stress points. (true/false)

3. According to Lazarus, hassles typically account for more life stress than major life changes. (true/false)

4. Lazarus's approach to measuring hassles and uplifts considers individual perceptions of stressful events. (true/false)

5. Travis cannot decide whether to go out or stay home and study for his test. What kind of conflict does he have?
   a. approach-approach
   b. avoidance-avoidance
   c. approach-avoidance
   d. ambivalence-ambivalence

6. What factor or factors increase stress, according to research on the topic?
   a. predictability of the stressor
   b. unpredictability of the stressor
   c. predictability of and control over the stressor
   d. unpredictability of and lack of control over the stressor

7. Sources of workplace stress for women include
   a. sexual harassment.
   b. discrimination.
   c. balancing family and work demands.
   d. all of the above.

8. Victims of catastrophic events usually panic. (true/false)

9. Posttraumatic stress disorder is a prolonged and severe stress reaction that results when a number of common sources of stress occur simultaneously. (true/false)

10. The group that has received the most attention from researchers interested in the association between stress and racism is
   a. Native Americans.
   b. Hispanic Americans.
   c. Asian Americans.
   d. African Americans.

Responding to Stress (pp. 196–198)

11. The stage of the general adaptation syndrome marked by intense physiological efforts to adapt to the stressor is the (alarm, resistance) stage.

12. Susceptibility to illness increases during the (alarm, exhaustion) stage of the general adaptation syndrome.

13. Selye focused on the (psychological, physiological) aspects of stress; Lazarus focused on the (psychological, physiological) aspects of stress.

14. During secondary appraisal, a person
    a. evaluates his or her coping resources and considers options for dealing with the stressor.
    b. determines whether an event is positive, neutral, or negative.
    c. determines whether an event involves loss, threat, or challenge.
    d. determines whether an event causes physiological or psychological stress.

15. Coping aimed at reducing, modifying, or eliminating a source of stress is called (emotion-focused, problem-focused) coping; that aimed at reducing an emotional reaction to stress is called (emotion-focused, problem-focused) coping.

16. People typically use a combination of problem-focused and emotion-focused coping when dealing with a stressful situation. (true/false)

Health and Illness (pp. 198–205)

17. The biomedical model focuses on _____; the biopsychosocial model focuses on _____.
    a. illness; illness
    b. health and illness; illness
    c. illness; health and illness
    d. health and illness; health and illness

18. Most research has pursued the connection between the Type A behavior pattern and
    a. cancer.   c. stroke.
    b. coronary heart disease.   d. ulcers.

19. Recent research suggests that the most toxic component of the Type A behavior pattern is
    a. hostility.   c. a sense of time urgency.
    b. impatience.   d. perfectionism.

20. Viral STDs are those that can be effectively treated with antibiotics. (true/false)

21. HIV eventually causes a breakdown in the _____ system.
    a. circulatory   c. immune
    b. vascular   d. respiratory

22. The incidence of AIDS in the United States is highest among
    a. homosexuals and IV drug users.
    b. homosexuals and hemophiliacs.
    c. homosexuals and bisexuals.
    d. heterosexuals, IV drug users, and hemophiliacs.

23. Lowered immune response has been associated with
    a. stress.   c. stress and depression.
    b. depression.   d. neither stress nor depression.

24. Some research suggests that optimists are more stress-resistant than pessimists. (true/false)

25. Which of the following is not a dimension of psychological hardiness?
    a. a feeling that adverse circumstances can be controlled and changed
    b. a sense of commitment and deep involvement in personal goals
    c. a tendency to look on change as a challenge rather than a threat
    d. close, supportive relationships with family and friends

26. Social support tends to reduce stress but is unrelated to health outcomes. (true/false)

Lifestyle and Health (pp. 205–212)

27. Which is the most important factor leading to disease and death?
    a. unhealthy lifestyle
    b. a poor health care system
    c. environmental hazards
    d. genetic disorders

28. Which health-compromising behavior is responsible for the most deaths?
    a. overeating   c. lack of exercise
    b. smoking   d. excessive alcohol use

29. (Alcohol, Smoking) damages virtually every organ in the body.

30. To improve cardiovascular fitness, aerobic exercise should be done
    a. 15 minutes daily.
    b. 1 hour daily.
    c. 20 to 30 minutes daily.
    d. 20 to 30 minutes three or four times a week.

31. Alternative health treatments have proven to be just as effective as traditional approaches to illness. (true/false)

List at least two forces for each of the following:

1. Biological forces favoring health and wellness
2. Biological forces working against health and wellness
3. Psychological forces favoring health and wellness
4. Psychological forces working against health and wellness
5. Social forces favoring health and wellness
6. Social forces working against health and wellness

◆ SECTION THREE: Fill In the Blank

1. Medicine has been dominated by the _____ model, which focuses on illness rather than on health, whereas the _____ model asserts that both health and illness are determined by a combination of biological, psychological, and social factors.

2. The field of psychology that is concerned with the psychological factors that contribute to health, illness, and recovery is known as _____ _____.

3. The fight-or-flight response is controlled by the _____ and the endocrine glands.

4. The first stage of the general adaptation syndrome is the _____ stage.

5. The stage of the general adaptation syndrome during which the adrenal glands release hormones to help the body resist stressors is called the _____ stage.

6. Lazarus's theory is considered a _____ theory of stress and coping.

7. Noelle knew that her upcoming job interview would be difficult, so she tried to anticipate the kinds of questions she would be asked and practiced the best possible responses. Noelle was practicing _____ coping.

8. The most feared disease related to the immune system is _____.

9. The primary means of transmission of HIV is through sexual contact between _____.

10. Daily _____ are the "irritating, frustrating, distressing demands and troubled relationships that plague us day in and day out."

11. Tiffany is a psychologist who works with biologists and medical researchers to determine the effects of psychological factors on the immune system. Tiffany works in the field of _____.

12. People with the Type _____ behavior pattern have a strong sense of time urgency and are impatient, excessively competitive, hostile, and easily angered.

13. The effects of alcohol on _____ may continue for several months after an alcoholic stops drinking.

14. _____ appraisal is an evaluation of the significance of a potentially stressful event according to how it will affect one's well-being—whether it is perceived as irrelevant or as involving harm, loss, threat, or challenge.

15. African Americans may have a greater incidence of _____ _____ _____ than White Americans because of the stress associated with historical racism.

16. A _____ is any event capable of producing physical or emotional stress.

17. Cole wants to get a flu shot, but he is also very afraid of needles. He is faced with an _____-_____ conflict.

◆ SECTION FOUR: Comprehensive Practice Test

1. Stress consists of the threats and problems we encounter in life. (true/false)

2. Hans Selye developed the
   a. diathesis stress model.
   b. general adaptation syndrome model.
   c. cognitive stress model.
   d. conversion reaction model.

3. The fight-or-flight response is seen in the _____ stage of the general adaptation syndrome.
   a. alarm
   c. resistance
   b. exhaustion
   d. arousal

4. Lack of exercise, poor diet, and disease and injury are considered to be _____ forces that work against health and wellness.
   a. environmental
   c. biological
   b. psychological
   d. social

5. Charlotte has been looking for new bedroom furniture and has found two styles that she really likes. She is trying to decide which one she will purchase. Charlotte is experiencing an _____ conflict.
   a. approach-approach
   b. approach-avoidance
   c. avoidance-avoidance
   d. avoidance-approach

6. People's sense of control over a situation can have an important beneficial influence on how a stressor affects them even if they do not exercise that control. (true/false)

7. Posttraumatic stress disorder leaves some people more vulnerable to future mental health problems. (true/false)

8. Which of the following is not a variable in work stress?
   a. workload
   b. clarity of job description
   c. perceived equity of pay for work
   d. task variety

9. Research indicates that African Americans who are highly concerned about _____ are more sensitive to stressors than their peers who are less concerned.

10. Religious faith helps people cope with negative life events. (true/false)

11. Lazarus's term for the positive experiences that can serve to cancel out the effects of day-to-day hassles is
    a. stress assets.
    c. uplifts.
    b. coping mechanisms.
    d. appraisals.

12. Type B behavior patterns seem to be more correlated with heart disease than do Type A behavior patterns. (true/false)

13. B cells produce antibodies that are effective in destroying antigens that live _____ the body cells; T cells are important in the destruction of antigens that live _____ the body cells.
    a. outside; inside
    b. inside; outside

14. AIDS is caused by HIV, often called the AIDS virus. (true/false)

15. HIV weakens the immune system by attacking T cells. (true/false)

◆ SECTION FIVE: Critical Thinking

1. In your view, which is more effective for evaluating stress: the Social Readjustment Rating Scale or the Hassle Scale? Explain the advantages and disadvantages of each.

2. Prepare two arguments: one supporting the position that alcoholism is a genetically inherited disease, and the other supporting the position that alcoholism is not a medical disease but results from learning.

3. Choose several stress-producing incidents from your life and explain what problem-focused and emotion-focused coping strategies you used. From the knowledge you have gained in this chapter, list other coping strategies that might have been more effective.

Testing Your Understanding—Unit VI

Mastering the World of Psychology, Chapter 10: Health and Stress

Pages 187–197
CHECKING YOUR COMPREHENSION

Choose the best answer for each of the following questions.

1. According to the text, the Social Readjustment Rating Scale (SRRS) is a predictor of
   a. a person's ability to handle coping with disease.
   b. a person's chances to survive a major health problem.
   c. a person's cognitive sympathetic response to stress.
   d. a person's risk of suffering major health problems.

2. From the research regarding the Social Readjustment Rating Scale (SRRS), you can conclude that a person's stress level
   a. can change from year to year.
   b. can predict major health problems.
   c. can predict life-threatening illnesses.
   d. can indicate how individuals deal with stress.

3. The primary purpose of Figure 10.2 is to
   a. explain Americans' increased levels of stress.
   b. reveal additional lingering effects associated with September 11th.
   c. show reasons for Americans suffering from posttraumatic stress disorder (PTSD).
   d. illustrate the potential impact of prolonged and severe stress reactions.

Identify the following statements as true or false.

4. Hassles and uplifts may neutralize the effects of one another.

5. The text infers that those who suffer from posttraumatic stress disorder (PTSD) are unable to live normal lives.

6. Studies regarding hassles have revealed that they may be a better indicator of stress than major life events.

Answer the following questions.

7. Explain the three stages of Selye's general adaptation syndrome (GAS).

8. Describe the differences between the approach-approach conflict and the avoidance-avoidance conflict.

9. List the nine variables related to stress in the workplace.

Define each term as it is used in the chapter.

10. historical racism

11. survivor guilt

12. glucocorticoids

13. stressor

14. coping

Discussion and Critical Thinking Questions

1. What are some of the benefits and detriments of using the Social Readjustment Rating Scale (SRRS)?
2. The ability to navigate today's technology in the workplace has become a problem for some employees. Should technological knowledge be added as a variable in Albrecht's work stress variables? How could the absence of technological skills stress an employee?
3. Discuss the relationship between racism and stress. What is another qualifier other than race that may cause the same result noted in the text?

Pages 198–204
CHECKING YOUR COMPREHENSION

Choose the best answer for each of the following questions.

1. According to the text, what do the biomedical model and the biopsychosocial model have in common?
   a. They both include the use of health psychology.
   b. They both take biological factors into consideration.
   c. They both take social factors into consideration.
   d. They have both been recognized by physicians for many decades.

2. What do the authors infer regarding individuals who are Type B?
   a. They are not concerned with leading sedentary lives.
   b. They are able to deal with stress better than those with Type A.
   c. Their personality types directly relate to their low risk of coronary heart disease.
   d. They go through life hostile and angered by those around them.

3. Researcher Edith Chen suggests that
   a. a child living in poverty is more likely to have poor health.
   b. a child's race is a predetermination of future health.
   c. a male child will acquire fewer life-threatening illnesses than a female child.
   d. a female child is three times more likely to suffer from AIDS than a male child.

Identify the following statements as true or false.

4. An individual's personality can be both Type A and Type B.

5. Cancer patients require both medical and psychological treatment.

6. Hardiness is prevalent in healthy male executives who handle stress well.

Answer the following questions.

7. Explain why cancer is not a single illness but a collection of diseases.

8. List six factors that negatively affect the immune system.

9. Describe the effect social support has on people with illness.

Define each term as it is used in the chapter.

10. antibodies

11. hardiness

12. antigens

13. psychoneuroimmunology

14. lymphocytes

Discussion and Critical Thinking Questions

1. The text infers that individuals can control many factors that attribute to coronary heart disease. What questions would you ask someone who has been told he/she is at risk of coronary heart disease, and what advice would you give him/her?
2. Examine your answers to the questions in Try It 10.2, Type A or Type B. Explain some of the behaviors that you feel may be detrimental to your health. What are some changes that you can make that will decrease your risk of disease?
3. Health psychology is a new subfield of medical care. Why do you think this field of medicine has not been focused upon prior to the introduction of the biopsychosocial model of health?

Pages 205–215
CHECKING YOUR COMPREHENSION

Choose the best answer for each of the following questions.

1. According to the text, which of the following is not a negative consequence of smoking?
   a. chronic bronchitis and other respiratory problems
   b. death and injuries from fires caused by smoking
   c. a greater risk for anxiety and depression
   d. low birth weight and retarded fetal development in babies of smoking mothers

2. AIDS is a disease that is
   a. considered primarily an illness that infects mostly homosexual males.
   b. currently epidemic and is believed to have originated in Africa.
   c. transmitted 12 times more easily from infected women to men.
   d. sometimes accompanied with serious clinical depression.

3. Health professionals agree that
   a. lifestyle changes are more beneficial than alternative medicine.
   b. research has shown alternative medicine is helpful in fighting disease.
   c. aerobic exercise is a fundamental activity of alternative medicine.
   d. alternative medicine makes bones denser and stronger, preventing osteoporosis.

Identify the following statements as true or false.

4. Alcohol only damages the liver, causing cirrhosis, which kills 26,000 people each year.

5. Over the past 30 years, 15 million Americans have contracted an STD.

6. The text suggests that alternative medicine would be held in higher esteem if scientific research proves that it is a viable alternative to traditional medicine.

Answer the following questions.

7. Explain the two foolproof ways to protect oneself from becoming infected with an STD.

8. What is the major difference between viral STDs and bacterial STDs?

9. What type of information is used to support the author's knowledge regarding lifestyle changes in Table 10.2, Benefits of Lifestyle Changes?

Discussion and Critical Thinking Questions

1. Make a list of all of the physical activity you participated in during the last week. According to the text, do you think that your activities reveal that you are getting enough exercise? What specific changes can you make that will ensure you follow the guidelines in the text?
2. What are your thoughts regarding the introduction of an HIV-positive Muppet on *Sesame Street*? Do you feel it is necessary to include such harsh realities in children's television?

Chapter Review
END OF CHAPTER ANALYSIS

Choose the best answer for each of the following questions.

1. The chapter employs all of the following techniques for making the material easier to use except
   a. marginal annotations.
   b. graphics and visuals.
   c. boldface and highlighting.
   d. chapter outline.

2. The author would most probably agree with which of the following statements?
   a. People can take control of their health and make a difference in their future.
   b. People have to suffer with their illnesses and have no power over them at all.
   c. People need to realize that illnesses have no connection to their mental health.
   d. People have to exercise every day for more than 30 minutes to be healthy.

3. After reading the chapter, you should be able to answer all of the following questions except which one?
   a. What are some ways to prevent coronary heart disease?
   b. What is the relationship between the immune system and stress?
   c. How does a person's cultural background affect his or her personality type?
   d. How does long-term tobacco and alcohol use affect an individual's health?

Group Projects

1. After taking the AIDS Quiz (Try It 10.3), discuss the statements you answered incorrectly. Discuss with the other members of the group how you learned about AIDS. What do you think our government and our educational systems can do to prevent more people from acquiring AIDS?

2. Survey your classmates regarding the different factors of living a healthy lifestyle discussed in the chapter. After you tabulate the responses, discuss whether the class overall has healthy lifestyles and what changes should be made to ensure future health.

3. In our society there are many organizations that teach the public about the connection between health and stress, such as The American Heart Association (www.americanheart.org) and The Campaign for Tobacco-Free Kids (www.tobaccofreekids.org). Investigate one of these organizations on the Internet and discuss how it supports the information in the text.

Journal Ideas

1. Using information from the chapter, write a plan that outlines how you need to change your lifestyle to accommodate healthy living.

2. Write a letter to a friend explaining how an unhealthy lifestyle is damaging his or her future. Support your ideas with facts, statistics, and proven research from the chapter.

PIANO • VOCAL • GUITAR

W9-AAK-383

THE BEST WEDDING SONGS EVER

ISBN 0-634-07395-8

HAL•LEONARD®
CORPORATION

7777 W. BLUEMOUND RD. P.O. BOX 13819 MILWAUKEE, WI 53213

Visit Hal Leonard Online at
www.halleonard.com

THE BEST WEDDING SONGS EVER

CONTENTS

AIR
from WATER MUSIC

By GEORGE FRIDERIC HANDEL

ALL I ASK OF YOU
from THE PHANTOM OF THE OPERA

Music by ANDREW LLOYD WEBBER
Lyrics by CHARLES HART
Additional Lyrics by RICHARD STILGOE

No more talk of dark-ness, for-get these wide-eyed fears: I'm

here, noth-ing can harm you, my words will warm and calm you.

Let me be your free-dom, let day-light dry your tears: I'm

here, with you, be-side you, to guard you and to guide you.

CHRISTINE:

Say you love me ev-ery wak-ing mo-ment, turn my head with talk of sum-mer-time.

Say you need me with you now and al-ways;

pro-mise me that all you say is true, that's all I ask of

10

ALLEGRO MAESTOSO
from WATER MUSIC

By GEORGE FRIDERIC HANDEL

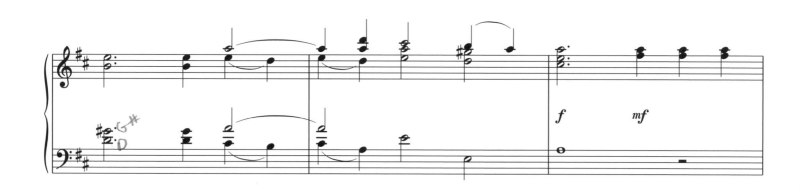

ALLEGRO MAESTOSO
from WATER MUSIC

By GEORGE FRIDERIC HANDEL

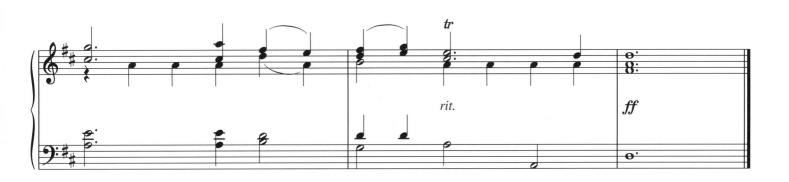

ALWAYS AND FOREVER

Words and Music by
ROD TEMPERTON

Al-ways and for-ev-er, _____ each mo-ment with
There'll al-ways be sun-shine _____ when I look at

you you _____
you. It's some-thing I can't ex-plain, _____ is just like a dream to ___ me _____

AVE MARIA

By FRANZ SCHUBERT

A - ve Ma - ri - a!

A - ve Ma - ri - a!

sim.

dim.

BECAUSE

Words by EDWARD TESCHEMACHER
Music by GUY D'HARDELOT

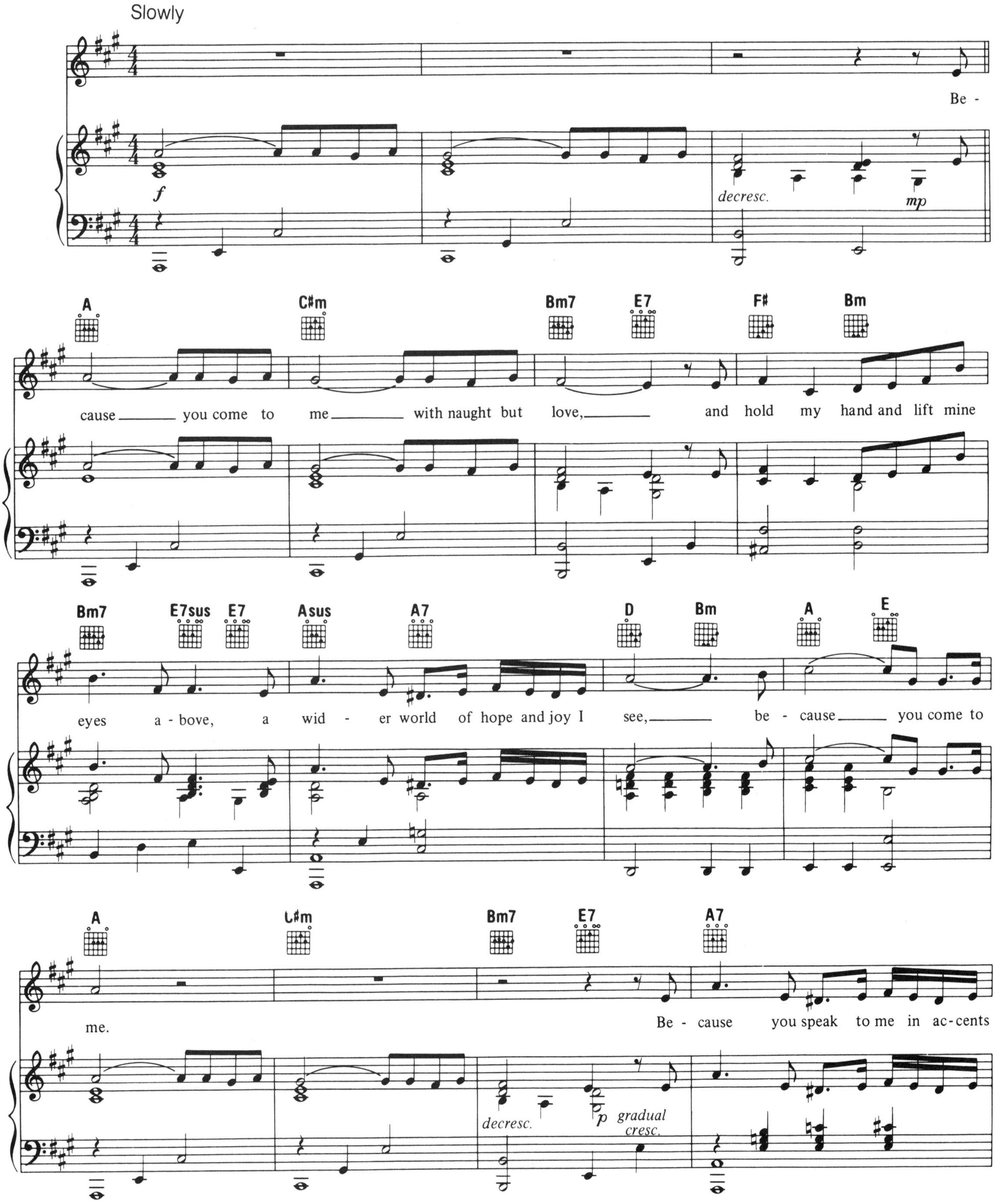
Slowly
f
decresc.
mp
Be -
A
C#m
Bm7
E7
F#
Bm
cause you come to me with naught but love, and hold my hand and lift mine
Bm7
E7sus
E7
Asus
A7
D
Bm
A
E
eyes a - bove, a wid - er world of hope and joy I see, be - cause you come to
A
C#m
Bm7
E7
A7
me. Be - cause you speak to me in ac-cents
decresc.
p
gradual cresc.

BEST THING THAT EVER HAPPENED TO ME

Words and Music by
JIM WEATHERLY

THE BEST YEARS OF MY LIFE

Words and Music by WILL JENNINGS
and STEPHEN ALLEN DAVIS

BRIDAL CHORUS
from LOHENGRIN

By RICHARD WAGNER

Moderato

BUTTERFLY KISSES

Words and Music by BOB CARLISLE
and RANDY THOMAS

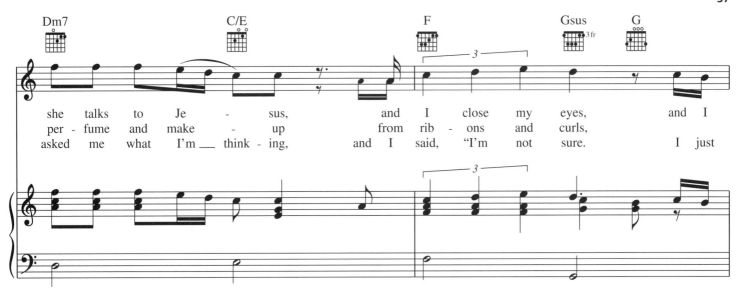

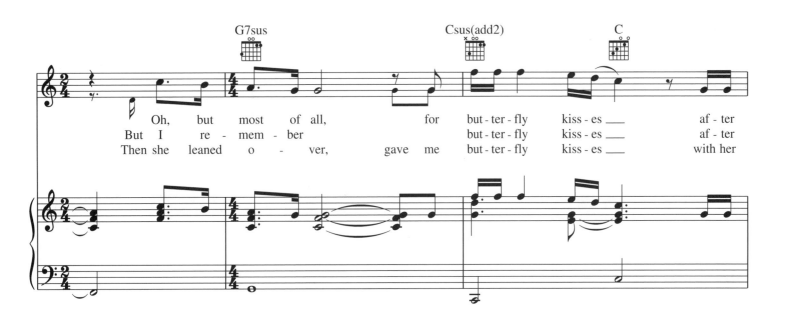

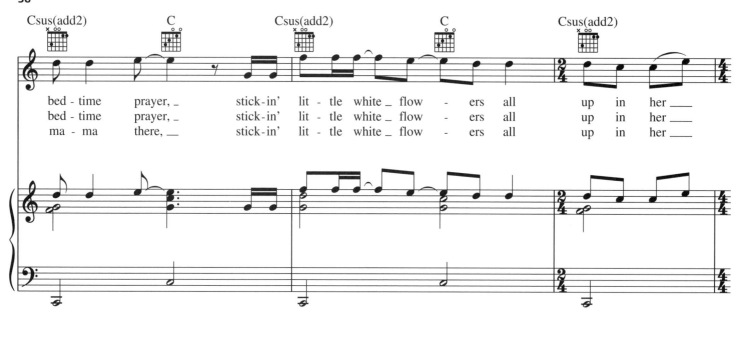

bed - time prayer, _ stick-in' lit - tle white _ flow - ers all up in her ___
bed - time prayer, _ stick-in' lit - tle white _ flow - ers all up in her ___
ma - ma there, __ stick-in' lit - tle white _ flow - ers all up in her ___

hair. "Walk be - side ___ the po - ny, dad - dy, it's
hair. "You know how much ___ I love __ you, dad - dy, but if
hair. "Walk me down _ the aisle, __ dad - dy, it's

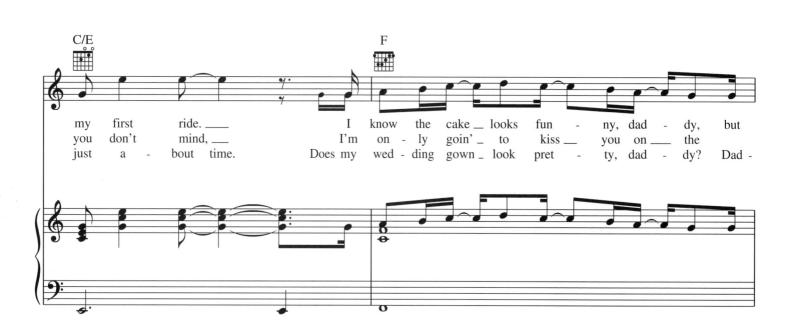

my first ride. ___ I know the cake _ looks fun - ny, dad - dy, but
you don't mind, __ I'm on - ly goin' _ to kiss __ you on __ the
just a - bout time. Does my wed - ding gown _ look pret - ty, dad - dy? Dad -

CANDLE ON THE WATER
from Walt Disney's PETE'S DRAGON

Words and Music by AL KASHA
and JOEL HIRSCHHORN

Smoothly

I'll be your can-dle on the wa-ter, my love for you will al-ways
I'll be your can-dle on the wa-ter 'til ev-'ry wave is warm and

burn. I know you're lost and drift-ing, but the clouds are lift-ing.
bright. My soul is there be-side you, let this can-dle guide you;

Don't give up; you have some-where to turn.
soon you'll see a gold-en stream of light.

CANON IN D

By JOHANN PACHELBEL

Adagio

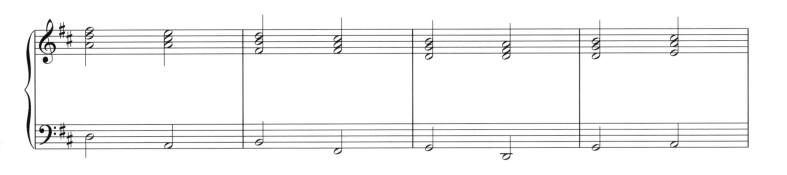

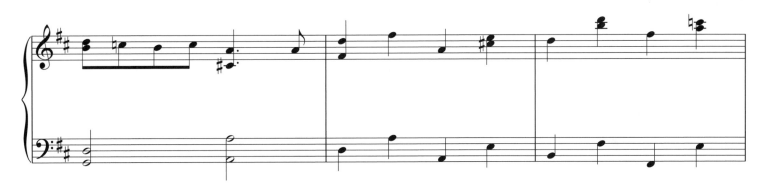

DESTINY

Words and Music by JIM BRICKMAN,
SEAN HOSEIN and DANE DEVILLER

Original key: D-flat major. This edition has been transposed down one half-step to be more playable.
* Male vocal written at pitch.

52

DEVOTED TO YOU

Words and Music by
BOUDLEAUX BRYANT

DON'T KNOW MUCH

Words and Music by BARRY MANN,
CYNTHIA WEIL and TOM SNOW

ENDLESS LOVE

from ENDLESS LOVE

Words and Music by
LIONEL RICHIE

THE GIFT

Words and Music by TOM DOUGLAS
and JIM BRICKMAN

Slow Ballad

Female: Hoo. _____

Win-ter snow is fall-ing __ down, chil-dren laugh-ing all a-round,

lights are turn-ing on, _____ like a fair-y tale __ come true. __

74

GROW OLD WITH ME

Words and Music by
JOHN LENNON

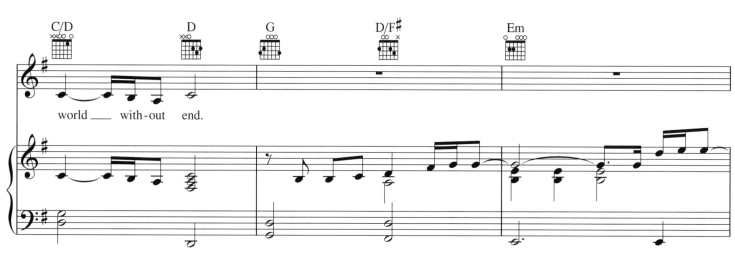

HERE AND NOW

Words and Music by TERRY STEELE
and DAVID ELLIOT

HOW BEAUTIFUL

Words and Music by
TWILA PARIS

(Everything I Do)
I DO IT FOR YOU

from the Motion Picture ROBIN HOOD: PRINCE OF THIEVES

Words and Music by BRYAN ADAMS,
ROBERT JOHN LANGE and MICHAEL KAMEN

way, ___ yeah. _____

Oh, you can't tell me it's not worth try - ing for. I can't

I HONESTLY LOVE YOU

Words and Music by PETER ALLEN
and JEFF BARRY

Lyrics:

May-be I hang a-round_ here a lit-tle more than I should; we
You don't_ have to an-swer; I see it in your eyes.

both know I got some-where else_ to go. But
May-be it was bet-ter left_ un-said. But

I PLEDGE MY LOVE

Words by DINO FEKARIS
Music by DINO FEKARIS
and FREDDIE PERREN

I LOVE YOU

from MEXICAN HAYRIDE

Words and Music by
COLE PORTER

I NEVER KNEW LOVE

Words and Music by WILL ROBINSON
and LARRY BOONE

I nev-er knew the pow-er ___ of a song ___
I nev-er un-der-stood the mean-ing of home ___

till I heard the mu-sic play - in' the day
till I pulled in-to ___ that old dirt drive af-ter

I SWEAR

Words and Music by FRANK MYERS
and GARY BAKER

I see the ques - tions in___ your eyes;___   I know what's weigh -
I'll give you ev - 'ry - thing___ I can;___   I'll build your dreams _

I WON'T LAST A DAY WITHOUT YOU

Words and Music by PAUL WILLIAMS
and ROGER NICHOLS

Day af-ter day ___ I must face a world ___ of strang-ers where I
So man-y times ___ when the cit-y seems ___ to be with-out a

don't be-long; ___ I'm not that strong. It's nice to know ___ that there's
friend-ly face, ___ a lone-ly place, it's nice to know ___ that you'll

some-one I ___ can turn to who will al-ways care; ___ you're
be there if ___ I need you, and you'll al-ways smile; ___ it's

I WILL BE HERE

Words and Music by
STEVEN CURTIS CHAPMAN

I'LL HAVE TO SAY I LOVE YOU IN A SONG

Words and Music by
JIM CROCE

IN MY LIFE

Words and Music by JOHN LENNON
and PAUL McCARTNEY

There are plac- es I'll re- mem- ber all my
But of all these friends and lov- ers there is

life, _____ though some have changed. __ Some for- ev- er, not for
no _____ one com- pares with you. ____ And these mem- 'ries lose their

bet- ter; some have gone _____ and some re- main. __ All these
mean- ing when I think of ___ love as some- thing new. __ Tho' I

JESU, JOY OF MAN'S DESIRING

By JOHANN SEBASTIAN BACH

Moderato

JUST THE TWO OF US

Words and Music by RALPH MacDONALD,
WILLIAM SALTER and BILL WITHERS

Lyrics:

I see the crys-tal rain-drops fall, and the beau-ty of it
We look for love; no time for tears. Wast-ed wa-ter's all that
I hear the crys-tal rain-drops fall on the win-dow down the

all is when the sun comes shin-ing through___ to make those rain-bows in my
is, and it don't make no flow-ers grow.___ Good things might come to those who
hall, and it be-comes the morn-ing dew.___ And dar-ling, when the morn-ing

mind, when I think of you some-time, and I want to spend___ some time with
wait but not for those who wait too late. We've got to go___ for all we
comes and I see the morn-ing sun. I want to be___ the one with

you.___ Just___ the two of us, we can make it if___ we try.___ Just the
know.___
you.___

two of us. (Just the two___ of us.) Just___ the two of us build-ing

cas-tles in — the sky. — Just the two of us, you and I. —

Just the

LARGO
from XERXES

By GEORGE FRIDERIC HANDEL

Larghetto

LONG AS I LIVE

Words and Music by WILL ROBINSON
and RICK BOWLES

world's been spin-ning 'round since time be-gan,
mat-ter if there's moun-tains you can't move

and when it stops, it's out of my hands.
or hard-er times than you thought you'd go through;

LOVE AND MARRIAGE

Words by SAMMY CAHN
Music by JAMES VAN HEUSEN

LONGER

Words and Music by
DAN FOGELBERG

158

THE LORD'S PRAYER

By ALBERT H. MALOTTE

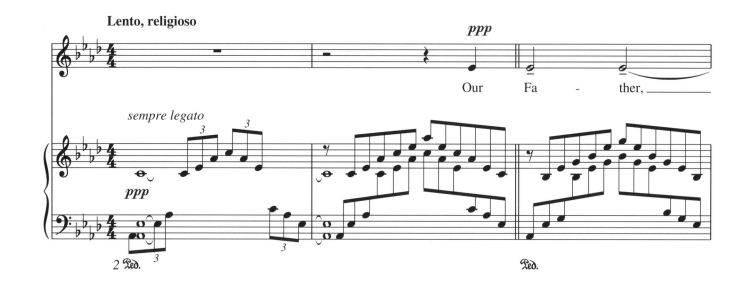

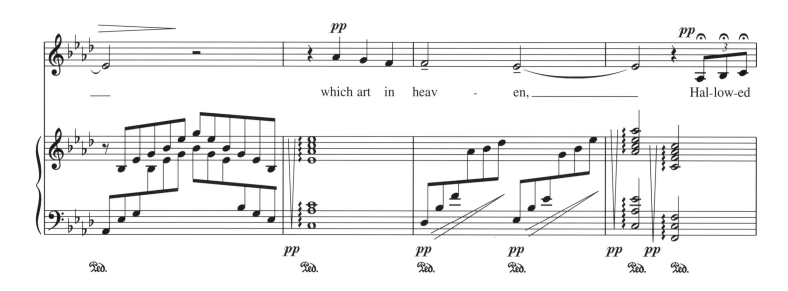

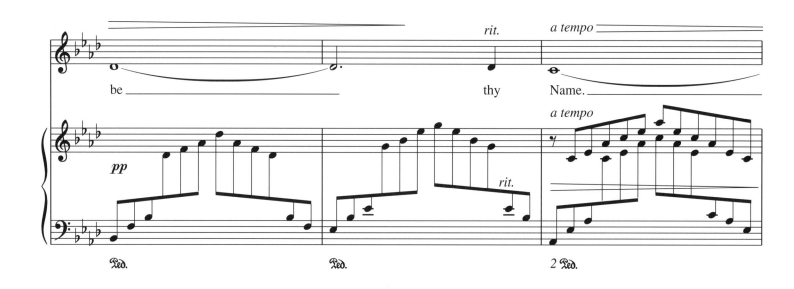

LOVE OF MY LIFE

Words and Music by JIM BRICKMAN
and TOM DOUGLAS

MAY YOU ALWAYS

Words and Music by LARRY MARKES
and DICK CHARLES

ME AND YOU

Words and Music by SKIP EWING
and RAY HERNDON

MEDITATION
from THAÏS

By JULES MASSENET

MORE
(Ti guarderò nel cuore)
from the film MONDO CANE

Music by NINO OLIVIERO and RIZ ORTOLANI
Italian Lyrics by MARCELLO CIORCIOLINI
English Lyrics by NORMAN NEWELL

MORE THAN WORDS

Words and Music by NUNO BETTENCOURT
and GARY CHERONE

Original key: F♯ major. This edition has been transposed up one half-step to be more playable.

MY HEART WILL GO ON

(Love Theme from 'Titanic')

from the Paramount and Twentieth Century Fox Motion Picture TITANIC

Music by JAMES HORNER
Lyric by WILL JENNINGS

190

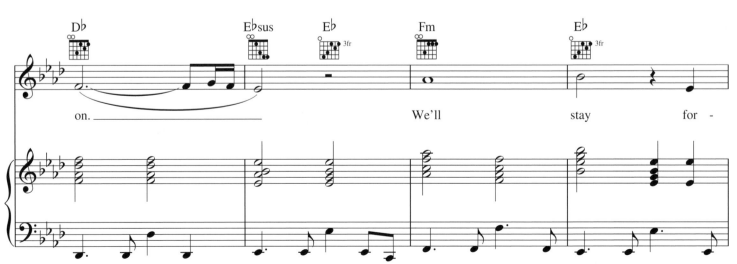

NOW AND FOREVER
(You and Me)

Words and Music by JIM VALLANCE,
RANDY GOODRUM and DAVID FOSTER

Moderately slow Rock

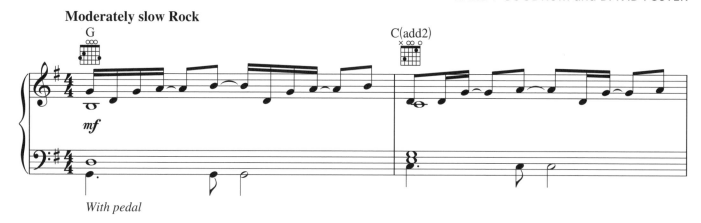

With pedal

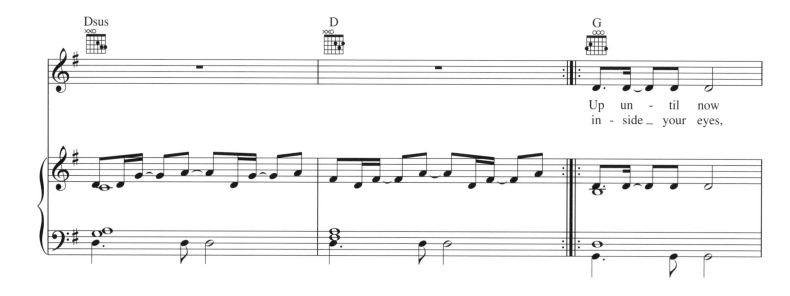

Up un - til now
in - side_ your eyes,

I've learned to live_ with - out love,
I can see mys - ter - ies there.

ODE TO JOY
from SYMPHONY NO. 9 IN D MINOR

By LUDWIG VAN BEETHOVEN

With spirit

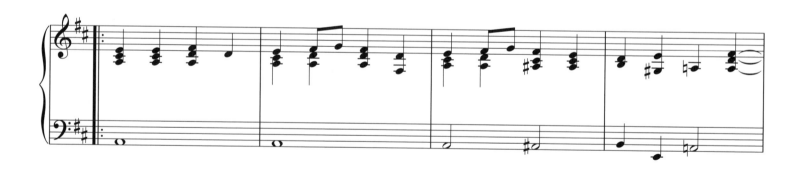

ONE IN A MILLION YOU

Words and Music by
SAM DEES

OPEN ARMS

Words and Music by STEVE PERRY
and JONATHAN CAIN

PERFECT UNION

Words and Music by JOHN ANDREW SCHREINER
and MATTHEW WARD

ROMEO AND JULIET

Fantasy Overture
"Love Theme"

By Pyotr Il'yich Tchaikovsky

Allegro giusto

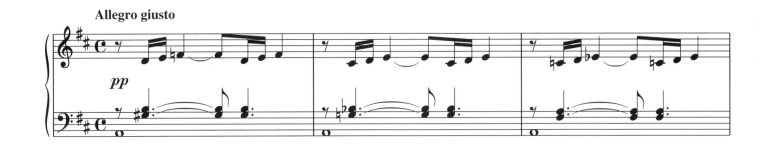

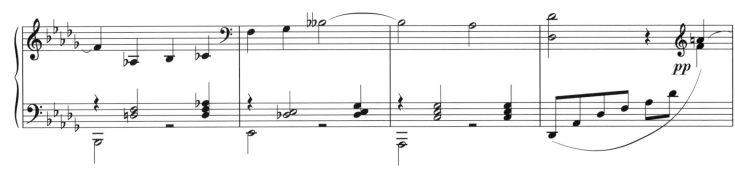

THIS IS THE DAY
(A Wedding Song)

Words and Music by
SCOTT WESLEY BROWN

This is the day _____ that the Lord ___ hath ___ made, _ That
This is the love _____ that the Lord ___ hath ___ made, _ That

I'm so ___ glad ___ He made you.
you and ___ I ___ we are one.

With

each ris- in' sun ___ you are here by my side, _ You are
Love's mys- ter- y ___ is un- fold- ing to- day, _

This is the day, _____

This is the day. _____

THROUGH THE YEARS

Words and Music by STEVE DORFF
and MARTY PANZER

TILL THE END OF TIME
(Based on Chopin's Polonaise)

Words and Music by BUDDY KAYE
and TED MOSSMAN

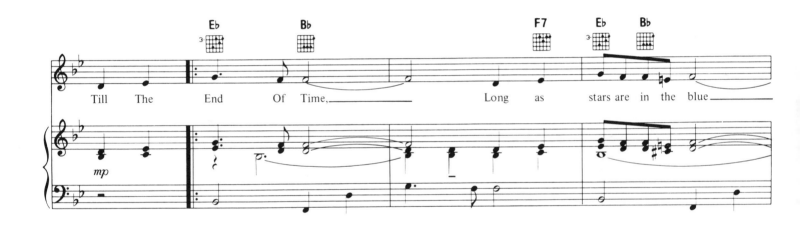

Till The End Of Time,_____ Long as stars are in the blue_____

_____ Long as there's a spring, a bird to sing I'll go on lov- ing

TRUE LOVE

from HIGH SOCIETY

Words and Music by
COLE PORTER

Moderately slow

TRUMPET VOLUNTARY

By JEREMIAH CLARKE

Andante con moto

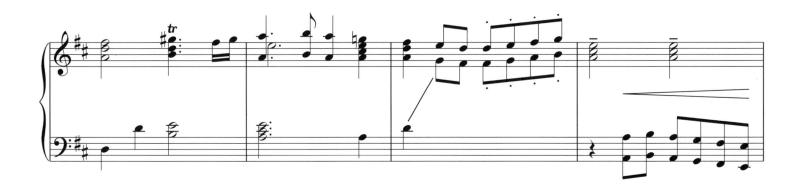

WE'VE ONLY JUST BEGUN

Words and Music by ROGER NICHOLS
and PAUL WILLIAMS

THE VOWS GO UNBROKEN
(Always True to You)

Words and Music by GARY BURR
and ERIC KAZ

WEDDING MARCH
from A MIDSUMMER NIGHT'S DREAM

By FELIX MENDELSSOHN

Allegro

D.S. al Fine

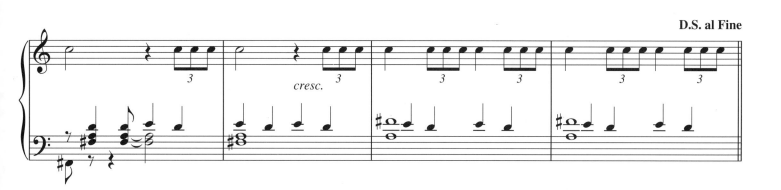

WEDDING PRAYER

Words and Music by
MARY RICE HOPKINS

WEDDING PROCESSIONAL
from THE SOUND OF MUSIC

Lyrics by OSCAR HAMMERSTEIN II
Music by RICHARD RODGERS

WEDDING PROCESSIONAL

from THE SOUND OF MUSIC

Lyrics by OSCAR HAMMERSTEIN II
Music by RICHARD RODGERS

For the entrance of the Bride

rit.

a tempo

WHAT A DIFFERENCE YOU'VE MADE IN MY LIFE

Words and Music by
ARCHIE JORDAN

WHEN YOU SAY NOTHING AT ALL

Words and Music by PAUL OVERSTREET
and DON SCHLITZ

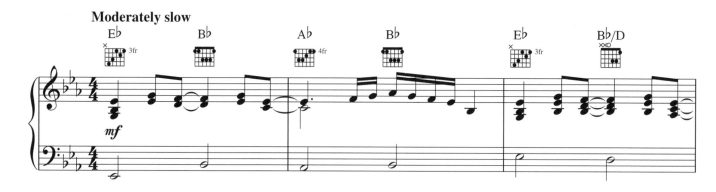

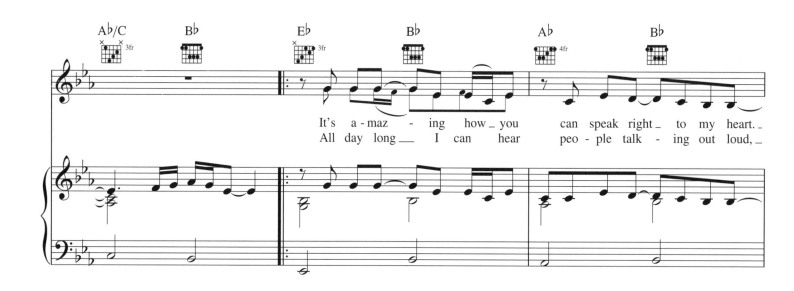

It's a-maz-ing how you can speak right to my heart.
All day long I can hear peo-ple talk-ing out loud,

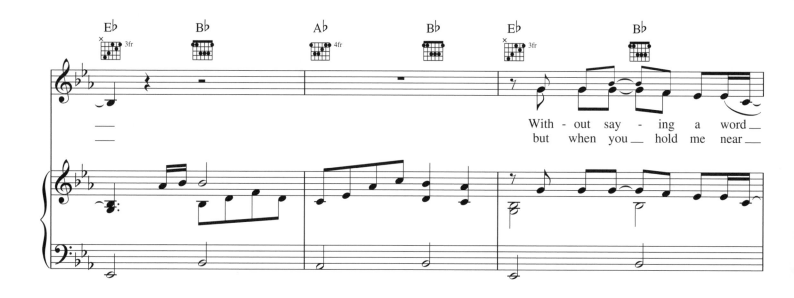

With-out say-ing a word
but when you hold me near

E♭ B♭ A♭ B♭
truth in your eyes say - ing you'll nev - er leave me. A
E♭ B♭ A♭ B♭
touch of your hand says you'll catch me if ev - er I fall.
A♭/C B♭/D E♭/G A♭
To Coda
1
B♭
Now you say it best when you say noth - ing at all.
E♭ B♭ A♭ B♭ E♭ B♭/D
3fr
4fr

WITH THIS RING

Words and Music by CLYDE OTIS
and VINCENT CORSO

YEARS FROM NOW

Words and Music by ROGER COOK
and CHARLES COCHRAN

YOU LIGHT UP MY LIFE

Words and Music by
JOSEPH BROOKS

YOU RAISE ME UP

Words and Music by BRENDAN GRAHAM
and ROLF LOVLAND

Moderately slow

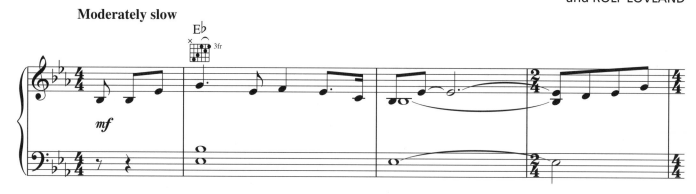

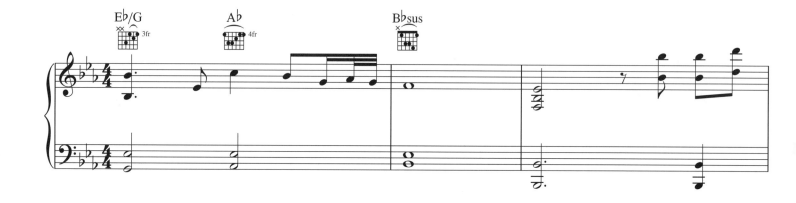

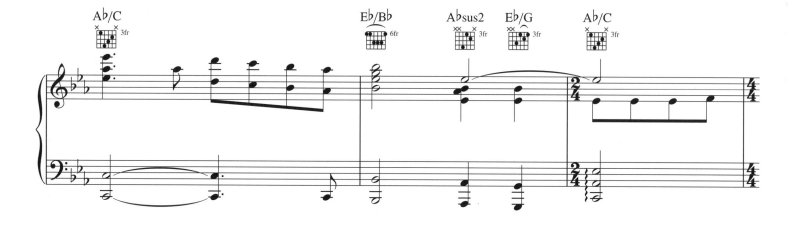

YOU'LL ACCOMP'NY ME

Words and Music by
BOB SEGER

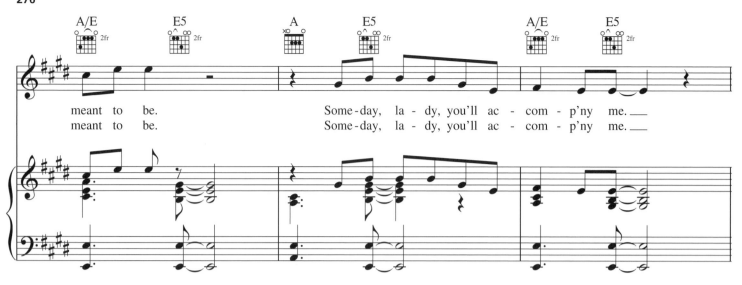

meant to be.
meant to be.

Some-day, la - dy, you'll ac - com - p'ny me. ___
Some-day, la - dy, you'll ac - com - p'ny me. ___

Some-day, la - dy, you'll ac - com - p'ny me ___
Some-day, la - dy, you'll ac - com - p'ny me. ___
Some-day, la - dy, you'll ac - com - p'ny me ___

out where the riv - ers meet the
It's writ - ten down some-where. It's
out where the riv - ers meet the

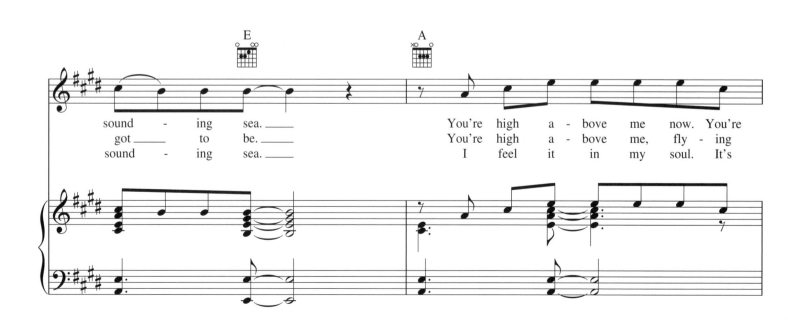

sound - ing sea. ___
got ___ to be. ___
sound - ing sea. ___

You're high a - bove me now. You're
You're high a - bove me, fly - ing
I feel it in my soul. It's

YOU'RE MY EVERYTHING

Lyric by MORT DIXON and JOE YOUNG
Music by HARRY WARREN

YOUR LOVE AMAZES ME

Words and Music by CHUCK JONES
and AMANDA HUNT-TAYLOR

I've seen the sev-en won-ders
I've seen a sun-set that would
I've prayed for mir-a-cles that

of the world. I've seen the beau-ty of dia-monds and pearls.
make you cry, and col-ors of a rain-bow reach-ing 'cross the sky,
nev-er came. I got down on my knees out in the pour-ing rain.

your love a - maz - es me. ___

Vocal ad lib.

Optional Ending

Repeat and Fade

YOU ARE THE SUNSHINE
OF MY LIFE

Words and Music by
STEVIE WONDER